BUILDING THE MYTH

BUILDING THE MYTH

Selected Speeches Memorializing
Abraham Lincoln

Edited by Waldo W. Braden

University of Illinois Press
Urbana and Chicago

©1990 by the Board of Trustees of the University of Illinois
Manufactured in the United States of America
C 5 4 3 2 1
This book is printed on acid-free paper.

Library of Congress Cataloging-in-Publication Data

Building the myth: selected speeches memorializing Abraham Lincoln / edited by
Waldo W. Braden.
  p. cm.
  Includes bibliographical references.
  ISBN 0-252-01734-X (alk. paper)
  1. Lincoln, Abraham, 1809–1865—Anniversaries, etc. 2. Lincoln,
Abraham, 1809–1865—Influence. 3. Presidents—United States—
Biography. I. Braden, Waldo Warder, 1911–
E457.7.M55 1990
973.7'092—dc20   90-30888
                                                                         CIP

Contents

Acknowledgments

I am well aware that I owe much to the Lincoln searchers who have come before me. I continue to be impressed and grateful for *The Collected Works of Abraham Lincoln,* edited by Roy P. Basler and his staff; *Lincoln Day by Day: A Chronology 1809–1865,* edited by Earl Schenck Miers; *The Lincoln Encyclopedia,* by Mark E. Neely, Jr.; and the numerous biographical recollections and studies.

I am much indebted to the staffs of the Louisiana State University Library, the University of Missouri Library, the Illinois State Historical Library, and the Missouri Historical Library. Harold Mixon and Owen Peterson of Louisiana State University and Gary Planck of the *Lincoln Herald* have been most helpful. Wayne Temple and Thomas Dyba have long served as inspirations. I drew heavily upon those who assisted me earlier with my book *Abraham Lincoln: Public Speaker.* Of course, it could never have been done without the skill and patience of my typists in Baton Rouge, Louisiana, and Caroline and Co., especially Regg Schilowsky in Columbia, Missouri.

The Eulogist
and the Lincoln Myth

Some Abraham Lincoln followers believe that he has approached sainthood. According to David Donald, the "Lincoln cult" has become "almost an American religion."[1] Another Lincoln authority, Roy P. Basler, thinks that as time passes, Lincoln "becomes more and more a national mythos. The certainty with which this mythos will continue to live depends upon how much Lincoln is able to stand reinterpretation." Although this prediction was made fifty years ago, the evidence is that the Lincoln legend will have an "indefinite life."[2] In *The Lincoln Image,* Harold Holzer, Gabor S. Boritt, and Mark E. Neely, Jr., have written: "This redefinition of Lincoln's place in American thought, his swift transcendence from history into folklore, was one of the more remarkable cultural phenomena of our history. It was the product of many influences, including religious fervor, superstition, the retrospective impact of Lincoln's own last public utterances, and popular art. Lincoln the man was swallowed by the myth, a myth neither the passage of time nor the challenge of revision has been able to tarnish."[3]

The darkness and anguish that came from the death of Abraham Lincoln suddenly transformed the earlier, maligned Old Abe into the personification of Father Abraham and the Savior of the Republic. Radical Republican Charles Sumner associated the dead leader with George Washington: "The work left undone by Washington was continued by Lincoln," who drew "a reluctant sword to save those great ideas, essential to the life and character of the Republic."[4] The vitriolic Lincoln critic Wendell Phillips admitted, "With all his shortcomings, we point proudly to him as the natural growth of democratic institutions." Phillips placed Lincoln "in that galaxy of Americans which makes our history the day star of the nations— Washington, Hamilton, Franklin, Jefferson, and Jay. History will add his name to the bright list."[5] These two statements were mild in comparison with what some other eulogists declared. Many saw Lincoln's death as apocalyptic, suggesting that he died for freedom and democratic ideals and that his death resembled that of Christ and portended better times.

The Rail-Splitter suddenly became the epic hero, yearned for by many Americans.[6] Many Americans today like to get close to where he lived and died. When admirers visit the Kentucky birthplace, the Springfield home, the Gettysburg battle site, the numerous statues, the Lincoln Memorial, or the Oak Ridge Cemetery tomb, they can pause to contemplate forces at work on the raw frontier of Kentucky, Indiana, and Illinois that produced this remarkable, self-educated Western lawyer and politician. At the Oak Ridge monument, they are immediately attracted to Gutzon Borglum's great head of Lincoln, mounted eye-level, at the entrance of the tomb. Upon seeing it, they cannot resist touching the nose, already made shiny by those who came earlier. When a replica of it was included in a traveling exhibit for display in Japan, the sponsors learned that the Japanese admirers of Lincoln responded much the same. How is it that he has outdistanced other presidents? Why has his birth date become more widely observed by memorial services than that of any other American? This simple, plain, angular man who in his time was thought to be ugly has become attractive and revered.[7]

At least six libraries have gathered his papers and memorabilia.[8] Collectors spend thousands of dollars to acquire mementoes or scraps of paper that contain his signature.[9] At present a research project is under way to gather every document, no matter how small, pertaining to his law practice in central Illinois.[10] Across the country, from Redlands, California, to New York City, to Winter Park, Florida, the faithful, sometimes calling their groups Lincoln fellowships, foster Lincoln activities, seeking speakers to inspire and provide fresh insights, and sponsor projects to glorify the memory of the man.[11] He continues to inspire conferences, critical studies, novels, dramas, movies, poetry, editorials, cartoons, statues, paintings, prints, and eulogies.

The extent and dimension of the Lincoln memorializing have exceeded by far that of any other American. Soon after Lincoln's death, the vocal critics and realists were silenced and the mythmakers gained control. They started building the Lincoln image that became deeply embedded in the American consciousness and consequently achieved the power of a highly persuasive symbol. This remarkable cultural phenomena has incorporated the efforts of hundreds of persons and dozens of organizations.

Several scholars have studied the 120 known photographs of Lincoln, the most recent being James Mellon in *The Face of Lincoln*.[12] William W. Betts has collected the best Lincoln poems. Holzer, Boritt, and Neely have analyzed the Lincoln prints in two splendid books. The Lincoln cartoons have been collected and discussed. In addition, dozens of pamphlets have explored special aspects of the Lincoln story.[13]

In *Lincoln in Marble and Bronze* F. Lauriston Bullard has accounted for eighty-seven statues, the work of fifty-six sculptors, presenting the Illinoisan in bronze and stone from youth to his assassination. He made the following observations about the dedications of these statues:

> For nearly every statue we record the origin of the movement for its erection, some account of the life and work of the sculptor, and the ceremonies of its dedication. In a surprising number of instances the dedication addresses have proved to be of high merit, and most of these are quite unknown.... If a Lincoln memorial is unveiled before an admiring throng, and dedicated with eulogies of the man and of the artist, it surely deserves better care over the years than some of these monuments have received. A few have been disfigured by the wear of weather and climate, and a few—but only a few—have been mutilated by vandals. Far the greater number, however, have had the watchful care of local Lincolnians, and these lovers of Lincoln number many thousands today, while the influence of Lincoln tourists is also a protective factor.

Bullard stirred sympathy for the poor orators who, after struggling to produce addresses "of high merit," have been forgotten. In spite of disfigurement and neglect, the lone bronze statues still invite attention, but the orations remain buried in dusty newspapers, fugitive pamphlets, and seldom-opened anthologies. Many of these oral efforts were more than the creations of village preachers, would-be Fourth of July orators, or tiresome elocutionists, they were the rhetorical efforts of distinguished American speakers.

Basler has discussed "how poets, writers of fiction, dramatists and occasionally biographers" have contributed to "a national legend or myth" about Lincoln. But with the exception of a brief mention of Ralph Waldo Emerson's eulogy of April 15, 1865, Basler had nothing to say about the contributions of the orators. It would seem that the Lincoln orators need to be rediscovered, restored, and reinterpreted.[14]

The demand for eulogies about Lincoln has continued until the present day. Seldom has a great commemoration not involved the combined efforts of several media. Always in this milieu the orator has taken a prominent part. At a dedication of a statue or a monument, a celebration, or an important Lincoln anniversary, the speaker is asked to present a eulogy or speech of presentation or acceptance. The orator attempts to capture in eloquent words what the artist had hoped to portray, what the sponsors hoped to preserve, and what the onlookers hoped to feel, thereby tying together all components of the occasion.

Since 1865 our most prominent American speakers have celebrated the memory of Lincoln, and they have delivered thousands of speeches. The motivation to produce eloquence about him has been at times almost overpowering. The speaker, honored by special invitation, has been given center stage; the occasion, well advertised, has always been dramatic: a cabin at Hodgenville, Kentucky, a picture of the signing of the Emancipation Proclamation, an anniversary of a document, or the erection of a statue or monument. The expectant audiences have been emotionally intense, adding fervor to the ritual and overt response. Participants have come fully intent upon promoting reverence, well aware of the Lincoln story, the historical context, and what previous eulogists had said. In this scenario the orator of the day indulged in oratorical flourish to heighten sentiment and emotion. The supreme test was whether the performer could avoid banality, overworked figures of speech, and stereotypes.

Admittedly, many of the eulogies have been ephemeral, and they do not compare to the poetry of Walt Whitman, Vachel Lindsay, and Edwin Markham or to the dramas of John Drinkwater and Robert Sherwood. But these epideictic pieces came from important rhetoricians experienced in public affairs, sensitive to the intimate feelings of the public, and gifted with the artistry to put into popular language memories about heroes and great events.

What is worthy of note is that the eulogists as a group have not received acclaim equal to that given to writers and artists. As far as

I know there have been no efforts to analyze the Lincoln eulogies as a genre of epideictic oratory or to fit them into the larger context of the developing Lincoln myth. It is true that a few fugitive anthologies of Lincoln speeches, never issued in large numbers and now almost forgotten, appeared many years ago.[15] A few speeches devoted to Lincoln were included in general collections or in collected works of key personalities such as Theodore Roosevelt, Adlai E. Stevenson, Booker T. Washington, and Woodrow Wilson. A few scattered articles discussed the sermons preached after the assassination.[16] But on the whole, eulogies about Lincoln have been bypassed or dismissed as mere oratory. Nevertheless, year after year additions to the speeches on Lincoln continue to emerge. The prominent Lincoln scholar Roy Basler, who did his share of speaking about the Illinois lawyer, dismissed much of the continuing demand as little more than idolatry: "Perhaps what most of Lincoln's admirers want in a Lincoln's birthday speech or sermon is to be indulged in patriotic sentimentality—an anecdotal sketch of the personality of Lincoln or a eulogy of his character. . . . Idolatry is perhaps the word for this, or a very near thing to it. . . . But let me ask, what is the use of this idolatry? What good is it aside from providing a sort of pious secular adjunct to, or substitute for, going to church and worshipping the person of Jesus?"[17] What did Basler mean by *idolatry*? Did he mean religious worship of an idol, implying excessive and blind adoration?

The question *what good is it* is really the thesis of this book. Is the label *idolatry* a fair one? It of course applies to the empty ritual that has many times become habitual and superficial, lacking in originality and tending toward mawkishness. But what can be said about the better rhetorical efforts, those coming from some of the distinguished speakers, people who have gained recognition in politics, the professions, and business? What part have the experts of the rhetorical art contributed to the growing Lincoln myth?

A hasty reading of the orations collected here may cause the casual reader to conclude that some of the speakers were florid, ornate, excessively emotional, and even grandiloquent. Such reactions are to be expected from those who have difficulty projecting themselves back into the original settings or fantasizing the Lincoln experience. Some also may confuse the *ceremonial* with *deliberative* and *forensic* speeches. Aristotle suggested that each had its specific purposes, its peculiar audience appeals, *topoi* (sources or methods), and materials. The *epideictic* (ceremonial, occasional, declamatory) is a speech of praise or blame; the *deliberative* (political, parliamentary) argues for the adoption of a course of action; the *forensic* (legal, judicial) argues whether a human act comes within the provisions of the law or edict (whether the accused is innocent or guilty).

"The ceremonial orator," explained Aristotle, "is, properly speaking, concerned with the present, since all men praise or blame in view of the state of things existing at the time, though they often find it useful also to recall the past and to make guesses at the future."[18] The twenty-three speeches collected here are mainly *epideictic* in purpose because the speakers sought to heighten appreciation for the president or one of his acts, such as the Cooper Institute Address, the Gettysburg Address, or the signing of the Emancipation Proclamation. Their auditors agreed with the speakers about the worth of Abraham Lincoln; they were not seeking proof of his greatness, but wanted assurance and emotional stimulation through eloquent and poetic language. Therefore the speakers turned to amplification, using comparison and contrast, or what Aristotle referred to as *topoi* of more or less ("Lincoln was greater than . . . because . . ."). Their principal supporting materials were narratives of the events of Lincoln's life, quotations from his speeches and writing, mythical episodes, quotations about Lincoln from his acquaintances, and the history of his times. The speakers' excellence was judged on how well they phrased their thoughts and caused their listeners to fantasize Lincoln's heroic acts. What was sought was not historical accuracy, but emotional relevance.

Understanding the nature and theory of the eulogy helps to know why the perspective of the eulogist is different from the poet, novelist, painter, or sculptor. They all draw from the same basic materials and generally have the same objectives, but they have different relations with the consumers (readers, viewers, listeners). Much of their differences in perspective comes from what might be referred to as *distance*. The artist, whether literary or graphic, communicates with a universal group, abstract, absent, unaccounted for, and remote. The poet or sculptor creates largely without direct interference or confrontation with readers, viewers, or critics.

The immediate audience of the speaker is present, may sometimes set forth instructions and requests, and is capable of letting the speaker know at once what is acceptable and unacceptable. When perceptive, the speaker profits from this feedback and adapts the speech to the listeners and to the ritual, customs, setting, pagentry, and even the hysteria of the moment. The speech, therefore, often becomes a reflection of public sentiments and tastes of a moment.

The speeches discussed here are not intended to be a true representative sample of the thousands of speeches devoted to Lincoln. Only three are clearly sermons, and more than half were delivered at dedicatory occasions. The speeches of George Bancroft, Shelby Cullom, Jonathan Dolliver, Booker T. Washington, and Mario Cuomo show an intermingling of deliberative and epideictic elements, for these speakers introduce pleas to promote their partisan causes, thus detracting from pure praise of Lincoln.

Short speeches were chosen so that as many speeches as possible could be included while at the same time keeping the volume within a reasonable length. Therefore some famous ceremonial speeches by Walt Whitman, George Bancroft, and Henry Watterson were excluded.[19] The speeches included are complete, though some may have been edited for publication. When a title was not available, I supplied one.

Speeches were chosen according to seven criteria:
1. Created by an important personality recognized as eloquent
2. Delivered on a memorable occasion (commemoration, dedication, or celebration)
3. Honored Lincoln and his work
4. Showed thoughtful conception, planning, composition, and polishing
5. Recognized by contemporaries as a significant statement about Lincoln
6. Encompassed within a form and length suitable for a book of limited scope
7. Demonstrated rhetorical originality.

Each speech is presented in the context in which it was delivered because an epideictic speech cannot stand alone. It is the result of the interaction of forces, involving time, place, prevailing customs, and the predisposition and expectations of the speaker and audience. The alert rhetorician, acting as a sensitive filter, draws substance from the context and creates a unified whole—a speech.

This book primarily focuses on the study of eulogies devoted to Abraham Lincoln, but it is much more. *In toto* it strives to comprehend the efforts to magnify the essence of a popular leader and to memorialize him for posterity through looking at the blend of artistry of marble and bronze and the orator's ephemeral rhetorical choices.

Those speeches delivered in the weeks following the assassination showed the marks of the fearful gloom that fell over the nation. The five speakers represented here in the first section could not escape the hysteria of the time. Perhaps Henry Ward Beecher best expressed their plight when he said, "For myself, I cannot yet command that quietness of spirit needed for a just and temperate delineation of a man whom goodness has made great. Leaving that . . . to some other occasion, I pass to some considerations aside from the martyr-President's character which may be fit for this hour's instruction" (40).

The time for speech preparation was brief. Before facing the citizens of Concord, Emerson had only four days for preparation. He perhaps faced less overt mourning than the other four: New Englanders, particularly the abolitionists, were less favorable toward Lincoln than many in other parts of the North. Prominent New England intellectuals, reformers, and poets had made some harsh judgments about Lincoln's conduct of the war and the freeing of the slaves.

The other four speakers could in no way avoid the emotionalism of the obsequies and the wearisome funeral journey westward. On the Sunday after Lincoln's death, Phillips Brooks had responded in his pulpit, but after further thought, he preached a revised, enlarged version a week later while the corpse lay in state at Independence Hall.[20]

On that same day Henry Ward Beecher, back from a long ocean voyage to and from Charleston, South Carolina, met his expectant congregation at his Plymouth Church in Brooklyn. When he said, "In one hour, under the blow of a single bereavement, joy lay without a pulse, without a gleam, or breath," he was describing his own bereavement as well as that of his listeners (39).

George Bancroft, a historian and diplomat who had won recognition for his eulogy of Andrew Jackson, became the official eulogist of the city of New York; his very selection was a part of the ostentation of the New Yorkers, or what Bancroft questionably called "unexampled emblems of deeply seated grief" (69). He gave what he referred to as "the duty of the hour," that is, a course of action, saying that the support of the new administration was a fitting memorial to the fallen president (70). Although Lincoln was honored, Bancroft was indirect and restrained.

In an atmosphere of hysteria Methodist bishop Matthew Simpson became what appeared to be the spokesman for the administration, particularly Secretary of War Edwin Stanton, who had appointed him; consequently, Simpson was caught up in the events of the hour that started in Washington and slowly moved westward with the funeral train and twelve public viewings of the corpse. At the first service in the East Room of the White House on April 19, 1865, he had offered a public prayer. When he faced the graveside service on May 4 at Oak Ridge Cemetery, Simpson carried a double burden, representing the Radical Republicans and honoring his dead friend; consequently what he said was most inclusive: a review of the public mourning; those who had died in the war; the character of Lincoln; the contributions of the army, navy, and Treasury Department; the Emancipation Proclamation; Lincoln's religious and family life; and a recommendation on how to punish the Confederates. Stanton must have been pleased, for Simpson gave a fitting close to the effort to make the assassination into a political weapon against the Democrats and the defiant South.

In these first speeches the disagreement over what Lincoln persona should persist was evident: the Western man versus the saintly president. Ralph Waldo Emerson and Phillips Brooks saw Lincoln as the result of frontier influences. His physical, mental, and moral characteristics were those of the West. Well acquainted with Illinois, Iowa, and Missouri, Emerson declared Lincoln "a plain man of the people," (30) a "native, aboriginal man" (31) who was not tainted by European learning, manners, and customs. The New England philosopher saw him as the incarnation of Western attitudes and virtues, or "the true history of the American people in his time" (33).

Following the same line, Phillips Brooks also commended the frontier influence. "All the conditions of his birth, his youth, his manhood . . . made him what he was. . . . His pioneer home in Indiana was a type of the pioneer land in which he lived. If ever there was a man who was a part of the time and country he lived in, this was he. . . . Abraham Lincoln was the type-man of the country. . . . This character . . . [is] of an American under the discipline of freedom" (52).

Underpinning this admiration of the West was the feeling that the true Americans were not New Englanders or Southerners, but Westerners who had developed deep feelings for freedom and democracy as they battled the hardships and challenges of the frontier. Likewise some argued that the lands in the West brought out virtues and strengths. These philosophers were critical of English and European education, literature, manners, and social systems. Brooks thought that slavery was "false and effete and old" (53). It represented the Old World, feudalism, and false pride of blood. The sympathy of the English aristocracy for the Confederacy had galled many Northerners and turned them westward for their model of an American.

Henry Ward Beecher and Matthew Simpson leaned toward apotheosizing Abraham Lincoln, seeing him heavenly sent and divinely guided. Beecher drew parallels between the death of "our faithful and sainted Lincoln" and Moses who saved Israel but was denied entrance into the promised land by God (38). Saying that the martyr "standest among the elect" (38), Beecher placed him "in the goodly company of Mount Zion" (38) where his "everlasting name in heaven, shall flourish in fragrance and beauty" (39). Bishop Simpson thought that "by the hand of God, he was especially singled out to guide our Government in these troublous times" and "that the hand of God may be traced in many of the events connected with his history" (79). Brooks also implied that Lincoln had divine blessing and direction. Near the end of his sermon, Brooks suggested that "God brought him up as he brought David up" (60). Calling him "The *Shepherd of the People,*" Brooks concluded that Lincoln spread before Americans "the love and fear of God" (60).

The eulogies delivered within the month following Lincoln's death set the pattern for later speeches. The themes found in these first eulogies continued to show up in later speeches; likewise they also found expression in poems, novels, plays, and statues.

The representatives and senators recognized that the gift of the historic Francis B. Carpenter painting, *The First Reading of the Emancipation Proclamation of President Lincoln,* was a generous and significant act that deserved a fitting ceremony, but one that required well-chosen words. The lapse of thirteen short years since Appomattox and the intervening Reconstruction was not long enough to erase the scars and ugly memories of the war. By 1878 the former Confederate states had returned to full status, the election of Hayes promised stability, and the U.S. House of Representatives was actually controlled by the Democrats. Now returning to Washington, Southern members of Congress came at the behest of constituencies dramatically affected by the Emancipation Proclamation. Many Southerners, though, were still unreconstructed. Some resented honoring the very act that symbolized their greatest defeat and humiliation. Some considered the great canvas little better than a propaganda device to help reelect Lincoln to a second term.[21] Well aware of these undercurrents, Elizabeth Thompson, the donor, had hoped that the presentation could be made into a dramatic demonstration of good will, a sign that reconciliation had been achieved.[22] Hence two speeches of acceptance—one from the North and the other from the South—were scheduled: the first from the eloquent and popular James Garfield, an ex-Union general and a Republican from Ohio, and the other from the highly revered former vice-president of the Confederacy, Alexander Stephens, a Democrat from Georgia.[23]

The two speakers showed their awareness that the sensitive issue, if not handled adroitly, could disrupt good feelings and the epideictic atmosphere. It is notable that Garfield referred to the "great and honest differences of opinion" about emancipation and the nearness to "the great events" that made it difficult "to understand its deep significance and to foresee its far-off consequences" (108). He wisely chose to amplify the character of Lincoln and what he stood for and not the act of signing the proclamation. Herein Garfield knew he was on safe ground because by this time Lincoln had been accepted as a symbol of reconciliation.

The invitation to ex-Confederate Stephens, an influencial and popular Southerner, was a master stroke in demonstrating that the acceptance of the painting had meaning beyond the painting itself and what it represented. Wisely declining to deliver the opening speech, Stephens was in a position to endorse what he approved of in Garfield's speech and to recall his friendship with Lincoln. Herein he showed his rhetorical skill of adjusting his ideas to people and people to his ideas, illustrating a definition of *rhetoric* formulated by Donald Bryant.[24] As a rhetorician, the Georgian wanted to provide his Southern listeners with a way to acknowledge the gift in good grace and honor Abraham Lincoln without endorsing what Southerners considered an infamous act. Stephens showed that he was a man of good will, a positive force toward reconciliation, but also a proud Southerner.

Appearing in a wheelchair, old and withered, Stephens in truth was himself a symbol of a broken but returning proud South. In his opening sentences, the diminutive Georgian endorsed what Garfield had said and declared his admiration for Lincoln. Stephens suggested that his purpose was "to bury, not to praise, to laud 'nor aught extenuate.' "[25] He did not make clear what he meant by this thesis sentence, but he set upon the task of rationalizing the Southern position and interpreting the Southern position on emancipation, slavery, and reconciliation. As a skillful rhetorician he provided Southerners with a way around Lincoln's signing of the Emancipation: Stephens suggested that Lincoln was primarily interested in saving the Union, now accepted by many Southerners as more commendable than freeing the slaves. Of course such was not the view of abolitionists and their Radical Republican supporters. Another part of his rationalization was his argument that the Southern states had voluntarily freed the slaves through the adoption of the Thirteenth Amendment, a painful act but one present Southern states' administrations would not deny. The implication was that what the former Confederate states had done as a legal act was more acceptable to them than an act of war that forced them to submit. Stephens also rationalized the institution of slavery, saying that it "was not an unmitigated evil," but an institution, the burden of which Southerners were glad to be freed from:

> Since the emancipation, since the former ruling race have been relieved of their direct heavy responsibility for the protection and welfare of their dependents, it has been common to speak of the colored race as 'the wards of the nation.' . . .
>
> Though it was the leading cause of the late terrible conflict of arms between the States, yet I think I may venture to affirm there is not one within the circle of my acquaintance, or in the whole southern country, who would now wish to see the old relation restored.[26]

Herein Stephens skillfully worked around the implications of the painting. Each speaker focused attention on Lincoln and not upon emancipation, upon reconciliation and not upon the past.

A speech about Lincoln or a memorial occasion supposedly to show respect for Abraham Lincoln on his birthday or at some other event did not necessarily mean that the primary motivation was to eulogize him. In many instances it only meant an opportunity to exploit the Lincoln image, to summon the faithful, to enlist the young, to recharge party sentiment, or to polish the Republican armor for battle. Thus important Lincoln dates or icons have been converted into crass persuasion at political extravaganzas. From the moment of Lincoln's death, Republican leadership started invoking his name to promote partisan purposes, to unite the party, to discredit the influence of the Democrats, and to silence disruptive factions. Republicans, regardless of their intraparty differences, held tightly to the Lincoln aura until the time of Franklin D. Roosevelt.[27]

No lesser Republican than Edwin Stanton, Lincoln's secretary of war, saw the value of "getting right" with Lincoln and set out to reap the full propaganda value from Lincoln's assassination, making it a powerful symbol with which to excoriate the Democrats, to ensure a harsh Reconstruction, and to make it difficult for Democratic office-seekers to win. When he arranged the long funeral journey with frequent stops for public viewing of the corpse, he knew that millions of Northerners would perceive his intent and become responsive to the "bloody shirt oratory" (holding Democrats responsible for Lincoln's death).[28] In the 1868 campaign for Ulysses S. Grant, Stanton moved a Pennsylvania audience by reading the Gettysburg Address and then concluded tearfully: "That is the voice of God speaking through the lips of Abraham Lincoln! . . . You hear the voice of Father Abraham here tonight. Did he die in vain? . . . Let us here, every one, with uplifted hands, declare before Almighty God that the precious gift of this great heritage, consecrated in the blood of our soldiers, shall never perish from the earth. Now—[and he uplifted his hands]—all hands to God. I swear it!"[29]

When the need arose many Republicans dramatized their personal association with or observations of the Illinois lawyer. Senator Joseph G. Cannon of Danville, most adept at name-dropping, gave little glimpses of his Lincoln connections, taking full advantage of the

Lincoln aura. On February 10, 1910, forty-five years after the assassination, he reminded a chamber of commerce dinner in Pittsburgh, Pennsylvania:

> One of the greatest achievements of Lincoln was that, through his partisanship, being a practical man, he led in the formation of the Republican party, that party which has been longer in power than any other in the history of the Republic. Its policies, which were Lincoln's policies, have dominated the Republic. . . .
>
> For more than a generation poets, orators, historians, artists, and architects have been trying to build enduring monuments to Lincoln, as men of less ability and pretension have been groping after means for expressing their appreciation in that way which touches all levels of humanity, a treasured memory of a plain man who was equal in wisdom, courage, and humanity to meet all the responsibilities placed upon him by his fellowmen; but to me the most fitting monument to Lincoln is the party he helped organize, and the achievements of the policies he helped develop for the lasting benefit of the whole country, East and West, North and South, white and black.[30]

Through the two terms of Ulysses S. Grant, the Radical Republicans maintained firm control over national policy and Reconstruction, but the election dispute between Hayes and Tilden in 1877, the nomination and election of moderate James A. Garfield over James G. Blaine in 1880, the civil service reform of Chester Arthur, the defeat of James G. Blaine in 1884, the election of Grover Cleveland—the first Democratic president since Buchanan in 1856—and the subsequent return of Democratic Southerners to the national scene were all signs that the GOP needed to energize the party with new appeals and programs. No longer were war memories or "bloody shirt" tactics effective in winning elections. Young Republican leadership, particularly in the Midwest, was flirting with populist reforms. One strategy to unite the GOP was the formation of Republican clubs, perhaps as many as 1,500 by 1888. The more prosperous groups established well-furnished club rooms, published attractive club magazines, maintained dining rooms, and carried on a full agenda of activities. Each year dinners on Lincoln's birthday became the climax of their programs. The Republican Club of the City of New York, prominent in the East, attracted the most famous speakers of the party. It preserved its

Lincoln speeches from 1887 through 1927 in two limited editions, privately published.[31]

More than celebrations to honor Lincoln, these annual occasions became great political rallies. A good example of the party antics was the fourth annual meeting in 1890 at which Shelby M. Cullom made a Lincoln speech. Three hundred attended the dinner at Delmonico's to honor the eighty-first anniversary of the birth of Abraham Lincoln. The enthusiastic banqueteers overflowed the main dining room into the annex. The walls were covered with the stars and stripes. Behind the speaker's chair hung a flag-draped, three-quarter portrait of Lincoln by William Marshall. The menu cards displayed pictures of Lincoln's birthplace cabin and the national capitol and also included a brief summary of Lincoln's career. At the long head table were seated twelve, including the club president Cephas Brainard, the five speakers, Chauncey M. Depew, John C. Fremont, and the committee members. The organization had widely scattered invitations to the governors of Rhode Island, Massachusetts, Vermont, and Connecticut and other Republican notables—Hannibal Hamlin, John G. Nicolay, John Hay, General William T. Sherman, former president Rutherford B. Hayes, and Theodore Roosevelt. "The enthusiasms of the assemblage" with "frequent vent" of the song "John Brown's Body" made it difficult for President Brainard to maintain decorum. The reporter for the New York *Tribune* said the club president "did not allow his hearers to forget that it was the Republican party which Lincoln adorned; that this was the Republican Club and that the present Republican Administration [Harrison] [was] going forward in patriotic and progressive lines." When Brainard mentioned the recent illness of James G. Blaine, a traditional favorite of the stalwarts, Chauncey M. Depew stood and shouted, "Gentlemen, three cheers for James G. Blaine," bringing the response, "three times three." Someone returned "three cheers" for "Our Chauncey." "Everybody was running wild" until the chair promised that Depew would speak after the five toasts (but Depew slipped out before they were finished).

The printed program included two quotations: the first from Shakespeare's Julius Caesar: "So mixed in him that nature might stand up and say to all the world. This was a man"; the second was one that Lincoln had written after his defeat by Douglas in 1858: "The fight must go on. The cause of civil liberty must not be surrendered at the end of one, or even one hundred defeats." In the first toast Cullom amplified these quotations much the way a preacher develops a text. The old Illinois warrior, Lincoln's personal friend, was cheered "loud and long," after each of his points. Following Cullom there were four other speakers: Representative Jonathan Dolliver from Iowa, Senator Cushman K. Davis of Minnesota, Senator Gideon C. Moody of South Dakota, and Rev. Samuel H. Virgen.[32]

The Cullom speech stirred enthusiasm because as one of the last living Lincoln acquaintances in Congress, Cullom himself had become a symbol. What Cullom lacked in rhetorical artistry and originality he achieved through his own *ethos* and his rapport with Lincoln. For the most part Cullom confined his remarks to praise of the sixteenth president's virtues and the inclusion of such loaded superlatives as "the savior of the Union and the liberator . . . of four millions of slaves"; and "no man . . . on the American continent [was] superior to Abraham Lincoln" (119). But when in his concluding sentences Cullom picked up on the dinner theme, "the fight must go on," he shifted to a deliberative purpose, highly appropriate for a Republican pep rally, but not artistic epideictic oratory; he waved the Republican banner and exploited the Lincoln legend, making his presentation little more than a stump speech.

A second Lincoln speech delivered at the nineteenth annual meeting of the Republican Club of the City of New York was that of Jonathan Dolliver, who returned in 1905 as a featured banquet speaker. On this second appearance the Iowa senator held to a ceremonial stance and worked into his presentation the deification of Lincoln, an emphasis that had become more popular after 1900. The Iowa senator suggested that Lincoln stood "apart because he bore the ark of the covenant" (132) and was a "mysterious personality, in the hands of the higher Powers" (126). Dolliver advanced Lincoln as a symbol for intersectional understanding, another appeal frequently heard after the Spanish-American War. However, like Cullom, Dolliver could not resist giving a deliberative appeal for a "square deal," the slogan for the Theodore Roosevelt administration.[33] Booker T. Washington also delivered a speech before the Republican Club of the City of New York in 1909. Although he gave passing praise to Lincoln, Washington pursued his usual emphasis upon black education, the same message of his frequent lectures throughout the North. The black

16

educator commended Lincoln for the Emancipation Proclamation and what it meant to blacks. He saw in Lincoln's action a broadening of his influence, a pushing "back [of] the boundaries of freedom everywhere," a sentiment expressed fifty years later by Martin Luther King, Jr, and also by Elihu Root, David Lloyd George, and Adlai Stevenson (154).

Memorializing Lincoln has been expressed through various media, including the efforts of sculptors and architects who have sought to capture in bronze and stone the spirit and meaning of Abraham Lincoln. But like those who have worked in other media, they too were perplexed over how to capture the essence of this simple man. No iconography of any other American, not even George Washington, has rivaled that of Lincoln, including statues, bas-relief panels, simple plaques, monuments, buildings, historical displays, and historical sites. Few memorials approach the spaciousness and magnificence of the Lincoln Memorial in Washington, D.C., or Mount Rushmore National Memorial. These as well as hundreds of others serve to extend the Lincoln mythos and continue to attract and indoctrinate visitors, especially young Americans. They have almost become altars, temples, and sacred places.[34]

These Lincoln remembrances were slow in coming. The deep feelings of the disciples were at first restrained by their attempts to mend the war wounds or by indecision about what was sublime enough to memorialize the man. It was quite evident that James Garfield hesitated to give full vent to his enthusiasm about Lincoln's achievements in his acceptance of the Carpenter painting in 1878 because he did not wish to offend Southern members of Congress. Furthermore, finding sufficient funds and qualified artists sometimes caused delays. An exception was, of course, Vinnie Ream's toga-draped Lincoln, sculpted in white stone, paid for by funds from Congress, and placed in the rotunda of the Capitol.[35] The early statues were largely paid for by private donations, often coming from children, veterans, business leaders, and patriotic groups. One of the most touching memorials was Thomas Ball's the *Emancipation Group* (the Freedmen's Monument), which was dedicated in Washington, D.C., April 14, 1876, eleven years after Lincoln's death.[36]

Prior to 1900, ten bronze and three stone Lincoln statues appeared.

In addition to two Ball figures, others were erected in San Francisco; Washington, D.C.; Brooklyn; New York City; Philadelphia; Springfield; Chicago; Rochester; New York; Edinburgh, Scotland; and Middlesex, New Jersey. The Saint-Gaudens standing figure in Lincoln Park, Chicago, has become the most revered of these and has had much to do with setting the image of Lincoln. Until at least 1911 most of the sculptors chose to present a bearded, formally dressed, standing presidential figure. Exceptions were the Randolph Rogers piece in Fairmont Park, Philadelphia, and Charles Niehaus's seated Lincoln in Muskegon, Michigan. Over forty years passed after Lincoln's death before Charles J. Mulligan dared present a rail-splitter Lincoln grasping an axe in Garfield Park in Chicago. The next rebel, George Grey Barnard, produced a statue of Lincoln as a young man for Lytle Park in Cincinnati, Ohio, in 1917. Most sculptors, paid by private subscription, were eager to please their sponsors, who wanted to remember a presidential Lincoln.[37]

The great Lincoln structures were also slow to be erected. Immediately after the funeral, the citizens of Springfield laid plans for a Lincoln mausoleum. Finally $250,000 was raised, $1,700 coming from Sunday school children and $28,000 from Union veterans, ground was broken in 1869, and the tomb was dedicated in October 1874, but it was twice rebuilt, being rededicated in 1901 and 1931.[38] At Hodgenville, Kentucky, the shabby little cabin, Lincoln's supposed birthplace, was covered by a building that resembled a Greek temple. The Lincoln Memorial in Washington, D.C., which did not appear until 1922, was discussed as early as 1867, but not until 1911 did President Taft sign the bill creating the commission to launch the project. Eleven years later Taft, then chief justice of the Supreme Court, made the speech of presentation.[39] Giving little more than an account of the planning and construction, Taft explained that before starting the project American architects and artists had to study architecture abroad and develop confidence in their abilities to create a temple worthy of Lincoln.

In 1920 a controversy over the Lincoln image reached a dramatic climax: Americans had an opportunity to vote on how they wanted Lincoln represented abroad. A committee, wishing to express a token of appreciation for one hundred years of friendship between the United States and Great Britain, decided to present a replica of the dignified Saint-Gaudens Lincoln statue to the British for Parliament Square. But before it could act the committee received a generous counterproposal to substitute a replica of Barnard's youthful Lincoln, recently installed in Lytle Park in Cincinnati. The concerned citizens faced the choice between a classic dignified presidential Lincoln "marked by grace and heroic manner" or "the Lincoln of the frontier, of the debate, and the circuit, the American type and symbol of democracy."[40] In an opinion poll the readers of the *Independent* expressed the overwhelming preference for the Saint-Gaudens by a vote of 9,820 to 1,207. The Philadelphia *Evening Telegraph* received 167,076 replies to its questionnaire: 98,112 favored the classic Lincoln to 2,016 for the frontier figure.[41] The published letters in the *Independent* suggested the intensity of the concern about the choice. A retired lieutenant colonel wrote: "Almost four years I was a Lincoln soldier. I shook hands with him in 1861, saw him at Antietam in 1862, saw him twice at Fredericksburg in 1863 and again in 1865, near Petersburg. Barnard may have the Lincoln soul in his younger manhood, but he has made a disgraceful botch of Lincoln the President, the kind of a Lincoln the world wants to hear about and remember."[42] Representing the other side, a second reader wrote:

> Our sculptor felt the spirit of democracy guiding the hand that made his Lincoln look like the same Lincoln who gave us the Gettysburg speech, like the same Lincoln of tender, loving, human sympathies and living soul, who looked out beyond the vanities of personal adornment. Barnard has gotten away from the sham fine tailored and well groomed Lincoln and given us back the homespun, cowhide-booted, democratic Lincoln; he has told us that Lincoln's wedges and maul were more potent at rail splitting than was the hammer of Thor at splitting the thunders of Jove.[43]

Elihu Root presented the Saint-Gaudens statue for Parliament Square; the Barnard statue was given to the city of Manchester.

Another facet of the memorializing of Abraham Lincoln, so evident in many eulogies, has been the enshrining of the man's words and eloquence, particularly in his Farewell Address, the Gettysburg Address, the Second Inaugural Address, the Emancipation Proclamation, the annual messages, and letters. His quotations that fill complete volumes are repeated in speeches, editorials, and cartoons.[44] They provide Americans with folk wisdom that expresses the ideals of the nation. In the United States Senate and House of Representatives it became a custom on February 12 to have a member read the Gettysburg Address or the Second Inaugural Address. Likewise a part of the ritual at Lincoln dinners was to have someone recite one of his speeches. In the National Military Park at Gettysburg is the Lincoln Speech Memorial, perhaps the only monument to an address in the country. Dedicated in 1912, this bronze and granite exedra has a bronze Lincoln bust by Henry Kirke Brown at the center and on each flank a portion of the address on plaques.[45] Of course, the Gettysburg Address and the Second Inaugural Address appear on the walls of the Lincoln Memorial in Washington. The Gettysburg Address is inscribed in full or in part on the bases of several statues, including the marble shaft back of the Lincoln figure by Daniel Chester French on the capitol grounds at Lincoln, Nebraska, and also on the base stand of the Alfonso Pelzer figure at the Idaho Soldiers' Home in Boise, Idaho.[46]

Portions of it have appeared on a postage stamp, postcards, murals, placards, and lithographs. It is included in full in school readers, public speaking books, anthologies, biographies, and histories. School children frequently memorize and recite it. The little address has been translated into at least twenty-nine foreign languages,[47] and five full-length books discuss its origins, composition, languages and delivery.[48] In his address of November 19, 1951, Adlai E. Stevenson spoke of the Gettysburg Address as "the whole pith and substance of Lincoln's political philosophy" (221). It seemed most fitting therefore to have William Jennings Bryan and William Borah, speakers of distinction who had both been reared in southern Illinois, commend Lincoln for his speaking and rhetoric. Experienced in facing the citizens, they saw Lincoln's greatness through his important speeches. Bryan said to his Illinois listeners, "His Gettysburg speech is not surpassed, if equalled, in beauty, simplicity, force, and appropriateness by any speech of the same length of any language. It is the world's model of eloquence, elegance, and condensation. He might safely rest his reputation as an orator on that speech alone" (143).

The individualistic Idaho senator viewed Lincoln as the essence of democracy, calling him one of the few "tribunes of the people" (170) who stimulated "the public conscience," (170) "aroused public sentiment . . . marshalled the righteousness of the nation . . . crystallized the best . . . in men . . . [and] directed it through the channels of government. . . . In the affairs of government . . . he stands apart, its voice, and conscience—a great apostolic figure" (171). Contributing to a mythical interpretation, Borah suggested that "sacred writers, had he lived in those days, would have placed him among their seers and prophets and invested him with hidden powers of the mystic world. Antiquity would have clothed such a being with the attributes of deity. He was one of the moral and intellectual giants of the earth" (174). Borah, who was a sensitive and artful speaker, probably recognized that he was using a hyperbole, but he wanted to affirm that the frontier lawyer personified the essence of democracy and self-government.

Other speakers represented here found inspiration in Lincoln's words and thoughts. Joseph H. Choate paid homage to the Cooper Institute Address, which he termed "a full outpouring of his love of justice and liberty . . . on that lofty issue of right and wrong" (148). Booker T. Washington and Adlai E. Stevenson were inspired to speak about the Emancipation Proclamation. Stevenson thought that the document "gave courage to the oppressed from the Thames to the Ganges. . . . It was an application of the basic tenets of the nation" (226).

The twenty-three speeches of this volume demonstrate how Lincoln's words have become a testament of the democratic ideas. The Gettysburg Address produced "a government of the people, by the people, and for the people." The Emancipation Proclamation has become "a *mighty* impulse throughout the globe" for freedom seekers (228). The Second Inaugural Address has popularized the noble sentiment, "with malice toward none, with charity for all."

NOTES

1. David Donald, *Lincoln Reconsidered,* 2d ed. (New York: Random, 1959), 144.

2. Roy P. Basler, *The Lincoln Legend* (Boston: Houghton Mifflin, 1935), 296.

3. Harold Holzer, Gabor S. Boritt, and Mark E. Neely, Jr., *The Lincoln Image: Abraham Lincoln and the Popular Print* (New York: Scribner's, 1984), 149.

4. Speech delivered before the municipal authorities of Boston, June 1,

1865. *Charles Sumner: His Complete Works,* 20 vols. (New York: Negro University Press, 1969), 13:237–95.

5. Wendell Phillips, *Speeches, Lectures and Letters,* 2d ser. (Boston: Lee and Shepard, 1894), 446–53.

6. David Donald, *Lincoln Reconsidered,* 144–46.

7. *Lincoln Lore* 1672 (June 1977). Roy P. Basler, *A Touchstone for Greatness* (Westport, Conn.: Greenwood, 1973), 247.

8. Brown University, Providence, R.I.; Lincoln Memorial University, Harrogate, Tenn.; Library of Congress, Washington, D.C.; Louis A. Warren Lincoln Library and Museum, Fort Wayne, Ind.; Illinois State Historical Library, Springfield; Huntington Library, San Marino, Calif.

9. *Lincoln Newsletter,* Lincoln College, 7 (Spring 1988): 7.

10. "The Lincoln Legals, A Documentary History of the Law Practice of Abraham Lincoln, 1836-1861," a project of the Illinois Historic Preservation Agency.

11. Gary R. Planck, "Lincoln Related Organizations 1987," *Lincoln Herald* 89 (Fall 1987): 123; Gary R. Planck "Lincoln Related Publications 1987," *Lincoln Herald* 89 (Winter 1987): 177.

12. Charles Hamilton and Lloyd Ostendorf, *Lincoln in Photographs: An Album of Every Known Pose* (Norman: University of Oklahoma Press, 1963); Frederick Meserve and Carl Sandburg, *The Photographs of Abraham Lincoln* (New York: Harcourt, 1944); James Mellon, ed., *The Face of Lincoln* (New York: Bonanza, 1979).

13. William W. Betts, Jr., ed., *Lincoln and the Poets* (Pittsburgh: University of Pittsburgh Press, 1965); Harold Holzer, Gabor S. Boritt, Mark E. Neely, Jr., *The Lincoln Image;* Harold Holzer, Gabor S. Boritt, Mark E. Neely, Jr., *Changing the Lincoln Image* (Fort Wayne: Louis A. Warren Lincoln Library and Museum, 1985). Rufus Rockwell Wilson, *Lincoln in Caricature* (New York: Horizon, 1953); William S. Walsh, ed., *Abraham Lincoln and London Punch* (New York: Moffat, Yard, 1909). For examples of pamphlets by Geoffrey C. Ward, see the boxed set entitled *Lincoln's Thought and the Present,* which contains *Lincoln and the Right to Rise: New Salem; Lincoln and His Family: The Lincoln Home; Lincoln and the Law: Lincoln's Law Office; Lincoln and the Union: The Great Western Depot; Lincoln, Slavery and Civil Rights: The Old State Capitol;* and *Lincoln and His Legend: The Lincoln Tomb* (Springfield, Ill.: Sangamon State University, 1978). Also see Thomas Dyba and George L. Painter, *Seventeen Years of Eighth and Jackson,* 2d ed. (Lisle, Ill.: Illinois Benedine College, 1985); Wayne C. Temple, *By Square and Compasses: The Building of Lincoln's Home and Its Saga* (Bloomington, Ill.: Ashlar, 1984).

14. F. Lauriston Bullard, *Lincoln in Marble and Bronze* (New Brunswick, N.J.: Rutgers University Press, 1952), 9–10; Basler, *Lincoln Legend,* 307.

15. Andrew Boyd, *Memorial Lincoln Bibliography, Being an Account of Books, Eulogies, Sermons, Portraits, Engravings, Medals, etc.* (Albany, N.Y.: Boyd, 1890); *Obsequies of Abraham Lincoln* (New York: Van Nostrand, 1865); *Addresses Delivered at the Lincoln Dinners of the Republican Club of the City of New York in Response to the*

Toast: Abraham Lincoln, 1887–1909 (New York: Republican Club of the City of New York, 1909); a second volume covered the years from 1910 to 1927; Nathan William MacChesney, *Abraham Lincoln, The Tribute of a Century 1809–1909* (Chicago: McClung, 1910); John G. Shea, *The Lincoln Memorial: A Record of the Life, Assassination, and Obsequies of the Martyred President* (New York: Bunce and Huntington, 1865).

16. Jay Monagham, "An Analysis of Lincoln's Funeral Sermons," *Indiana Magazine of History* 41 (Mar. 1945): 31–44; Charles J. Stewart, "Lincoln's Assassination and the Protestant Clergy of the North," *Journal of the Illinois State Historical Society* 54 (Autumn 1961): 268–93; Charles J. Stewart, "The Pulpit and the Assassination of Lincoln," *Quarterly Journal of Speech* 50 (Oct. 1964): 299–307; Charles J. Stewart, "The Pulpit in Time of Crisis: 1865 and 1963," *Speech Monographs* 33 (Nov. 1965): 427–34.

17. Roy P. Basler, *A Touchstone for Greatness*, 247.

18. W. Rhys Roberts, ed., *Aristotle* (New York: Random, 1954), 32–36.

19. Walt Whitman, "Death of Abraham Lincoln," in William E. Barton, ed., *Abraham Lincoln and Walt Whitman* (Indianapolis: Bobbs-Merrill, 1928), 216–29; George Bancroft, "Abraham Lincoln," in *Memorial Addresses before Two Houses of Congress* (Washington, D.C.: Government Printing Office, 1903), 9–76; Henry Watterson, "Abraham Lincoln," in *Modern Eloquence,* ed. Ashley Thorndike, 15 vols., (New York: Modern Eloquence Corp., 1923), 5: 376–403.

20. Bayard S. Clark, "A Sermon by Phillips Brooks on the Death of Abraham Lincoln," *Historical Magazine of the Protestant Episcopal Church* 49 (Mar. 1980): 37–49.

21. Mark E. Neely, Jr., *The Abraham Lincoln Encyclopedia* (New York: McGraw-Hill, 1982), 47–48.

22. Stephen Robert Guempel, *A Rhetorical Analysis of Selected Ceremonial Speeches of Alexander H. Stephens, 1875–1883* (M.A. thesis, Louisiana State University, 1975), 51–53, 127–36.

23. *Congressional Record,* 45th Cong., 2d sess., 1878. Vol. 7, pt. 1, pp. 968–71.

24. Donald C. Bryant, "Aspects of the Rhetorical Tradition: The Intellectual Foundation," *Quarterly Journal of Speech* 37 (Apr. 1950): 169–76.

25. *Congressional Record,* 968–69.

26. Ibid., 970–71.

27. *Lincoln Lore* 1648 (June 1975).

28. Victor Searcher, *Farewell to Lincoln* (Nashville: Abingdon, 1965), 59–64; Geoffrey C. Ward, *Lincoln and His Legend: The Lincoln Tomb* (Springfield: Sangamon State University), 4–31.

29. Frank Abial Flower, *Edwin McMasters Stanton: The Autocrat of Rebellion, Emancipation and Reconstruction* (New York: W. W. Wilson, 1905), 395.

30. *Congressional Record,* 61st Cong., 2d sess., 1878. Vol. 45, pt. 9, App., 15–19.

31. *North American Review* 376 (March 1888): 241–65; *Addresses Delivered at the Lincoln Dinners . . . 1887–1909; Addresses Delivered at the Lincoln Dinners of the*

National Republican Club in Response to the Toast: Abraham Lincoln, 1910–1927 (New York: National Republican Club, 1927).

32. *New York Times,* Feb. 13, 1980; New York *Tribune,* Feb. 13, 1890. For an account of the 1903 dinner, see Donald, *Lincoln Reconsidered,* 10–12.

33. *New York Times,* Feb. 14, 1905.

34. Donald, *Lincoln Reconsidered,* 144–46.

35. Maurine Whorton Redway and Dorothy Kendall Bracken, *Marks of Lincoln on Our Land* (New York: Hastings, 1957), 87–90.

36. Frederick Douglass, *Oration Delivered on the Occasion of the Unveiling of the Freedmen's Monument in Memory of Abraham Lincoln in Lincoln Park, Washington, D.C., April 14, 1876* (Washington, D.C.: Gibson Brothers, 1876). Deposited in the Illinois State Historical Library, Springfield, Ill.

37. Bullard, *Lincoln in Marble and Bronze,* 44–72; *Lincoln Lore* 1488 (Feb. 1962).

38. Mark E. Neely, Jr., *The Abraham Lincoln Encyclopedia,* 309–10; Redway and Bracken, *Marks of Lincoln,* 107–11.

39. *Ibid.,* 111–16.

40. Roy P. Basler, *The Lincoln Legend,* 285–90.

41. *Independent* 92 (Dec. 29, 1917): 591–601; Bullard, *Lincoln in Marble and Bronze,* 228–41.

42. J. A. Watrous, *Independent* 92 (Dec. 29, 1917): 600.

43. Kathleen Boyd, *Independent* 92 (Dec. 29, 1917): 591.

44. Archer H. Shaw, ed., *The Lincoln Encyclopedia: The Spoken Key and Written Word* (New York: Macmillan, 1950); Fred Kerner, ed., *A Treasury of Lincoln Quotations* (New York: Doubleday, 1965).

45. Redway and Bracken, *Marks of Lincoln,* 101–3.

46. Bullard, *Lincoln in Marble and Bronze,* 104.

47. Roy P. Basler, *Lincoln's Gettysburg Address in Translation* (Washington, D.C.: Library of Congress, 1972).

48. William E. Barton, *Lincoln at Gettysburg* (Indianapolis: Bobbs-Merrill, 1930); Henry Sweetser Burrage, *Gettysburg and Lincoln* (New York: Putnam's, 1906); Orton H. Carmichael, *Lincoln's Gettysburg Address* (New York: Abingdon, 1917); Henry Eyster Jacobs, *Lincoln's Gettysburg World Message* (Philadelphia: United Lutheran, 1919); Louis A. Warren, *Lincoln's Gettysburg Declaration* (Fort Wayne, Ind.: Lincoln National Life Foundation, 1964).

PART ONE

Funeral and Cortege

"Though three weeks have passed the nation has scarcely breathed easily yet. A mournful silence is abroad upon the land," lamented Bishop Matthew Simpson at the Lincoln interment in Springfield. Never had a public ceremony, so solemn and grim, equaled the anguish that resulted from the assassination. Outside the White House silent mourners extended for a quarter of a mile, waiting to pass by the coffin, and finally 25,000 viewed the body.[1] After six days of obsequies, the funeral train started its westward, winding journey.

ITINERARY AND MILEAGE

First day—Friday, April 21: Washington to Baltimore, 38 miles, Baltimore and Ohio R.R.; Baltimore to Harrisburg, 85 miles, Northern Central R.R.

Second day—Saturday, April 22: Harrisburg to Philadelphia, 106 miles, Pennsylvania R.R.

Third day—Sunday, April 23: At Independence Hall, Philadelphia.

Fourth day—Monday, April 24: Philadelphia to New York, 86 miles from Kensington Station via Philadelphia and Trenton R.R., Camden and Amboy R.R., New Jersey Transportation Co., and ferryboat across Hudson River from Jersey City to New York.

Fifth day—Tuesday, April 25: New York City to Albany, 141 miles, Hudson River R.R. from 30th St. Station to East Albany and by ferryboat across Hudson River to Albany.

Sixth day—Wednesday, April 26: Albany to Buffalo, 298 miles, New York Central R.R.

Seventh day—Thursday, April 27: Buffalo to Cleveland, 183 miles, Buffalo and State Line R.R., Erie and Northeast R.R. and Cleveland, Painesville, and Ashtabula R.R. to Euclid Ave. Station of Cleveland and Pittsburgh R.R.

Eighth day—Friday, April 28: Cleveland to Columbus, 135 miles, Cleveland, Columbus, and Cincinnati Rwy.

Ninth day—Saturday, April 29: Columbus to Indianapolis, 187

miles, Columbus and Indianapolis Rwy. and Indiana Central
R.R.
Tenth day—Sunday, April 30: Indianapolis to Chicago, 210 miles,
Indianapolis and Lafayette R.R., Louisville, New Albany and
Chicago R.R., Michigan Central R.R. and Illinois Central R.R.
Eleventh day—May 1: At Cook County Courthouse, Chicago.
Twelfth day—May 2 [and 3]: Chicago to Springfield, 184 miles, St.
Louis, Alton, and Chicago R.R.[2]

Along the 1,634-mile trip that retraced the route that had brought
Lincoln to Washington in 1861 (only Pittsburgh and Cincinnati were
bypassed and Chicago was added), citizens prostrated themselves,
showing the depth of their sadness. The slow, black-draped train
paused at principal cities to permit the public viewing of the open
casket at central places—the state houses at Harrisburg, Albany,
Columbus, and Indianapolis, the Exchange in Baltimore, Independence Hall in Philadelphia, city hall in New York City, St. James Hall
in Buffalo, a structure erected especially for the occasion in Cleveland,
and the Cook County Courthouse in Chicago. Long lines of sober
dignitaries, slow-moving military units, flag bearers, dirgeful marching
bands, and weeping young women dressed in white accompanied the
hearse drawn by a team of six to ten horses along the route filled with
spectators who crowded every available space on doorsteps, balconies,
windows, housetops, and trees. Black-draped buildings, newly con-
structed arches, tolling bells, gun volleys, and funeral hymns intensified
the outpouring of raw emotion. Newspapers were bordered in black.

At Independence Hall, Philadelphia, waiting lines of mourners
extended three miles. In New York City, day and night, an average of
eighty persons each minute for a total of 60,000 passed the bier.
According to the Chicago *Tribune,* 120,000 viewed the sad display at
the Cook County Courthouse, passing at the rate of 7,000 per hour.
Finally on May 3 and 4, 75,000 viewed the remains in Springfield.
Public outpouring drained the emotions of the stricken.[3] How appropriate were the words of Rev. P. D. Gurley, the president's former pastor,
at the final benediction:

> "Rest, noble martyr, rest in peace.
> Rest with the true and brave."[4]

1. William T. Coggeshall, *The Journey of Abraham Lincoln from Springfield to Washington, 1861 and from Washington to Springfield, 1865* (Columbus: Ohio State Journal, 1865), 110, 165; *The Assassination and History of the Conspiracy* (New York: Hobbs, Dorman, 1965).

2. Victor Searcher, *Farewell to Lincoln* (Nashville: Abingdon, 1965), 291, reprinted with permission. ©1965 Victor Searcher.

3. William T. Coggeshall, *The Journey of Abraham Lincoln,* 165, 185, 214, 250, 298; Mark E. Neely, Jr., *The Abraham Lincoln Encyclopedia* (New York: McGraw-Hill, 1982), 121–22.

4. *The Assassination and History of the Conspiracy,* 142.

A Plain Man of the People

UNITARIAN CHURCH
CONCORD, MASSACHUSETTS
APRIL 19, 1865

At the time Lincoln's body was passing westward, the citizens of Concord, Massachusetts, assembled at the Unitarian Church and sought solace from their sage, Ralph Waldo Emerson, who they hoped could interpret the meaning of the "ghastly blow." The assignment became a dramatic challenge to the philosopher who earlier, like many other antislavery intellectuals, had thought that President Lincoln had been slow and timid in declaring emancipation and prosecuting the war. But as the struggle moved along, Emerson began to understand the Westerner, whom he finally declared to be "a sincerely upright and intelligent man."[1] Organizing his eulogy around a narrative sequence, Emerson presented Lincoln in a Western mythological motif, portraying him as "a plain man of the people," "a middle-class president," and "thoroughly American" (not "spoiled by English insularity or French dissipation"). To Emerson, Lincoln was a prototype of the typical Western man: "a man without vices," who was affable, compassionate, cheerful, courageous, diligent, fair, firm, honest, modest, long-headed, good natured, good humored, and pleasant. Emerson saw in the Illinoisan "the true history of the American people in his time." Herein the philosopher had anticipated the thinking of Frederick Jackson Turner about the influence of the legendary frontier upon the American character. Emerson saw in Lincoln a frontier hero who personified the democratic virtues.[2] He sought to comfort anguish through an apocalyptic interpretation of Lincoln's death and suggested that "serene Providence" makes "its own instruments, creates the man for the time, trains him in poverty, inspires his genius, and arms him for his task." Emerson prefigured the future with the suggestion that the murdered president may "serve his country even more by his death than by his life."

28

A comparison of what Emerson said with what Beecher and Brooks preached reveals a marked difference in approaches. Emerson, less the preacher in the traditional sense, did not offer suggestions about future action: he left to his listeners thoughts about what programs Lincoln's memory inspired.

1. Ralph L. Rusk, *The Life of Ralph Waldo Emerson* (New York: Scribner's, 1949), 427.

2. David D. Anderson, "Emerson and Lincoln," *Lincoln Herald* 66 (Winter 1958): 123–28.

The speech is reprinted from Ralph Waldo Emerson, *Miscellanies* (Boston: Houghton Mifflin, 1904), 329.

We meet under the gloom of a calamity which darkens down over the minds of good men in all civil society, as the fearful tidings travel over sea, over land, from country to country, like the shadow of an uncalculated eclipse over the planet. Old as history is, and manifold as are its tragedies, I doubt if any death has caused so much pain to mankind as this has caused, or will cause, on its announcement; and this, not so much because nations are by modern arts brought so closely together, as because of the mysterious hopes and fears which, in the present day, are connected with the name and institutions of America.

In this country, on Saturday, every one was struck dumb, and saw at first only deep below deep, as he meditated on the ghastly blow. And perhaps, at this hour, when the coffin which contains the dust of the President sets forward on its long march through mourning states, on its way to his home in Illinois, we might well be silent, and suffer the awful voices of the time to thunder to us. Yes, but that first despair was brief: the man was not so to be mourned. He was the most active and hopeful of men; and his work had not perished: but acclamations of praise for the task he had accomplished burst out into a song of triumph, which even tears for his death cannot keep down.

The President stood before us as a man of the people. He was thoroughly American, had never crossed the sea, had never been spoiled by English insularity or French dissipation; a quite native, aboriginal man, as an acorn from the oak; no aping of foreigners, no frivolous accomplishments, Kentuckian born, working on a farm, a flatboatman, a captain in the Black Hawk War, a country lawyer, a representative in the rural legislature of Illinois;—on such modest foundations the broad structure of his fame was laid. How slowly, and yet by happily prepared steps, he came to his place. All of us remember—it is only a history of five or six years—the surprise and the disappointment of the country at his first nomination by the convention at Chicago. Mr. Seward, then in the culmination of his good fame, was the favorite of the Eastern States. And when the new and comparatively unknown name of Lincoln was announced (notwithstanding the report of the acclamations of that convention), we heard the result coldly and sadly. It seemed too rash, on a purely local reputation, to build so grave a trust in such anxious times; and men naturally talked of the chances in politics as incalculable. But it turned out not to be chance. The profound good opinion which the people of Illinois and of the West had conceived of him, and which they had imparted to their colleagues, that they also might justify themselves to their constituents at home, was not rash, though they did not begin to know the riches of his worth.

A plain man of the people, an extraordinary fortune attended him. He offered no shining qualities at the first encounter; he did not offend by superiority. He had a face and manner which disarmed suspicion, which inspired confidence, which confirmed good will. He was a man without vices. He had a strong sense of duty, which it was very easy for him to obey. Then, he had what farmers call a long head; was excellent in working out the sum for himself; in arguing his case and convincing you fairly and firmly. Then, it turned out that he was a great worker; had prodigious faculty of performance; worked easily. A good worker is so rare; everybody has some disabling quality. In a host of young men that start together and promise so many brilliant leaders for the next age, each fails on trial; one by bad health, one by conceit, or by love of pleasure, or lethargy, or an ugly temper,—each has some disqualifying fault that throws him out of the career. But this man was sound to the core, cheerful, persistent, all right for labor, and liked nothing so well.

Then, he had a vast good nature, which made him tolerant and accessible to all; fair-minded, leaning to the claim of the petitioner; affable, and not sensible to the affliction which the innumerable visits paid to him when President would have brought to any one else. And how this good nature became a noble humanity, in many a tragic case which the events of the war brought to him, every one will remember; and with what increasing tenderness he dealt when a whole race was thrown on his compassion. The poor negro said of him, on an impressive occasion, "Massa Linkum am eberywhere."

Then his broad good humor, running easily into jocular talk, in which he delighted and in which he excelled, was a rich gift to this wise man. It enabled him to keep his secret; to meet every kind of man and every rank in society; to take off the edge of the severest decisions; to mask his own purpose and sound his companion; and to catch with true instinct the temper of every company he addressed. And, more than all, it is to a man of severe labor, in anxious and exhausting crises, the natural restorative, good as sleep, and is the protection of the overdriven brain against rancor and insanity.

He is the author of a multitude of good sayings, so disguised as pleasantries that it is certain they had no reputation at first but as jests; and only later, by the very acceptance and adoption they find in the mouths of millions, turn out to be the wisdom of the hour. I am sure if this man had ruled in a period of less facility of printing, he would have become mythological in a very few years, like Aesop or Pilpay, or one of the Seven Wise Masters, by his fables and proverbs. But the weight and penetration of many passages in his letters, messages and speeches, hidden now by the very closeness of their application to the moment, are destined hereafter to wide fame. What pregnant definitions; what unerring common sense; what foresight; and, on great occasion, what lofty, and more than national, what humane tone! His brief speech at Gettysburg will not easily be surpassed by words on any recorded occasion. This, and one other American speech, that of John Brown to the court that tried him, and a part of Kossuth's speech at Birmingham, can only be compared with each other, and with no fourth.

His occupying the chair of state was a triumph of the good sense of mankind, and of the public conscience. This middle-class country had got a middle-class president, at last. Yes, in manners and sympathies, but not in powers, for his powers were superior. This man grew according to the need. His mind mastered the problem of the day; and as the problem grew, so did his comprehension of it. Rarely was man so fitted to the event. In the midst of fears and jealousies, in the Babel of counsels and parties, this man wrought incessantly with all his might and all his honesty, laboring to find what the people wanted, and how to obtain that. It cannot be said there is any exaggeration of his worth. If ever a man was fairly tested, he was. There was no lack of resistance, nor of slander, nor of ridicule. The times have allowed no state secrets; the nation has been in such ferment, such multitudes had to be trusted, that no secret could be kept. Every door was ajar, and we know all that befell.

Then, what an occasion was the whirlwind of the war. Here was place for no holiday magistrate, no fair-weather sailor; the new pilot was hurried to the helm in a tornado. In four years,—four years of battle-days,—his endurance, his fertility of resources, his magnanimity, were sorely tried and never found wanting. There, by his courage, his justice, his even temper, his fertile counsel, his humanity, he stood a heroic figure in the centre of a heroic epoch. He is the true history of the American people in his time. Step by step he walked before them; slow with their slowness, quickening his march by theirs, the true representative of this continent; an entirely public man; father of his country, the pulse of twenty millions throbbing in his heart, the thought of their minds articulated by his tongue.

Adam Smith remarks that the axe, which in [Arnold] Houbraken's portraits of British kings and worthies is engraved under those who have suffered at the block, adds a certain lofty charm to the picture. And who does not see, even in this tragedy so recent, how fast the terror and ruin of the massacre are already burning into glory around the victim? Far happier this fate than to have lived to be wished away; to have watched the decay of his own faculties; to have seen—perhaps even he—the proverbial ingratitude of statesmen; to have seen mean men preferred. Had he not lived long enough to keep the greatest promise that ever man made to his fellow men,—the practical abolition of slavery? He had seen Tennessee, Missouri and Maryland emancipate their slaves. He had seen Savannah, Charleston and Richmond surrendered; had seen the main army of the rebellion lay down its arms. He had conquered the public opinion of Canada, England and France. Only Washington can compare with him in fortune.

And what if it should turn out, in the unfolding of the web, that he had reached the term; that this heroic deliverer could no longer serve us; that the rebellion had touched its natural conclusion, and what remained to be done required new and uncommitted hands,—a new spirit born out of the ashes of the war; and that Heaven, wishing to show the world a completed benefactor, shall make him serve his country even more by his death than by his life? Nations, like kings, are not good by facility and complaisance. "The kindness of kings consists in justice and strength." Easy good nature has been the dangerous foible of the Republic, and it was necessary that its enemies should outrage it, and drive us to unwonted firmness, to secure the salvation of this country in the next ages.

The ancients believed in a serene and beautiful Genius which ruled in the affairs of nations; which, with a slow but stern justice, carried forward the fortunes of certain chosen houses, weeding out single offenders or offending families, and securing at last the firm prosperity of the favorites of Heaven. It was too narrow a view of the Eternal Nemesis. There is a serene Providence which rules the fate of nations, which makes little account of time, little of one generation or race, makes no account of disasters, conquers alike by what is called defeat or by what is called victory, thrusts aside enemy and obstruction, crushes everything immoral as inhuman, and obtains the ultimate triumph of the best race by the sacrifice of everything which resists the moral laws of the world. It makes its own instruments, creates the man for the time, trains him in poverty, inspires his genius, and arms him for his task. It has given every race its own talent, and ordains that only that race which combines perfectly with the virtues of all shall endure.

A New Impulse of Patriotism for His Sake

The assassination of Abraham Lincoln stirred anticipation among the members of the Plymouth Church in Brooklyn, New York. They knew that their eloquent pastor, Henry Ward Beecher, could be counted upon to soothe their anguish. At the service on April 23 they crowded the hall, filling the pews and the added chairs in the aisles and on the platform. Scores unable to gain entrance listened outside.

The occasion was a sad one for the preacher who had felt close to Lincoln. When the Illinois politician came to New York for his Cooper Institute speech in February of 1860, he attended a Beecher service. On several occasions Beecher had strengthened the resolve of Lincoln to see the war to its end. The minister had long been a Republican supporter, and had campaigned for the party in 1860 and 1864. Beecher had just addressed the flag-raising ceremony at Fort Sumter, South Carolina, on April 14, in what the *New York Times* termed, "his matchless, eloquent, and effective manner."[1] While returning to New York by steamer, Beecher first heard the startling news of Lincoln's death. When he disembarked he hurried to prepare a last-minute manuscript for his Easter sermon.

The pulpit orator spoke from Deut. 34:1–5, which relates how, after leading Moses to the top of Mount Pisgah to view the promised land of Canaan before his death, the Lord said: "I have let you see it with your eyes but you shall not go over there." The analogy between Moses and Lincoln seemed appropriate, and Beecher emphasized the parallel: "Again a great leader of the people has passed through toil, sorrow, battle, and war, and come near to the promised land of peace, into which he might not pass over."

The presentation was apocalyptic. In describing the assassination and its cause, Beecher vividly presented the crisis phase by his denunciation of slavery as harsh, devastating, and the cause of Lincoln's death in the hour of victory. Herein Beecher proclaimed the new day: "This Nation . . . stands, four-square, more solid, to-day, than any pyramid in Egypt. . . . Men hate slavery and love liberty with stronger hate and love to-day than ever before." The eulogy, that now seems long and wearisome in detail, assured the sad listeners that Lincoln had not died in vain. Amplifying the Lincoln influence, Beecher predicted, "Men will receive a new impulse of patriotism for his sake, and will guard with zeal the whole country which he loved so well."

1. *New York Times,* April 14, 1865, as quoted in Halford R. Ryan, "Henry Ward Beecher," in *American Orators before 1900,* ed. Bernard K. Duffy and Halford R. Ryan (Westport, Conn.: Greenwood, 1987), 38–39.

The speech is reprinted from Newell Dwight Hillis, ed., *Lectures and Orations by Henry Ward Beecher* (New York: Fleming H. Revell, 1913), 263–83.

There is no historic figure more noble than that of the Jewish lawgiver. After so many thousand years the figure of Moses is not diminished, but stands up against the background of early days distinct and individual as if he had lived but yesterday. There is scarcely another event in history more touching than his death. He had borne the great burdens of state for forty years, shaped the Jews to a nation, filled out their civil and religious polity, administered their laws, guided their steps, or dealt with them in all their journeyings in the wilderness; had mourned in their punishment, kept step with their march, and led them in wars until the end of their labours drew nigh. The last stage was reached. Jordan, only, lay between them and the "promised land."

The Promised Land! O what yearnings had heaved his breast for that divinely foreshadowed place! He had dreamed of it by night, and mused by day; it was holy and endeared as God's favoured spot. It was to be the cradle of an illustrious history. All his long, laborious, and now weary life, he had aimed at this as the consummation of every desire, the reward of every toil and pain. Then came the word of the Lord to him: "Thou mayest not go over. Get thee up into the mountain; look upon it; and die!"

From that silent summit the hoary leader gazed to the north, to the south, to the west with hungry eyes. The dim outlines rose up. The hazy recesses spoke of quiet valleys between hills. With eager longing, with sad resignation, he looked upon the promised land. It was now to him a forbidden land. This was but a moment's anguish; he forgot all his personal wants, and drank in the vision of his people's home. His work was done. There lay God's promise, fulfilled. There was the seat of coming Jerusalem; there the city of Judah's King; the sphere of judges and prophets; the Mount of sorrow and salvation; the nest whence were to fly blessings innumerable to all mankind. Joy chased sadness from every feature, and the prophet laid him down, and died.

Again a great leader of the people has passed through toil, sorrow, battle, and war, and come near to the promised land of peace, into which he might not pass over. Who shall recount our martyr's sufferings for this people! Since the November of 1860, his horizon has been black with storms. By day and by night he trod a way of danger and darkness. On his shoulders rested a government dearer to him than his own life. At its integrity millions of men at home were striking; upon it foreign eyes lowered. It stood like a lone island in a sea full of storms; and every tide and wave seemed eager to devour it. Upon thousands of hearts great sorrows and anxieties have rested, but not on one, such, and in such measure, as upon that simple, truthful, noble soul, our faithful and sainted Lincoln. Never rising to the enthusiasm of more impassioned natures in hours of hope, and never sinking with the mercurial in hours of defeat to the depths of despondency, he held on with unmovable patience and fortitude, putting caution against hope that it might not be premature, and hope against caution that it might not yield to dread and danger. He wrestled ceaselessly, through four black and dreadful purgatorial years, wherein God was cleansing the sins of His people as by fire.

At last the watcher beheld the gray dawn for the country. The mountains began to give forth their forms from out of the darkness; and the East came rushing towards us with arms full of joy for all our sorrows. Then it was for him to be glad exceedingly, that had sorrowed immeasurably. Peace could bring to no other heart such joy, such rest, such honour, such trust, such gratitude. But he looked upon it as Moses looked upon the promised land.

Then the wail of a nation proclaimed that he had gone from among us.

Not thine the sorrow, but ours, sainted soul! Thou hast indeed entered into the promised land, while we are yet on the march. To us remain the rocking of the deep, the storm upon the land, days of duty and nights of watching; but thou art sphered high above all darkness and fear, beyond all sorrow and weariness. Rest, O weary heart! Rejoice exceedingly, thou that hast enough suffered! Thou hast beheld Him who invisibly led thee in this great wilderness. Thou standest among the elect. Around thee are the royal men that have ennobled human life in every age. Kingly art thou, with glory on thy brow as a diadem. And joy is upon thee forevermore. Over all this land, over all the little cloud of years that now from thine infinite horizon moves back as a speck, thou art lifted up as high as a star is above the clouds, that hide us but never reach it. In the goodly company of Mount Zion thou shalt find that rest which thou hast sorrowing sought here in vain; and thy name, an everlasting name in heaven, shall flourish in fragrance and beauty as long as men shall last upon the earth, or hearts remain, to revere truth, fidelity, and goodness.

Never did two such orbs of experience meet in one hemisphere, as the joy and the sorrow of the same week in this land. The joy of final victory was as sudden as if no man had expected it, and as entrancing as if it had fallen a sphere from heaven. It rose up over sobriety, and swept business from its moorings, and ran down through the land in irresistible course. Men embraced each other in brotherhood that were strangers in the flesh. They sang, or prayed, or, deeper yet, many could only think thanksgiving and weep gladness. That peace was sure; that our government was firmer than ever; that the land was cleansed of plague; that the ages were opening to our footsteps, and we were to begin a march of blessings; that blood was staunched, and scowling enmities were sinking like storms beneath the horizon; that the dear fatherland, nothing lost, much gained, was to rise up in unexampled honour among the nations of the earth,—these thoughts, and that undistinguishable throng of fancies, and hopes, and desires, and yearnings, that filled the soul with tremblings like the heated air of midsummer days,—all these kindled up such a surge of joy as no words may describe.

In one hour, under the blow of a single bereavement, joy lay without a pulse, without a gleam, or breath. A sorrow came that swept through the land as huge storms sweep through the forest and field, rolling thunder along the sky, dishevelling the flowers, daunting every singer in thicket or forest, and pouring blackness and darkness across the land and upon the mountains. Did ever so many hearts, in so brief a time, touch two such boundless feelings? It was the uttermost of joy; it was the uttermost of sorrow;—noon and midnight without a space between!

The blow brought not a sharp pang. It was so terrible that at first it stunned sensibility. Citizens were like men awakened at midnight by an earthquake, and bewildered to find everything that they were accustomed to trust wavering and falling. The very earth was no longer solid. The first feeling was the least. Men waited to get straight to feel. They wandered in the streets as if groping after some impending dread, or undeveloped sorrow, or some one to tell them what ailed them. They met each other as if each would ask the other, "Am I awake, or do I dream?" There was a piteous helplessness. Strong men bowed down and wept. Other and common griefs belonged to some one in chief; this belonged to all. It was each and every man's. Every virtuous household in the land felt as if its first-born were gone. Men were bereaved, and walked for days as if a corpse lay unburied in their dwellings. There was nothing else to think of. They could speak of nothing but that; and yet, of that they could speak only falteringly. All business was laid aside. Pleasure forgot to smile. The great city for nearly a week ceased to roar. The huge Leviathan lay down and was still. Even avarice stood still, and greed was strangely moved to generous sympathy and universal sorrow. Rear to his name monuments, found charitable institutions, and write his name above their lintels; but no monument will ever equal the universal, spontaneous, and sublime sorrow that in a moment swept down lines and parties, and covered up animosities, and in an hour brought a divided people into unity of grief and indivisible fellowship of anguish.

For myself, I cannot yet command that quietness of spirit needed for a just and temperate delineation of a man whom goodness has made great. Leaving that, if it please God, to some other occasion, I pass to some considerations aside from the martyr-President's character which may be fit for this hour's instruction.

And first, let us not mourn that his departure was so sudden, nor fill our imagination with horror at its method. Men, long eluding and evading sorrow, when at last they are overtaken by it seem enchanted and seek to make their sorrow sorrowful to the very uttermost, and to bring out every drop of suffering which they possibly can. This is not Christian, though it may be natural. When good men pray for deliverance from sudden death, it is only that they may not be plunged without preparation, all disrobed, into the presence of their Judge. When one is ready to depart suddenness of death is a blessing. It is a painful sight to see a tree overthrown by a tornado, wrenched from its foundations, and broken down like a weed; but it is yet more painful to see a vast and venerable tree lingering with vain strife against decay, which age and infirmity have marked for destruction. The process by which strength wastes, and the mind is obscured, and the tabernacle is taken down, is humiliating and painful; and it is good and grand when a man departs to his rest from out of the midst of duty, full-armed and strong, with pulse beating time. For such a one to go suddenly, if he be prepared to go, is but to terminate a most noble life in its most noble manner. Mark the words of the Master:

"Let your loins be girded about, and your lights burning; and ye yourselves like unto men that wait for their lord, when he will return from the wedding; that when he cometh and knocketh, they may open unto him immediately. Blessed are those servants whom the Lord when He cometh shall find watching" [Luke 12:37].

Not they that go in a stupor, but they that go with all their powers about them, and wide-awake, to meet their Master, as to a wedding, are blessed. He died watching. He died with his armour on. In the midst of hours of labour, in the very heart of patriotic consultations, just returned from camps and counsels, he was stricken down. No fever dried his blood. No slow waste consumed him. All at once, in full strength and manhood, with his girdle tight about him, he departed; and walks with God.

Nor was the manner of his death more shocking, if we divest it of the malignity of the motives which caused it. The mere instrument itself is not one that we should shrink from contemplating. Have not thousands of soldiers fallen on the field of battle by the bullets of the enemy? Is being killed in battle counted to be a dreadful mode of dying? It was as if he had died in battle. Do not all soldiers that must fall ask to depart in the hour of battle and of victory? He went in the hour of victory.

There has not been a poor drummer-boy in all this war that has fallen for whom the great heart of Lincoln would not have bled; there has not been one private soldier, without note or name, slain among thousands and hid in the pit among hundreds, without even the memorial of a separate burial, for whom the President would not have wept. He was a man from the common people who never forgot his kind. And now that he who might not bear the march, and the toil, and the battle with these humble citizens has been called to die by the bullet, as they were, do you not feel that there was a peculiar fitness to his nature and life that he should in death be joined with them in a final common experience to whom he had been joined in all his sympathies?

For myself, when any event is susceptible of a higher and nobler garnishing, I know not what that disposition is that should seek to drag it down to the depths of gloom, and write it all over with the

41

scrawls of horror or fear. I let the light of nobler thoughts fall upon his departure, and bless God that there is some argument of consolation in the matter and manner of his going, as there was in the matter and manner of his staying.

Then, again, this blow was but the expiring rebellion. As a miniature gives all the form and features of its subject, so, epitomized in this foul act, we find the whole nature and disposition of slavery. It begins in a wanton destruction of all human rights, and in a desecration of all the sanctities of heart and home; and it is the universal enemy of mankind, and of God, who made man. It can be maintained only at the sacrifice of every right moral feeling in its abettors and upholders. I deride him who points me to any one bred amid slavery, believing in it, and willingly practicing it, and tells me that he is a man. I shall find saints in perdition sooner than I shall find true manhood under the influences of so accursed a system as this. It is a two-edged sword, cutting both ways, violently destroying manhood in the oppressed, and insidiously destroying manhood in the oppressor. The problem is solved, the demonstration is completed in our land. Slavery wastes its victims, and it destroys the masters. It kills public morality, and the possibility of it. It corrupts manhood in its very centre and elements. Communities in which it exists are not to be trusted. They are rotten. Nor can you find timber grown in this accursed soil of iniquity that is fit to build our Ship of State, or lay the foundation of our households. The patriotism that grows up under this blight, when put to proof, is selfish and brittle; and he that leans upon it shall be pierced. The honour that grows up in the midst of slavery is not honour, but a bastard quality that usurps the place of its better, only to disgrace the name. And, as long as there is conscience, or reason, or Christianity, the honour that slavery begets will be a byword and a hissing. The whole moral nature of men reared to familiarity and connivance with slavery is death-smitten. The needless rebellion; the treachery of its leaders to oaths and solemn trusts; their violation of the commonest principles of fidelity, sitting in senates, in councils, in places of public confidence only to betray and to destroy; the long, general, and unparallelled cruelty to prisoners, without provocation, and utterly without excuse; the unreasoning malignity and fierceness,—these all mark the symptoms of that disease of slavery, which is a deadly poison to soul and body.

I do not say that there are not single natures, here and there, scattered through the vast wilderness which is covered with this poisonous vine, who escaped the poison. There are; but they are not to be found among the men that believe in it, and that have been moulded by it. They are the exceptions. Slavery is itself barbarity. That nation which cherishes it is barbarous; and no outside tinsel or glitter can redeem it from the charge of barbarism. And it was fit that its expiring blow should be such as to take away from men the last forbearance, the last pity, and fire the soul with an invincible determination that the breeding-ground of such mischiefs and monsters shall be utterly and forever destroyed.

We needed not that he should put on paper that he believed in slavery, who, with treason, with murder, with cruelty infernal, hovered around that majestic man to destroy his life. He was himself but the long sting with which slavery struck at liberty; and he carried the poison that belonged to slavery. As long as this Nation lasts, it will never be forgotten that we have had one martyred President—never! Never, while time lasts, while heaven lasts, while hell rocks and groans, will it be forgotten that slavery, by its minions, slew him, and in slaying him made manifest its whole nature and tendency.

But another thing for us to remember is that this blow was aimed at the life of the Government and of the Nation. Lincoln was slain; America was meant. The man was cast down; the Government was smitten at. It was the President who was killed. It was national life, breathing freedom and meaning beneficence, that was sought. He, the man of Illinois, the private man, divested of robes and the insignia of authority, representing nothing but his personal self, might have been hated; but that would not have called forth the murderer's blow. It was because he stood in the place of Government, representing government and a government that represented right and liberty, that he was singled out.

This, then, is a crime against universal government. It is not a blow at the foundations of our Government, more than at the foundations of the English government, of the French government, of every compacted and well-organized government. It was a crime against mankind. The whole world will repudiate and stigmatize it as a deed without a shade of redeeming light. For this was not the oppressed, goaded to extremity, turning on his oppressor. Not even the shadow of a cloud of wrong has rested on the South, and they know it right well.

In a council held in the city of Charleston, just preceding the attack on Fort Sumter, two commissioners were appointed to go to Washington; one on the part of the army from Fort Sumter, and one on the part of the Confederates. The lieutenant that was designated to go for us said it seemed to him that it would be of little use for him to go, as his opinion was immovably fixed in favour of maintaining the government in whose service he was employed. Then Governor Pickens took him aside, detaining for an hour and a half the railroad train that was to convey them on their errand. He opened to him the whole plan and secrets of the Southern conspiracy, and said to him, distinctly and repeatedly (for it was needful, he said, to lay aside disguises), that the South had never been wronged, and that all their pretenses of grievance in the matter of tariffs, or anything else, were invalid. "But," said he, "we must carry the people with us; and we allege these things, as all statesmen do many things they do not believe, because they are the only instruments by which the people can be managed." He then and there declared that it had simply come to this: that the two sections of country were so antagonistic in ideas and policies that they could not live together; that it was foreordained that, on account of differences in ideas and policies, Northern and Southern men must keep apart. This is testimony which was given by one of the leaders in the Rebellion, and which will probably, ere long, be given under hand and seal to the public. So the South has never had wrongs visited upon it except by that which was inherent in it.

This was not, then, the avenging hand of one goaded by tyranny. It was not a despot turned on by his victim. It was the venomous hatred of liberty wielded by an avowed advocate of slavery. And, though there may have been cases of murder in which there were shades of palliation, yet this murder was without provocation, without temptation, without reason, sprung from the fury of a heart cankered to all that was just and good, and corrupted by all that was wicked and foul.

The blow, however, has signally failed. The cause is not stricken; it is strengthened. This Nation has dissolved—but in tears only. It stands, four-square, more solid, to-day, than any pyramid in Egypt. This people are neither wasted, nor daunted, nor disordered. Men hate slavery and love liberty with stronger hate and love to-day than ever before. The Government is not weakened, it is made stronger. How naturally and easily were the ranks closed! Another stepped forward, in the hour that the one fell, to take his place and his mantle; and I utter my trust that he will be found a man true to every instinct of liberty; true to the whole trust that is reposed in him; vigilant of the Constitution; careful of the laws; wise for liberty in that he himself, through his life, has known what it was to suffer from the stings of slavery, and to prize liberty from bitter personal experiences.

Where could the head of government in any monarchy be smitten down by the hand of an assassin, and the funds not quiver nor fall one-half of one per cent.? After a long period of national disturbance, after four years of drastic war, after tremendous drafts on the resources of the country, in the height and top of our burdens, the heart of this people is such that now, when the head of government is stricken down, the public funds do not waver, but stand as the granite ribs in our mountains. Republican institutions have been vindicated in this experience as they never were before; and the whole history of the last four years, rounded up by this cruel stroke, seems now in the providence of God to have been clothed with an illustration, with a sympathy, with an aptness, and with a significance, such as we never could have expected or imagined. God, I think, has said, by the voice of this event, to all nations of the earth, "Republican liberty, based upon true Christianity, is firm as the foundation of the globe."

Even he who now sleeps has, by this event, been clothed with new influence. Dead, he speaks to men who now willingly hear what before they refused to listen to. Now, his simple and weighty words will be gathered like those of Washington, and your children and your children's children shall be taught to ponder the simplicity and deep wisdom of utterances which, in their time, passed, in the party heat, as idle words. Men will receive a new impulse of patriotism for his sake, and will guard with zeal the whole country which he loved so well; I swear you, on the altar of his memory, to be more faithful to the country for which he has perished. Men will, as they follow his hearse, swear a new hatred to that slavery against which he warred, and which in vanquishing him has made him a martyr and a conqueror; I swear you, by the memory of this martyr, to hate slavery with an unappeasable hatred. Men will admire and imitate his unmoved firmness, his inflexible conscience for the right, and yet his gentleness, as tender as a woman's, his moderation of spirit, which not all the heat of party could inflame, nor all the jars and disturbances of this country shake out of its place; I swear you to an emulation of his justice, his moderation and his mercy.

You I can comfort; but how can I speak to that twilight million to whom his name was as the name of an angel of God? There will be wailing in places which no ministers shall be able to reach. When, in hovel and in cot, in wood and in wilderness, in the field throughout the South, the dusky children, who looked upon him as that Moses whom God sent before them to lead them out of the land of bondage, learn that he has fallen, who shall comfort them? Oh, Thou Shepherd of Israel, that didst comfort Thy people of old, to Thy care we commit the helpless, the long-wronged, and grieved!

And now the martyr is moving in triumphal march, mightier than when alive. The Nation rises up at every stage of his coming. Cities and States are his pallbearers, and the cannon beats the hours with solemn progression. Dead—dead—dead—he yet speaketh! Is Washington dead? Is Hampden dead? Is David dead? Is any man dead that ever was fit to live? Disenthralled of flesh, and risen to the unobstructed sphere where passion never comes, he begins his illimitable work. His life now is grafted upon the Infinite, and will be fruitful as no earthly life can be. Pass on, thou that hast overcome! Your sorrows, O people, are his peace! Your bells, and bands, and muffled drums sound triumph in his ear. Wail and weep here; God makes it echo joy and triumph there. Pass on, thou victor!

Four years ago, O Illinois, we took from your midst an untried man, and from among the people; we return him to you a mighty conqueror. Not thine any more, but the Nation's; not ours, but the world's. Give him place, ye prairies! In the midst of this great Continent his dust shall rest, a sacred treasure to myriads who shall make pilgrimage to that shrine to kindle anew their zeal and patriotism. Ye winds, that move over the mighty places of the West, chant his requiem! Ye people, behold a martyr, whose blood, as so many articulate words, pleads for fidelity, for law, for liberty!

The Character, Life, and Death of Abraham Lincoln

HOLY TRINITY EPISCOPAL CHURCH
PHILADELPHIA, PENNSYLVANIA
APRIL 23, 1865

On Sunday, April 23, 1865, the third day of the funeral journey westward, while Lincoln's body lay in state at Independence Hall in Philadelphia, young Phillips Brooks, already recognized as a foremost minister, preached a memorial sermon at the Holy Trinity Episcopal Church where he served as pastor.[1]

In his analysis the pastor argued that "the nature of Slavery and the nature of Freedom, at last set against each other, [came] at last to open war." Brooks made the conflict a struggle between good and evil in which Lincoln the victim, the personification of what was "true and fresh and new," was "killed" by a feudalistic character, "false and effete and old." Symbolically the death of Lincoln represented the end of the evil of human slavery and and the triumph of God and freedom.

Brooks presented a striking contrast between the North and the South.

Spirit of North	Spirit of South
discipline of freedom	discipline of slavery
search for new ways	feudalism
true and fresh and new	false and effete and old
magnified labor	depreciated and despised labor
simple and direct	complex, full of sophistries and self-excuses
true and better nature	worse and falser nature
sacredness of free government	wickedness of treason

These virtues are the basic ingredients of the legendary West.

Expressing a grim determinism, Brooks lamented that "We take it for granted . . . that there is an essential connection between Mr.

47

Lincoln's character and his violent and bloody death. . . . He lived as he did, and he died as he did, because he was what he was." Brooks saw in Lincoln a man who was the natural result of the frontier or "the character of an American under the discipline of freedom." Herein he was anticipating Turner's thesis that the frontier shaped American distinctness and that the true Americans came from the Midwest. The historian David Donald has argued that "The Lincoln of Western legend represented a true folk-hero type." Both Brooks and Emerson subscribed to this popular belief.[2] This view of Lincoln was later developed by William Herndon, Carl Sandburg, and Robert Sherwood. Brooks was able to combine Lincoln as folk hero with Lincoln as defender of liberty, so he could conclude: "The cause that Abraham Lincoln died for shall grow stronger by his death,—stronger and sterner."

1. Brooks preached a shorter version of this sermon on April 16, but a week later he delivered this one; Bayard S. Clarke, "A Sermon on the Death of Abraham Lincoln," *Historical Magazine of the Protestant Episcopal Church* 49 (Mar. 1980): 37–49; Thomas H. Olbricht and Michael Casey, "Phillips Brooks," in *American Orators before 1900,* ed. Bernard K. Duffy and Halford R. Ryan (Westport, Conn.: Greenwood, 1987), 58–67.

2. David Donald, *Lincoln Reconsidered,* 2d ed., enlarged (New York: Random, 1961), 154–63.

The speech is reprinted from Phillip Brooks, *Addresses* (Boston: C. E. Brown, 1893), 166–96.

"He chose David also His servant, and took him away from the sheepfolds; that he might feed Jacob His people, and Israel His inheritance. So he fed them with a faithful and true heart, and ruled them prudently with all his power."—PSALM lxxviii, 71, 72, 73.

While I speak to you to-day, the body of the President who ruled this people, is lying, honored and loved, in our city. It is impossible with that sacred presence in our midst for me to stand and speak of ordinary topics which occupy the pulpit. I must speak of him to-day; and I therefore undertake to do what I had intended to do at some future time, to invite you to study with me the character of Abraham Lincoln, the impulses of his life and the causes of his death. I know how hard it is to do it worthily. But I shall speak with confidence, because I speak to those who love him, and whose ready love will fill out the deficiencies in a picture which my words will weakly try to draw.

We take it for granted, first of all, that there is an essential connection between Mr. Lincoln's character and his violent and bloody death. It is no accident, no arbitrary decree of Providence. He lived as he did, and he died as he did, because he was what he was. The more we see of events, the less we come to believe in any fate or destiny except the destiny of character. It will be our duty, then, to see what there was in the character of our great President that created the history of his life, and at last produced the catastrophe of his cruel death. After the first trembling horror, the first outburst of indignant sorrow, has grown calm, those are the questions which we are bound to ask and answer.

It is not necessary for me even to sketch the biography of Mr. Lincoln. He was born in Kentucky fifty-six years ago, when Kentucky was a pioneer State. He lived, as boy and man, the hard and needy life of a backwoodsman, a farmer, a river boatman and, finally, by his own effort at self education, of an active, respected, influential citizen, in the half-organized and manifold interests of a new and energetic community. From his boyhood up he lived in direct and vigorous contact with men and things, not as in older States and easier conditions with words and theories; and both his moral convictions and his intellectual opinions gathered from that contact a supreme degree of that character by which men knew him, that character which is the most distinctive possession of the best American nature, that almost indescribable quality which we call in general clearness or truth, and which appears in the physical structure as health, in the moral constitution as honesty, in the mental structure as sagacity, and in the region of active life as practicalness. This one character, with many sides, all shaped by the same essential force and testifying to the same inner influences, was what was powerful in him and decreed for him the life he was to live and the death he was to die. We must take no smaller view than this of what he was. Even his physical conditions are not to be forgotten in making up his character. We make too little always of the physical; certainly we make too little of it here if we lose out of sight the strength and muscular activity, the power of doing and enduring, which the backwoods boy inherited from generations of hard-living ancestors, and appropriated for his own by a long discipline of bodily toil. He brought to the solution of the question of labor in this country not merely a mind, but a body thoroughly in sympathy with labor, full of the culture of labor, bearing witness to the dignity and excellence of work in every muscle that work had toughened and every sense that work had made clear and true. He could not have brought the mind for his task so perfectly, unless he had first brought the body whose rugged and stubborn health was always contradicting to him the false theories of labor, and always asserting the true.

As to the moral and mental powers which distinguished him, all embraceable under this general description of clearness of truth, the most remarkable thing is the way in which they blend with one another, so that it is next to impossible to examine them in separation. A great many people have discussed very crudely whether Abraham Lincoln was an intellectual man or not; as if intellect were a thing always of the same sort, which you could precipitate from the other constituents of a man's nature and weigh by itself, and compare by pounds and ounces in this man with another. The fact is, that in all the simplest characters that line between the mental and moral natures is always vague and indistinct. They run together, and in their best combinations you are unable to discriminate, in the wisdom which is their result, how much is moral and how much is intellectual. You are unable to tell whether in the wise acts and words which issue from such a life there is more of the righteousness that comes of a clear conscience, or of the sagacity that comes of a clear brain. In more complex characters and under more complex conditions, the moral and the mental lives come to be less healthily combined. They co-operate, they help each other less. They come even to stand over against each other as antagonists; till we have that vague but most melancholy notion which pervades the life of all elaborate civilization, that goodness and greatness, as we call them, are not to be looked for together, till we expect to see and so do see a feeble and narrow conscientiousness on the one hand, and a bad, unprincipled intelligence on the other, dividing the suffrages of men.

It is the great boon of such characters as Mr. Lincoln's, that they reunite what God has joined together and man has put asunder. In him was vindicated the greatness of real goodness and the goodness of real greatness. The twain were one flesh. Not one of all the multitudes who stood and looked up to him for direction with such a loving and implicit trust can tell you to-day whether the wise judgments that he gave came most from a strong head or a sound heart. If you ask them, they are puzzled. There are men as good as he, but they do bad things. There are men as intelligent as he, but they do foolish things. In him goodness and intelligence combined and made their best result of wisdom. For perfect truth consists not merely in the right constituents of character, but in their right and intimate conjunction. This union of the mental and moral into a life of admirable simplicity is what we most admire in children; but in them it is unsettled and unpractical. But when it is preserved into manhood, deepened into reliability and maturity, it is that glorified childlikeness, that high and reverend simplicity, which shames and baffles the most accomplished astuteness and is chosen by God to fill his purposes when he needs a ruler for his people, of faithful and true heart, such as he had who was our President.

Another evident quality of such a character as this will be its freshness or newness; if we may so speak. Its freshness or readiness—call it what you will—its ability to take up new duties and do them in a new way, will result of necessity from its truth and clearness. The simple natures and forces will always be the most pliant ones. Water bends and shapes itself to any channel. Air folds and adapts itself to each new figure. They are the simplest and the most infinitely active things in nature. So this nature, in very virtue of its simplicity, must be also free, always fitting itself to each new need. It will always start from the most fundamental and eternal conditions, and work in the straightest even although they be the newest ways, to the present prescribed purpose. In one word, it must be broad and independent and radical. So that freedom and radicalness in the character of Abraham Lincoln were not separate qualities, but the necessary results of his simplicity and childlikeness and truth.

Here then we have some conception of the man. Out of this character came the life which we admire and the death which we lament to-day. He was called in that character to that life and death. It was just the nature, as you see, which a new nation such as ours ought to produce. All the conditions of his birth, his youth, his manhood, which made him what he was, were not irregular and exceptional, but were the normal conditions of a new and simple country. His pioneer home in Indiana was a type of the pioneer land in which he lived. If ever there was a man who was a part of the time and country he lived in, this was he. The same simple respect for labor won in the school of work and incorporated into blood and muscle; the same unassuming loyalty to the simple virtues of temperance and industry and integrity; the same sagacious judgment which had learned to be quick-eyed and quick-brained in the constant presence of emergency; the same direct and clear thought about things, social, political, and religious, that was in him supremely, was in the people he was sent to rule. Surely, with such a type-man for ruler, there would seem to be but a smooth and even road over which he might lead the people whose character he represented into the new region of national happiness and comfort and usefulness, for which that character had been designed.

But then we come to the beginning of all trouble. Abraham Lincoln was the type-man of the country, but not of the whole country. This character which we have been trying to describe was the character of an American under the discipline of freedom. There was another American character which had been developed under the influence of slavery. There was no one American character embracing the land. There were two characters, with impulses of irrepressible and deadly conflict. This citizen whom we have been honoring and praising represented one. The whole great scheme with which he was ulti-mately brought in conflict, and which has finally killed him, represented the other. Beside this nature, true and fresh and new, there was another nature, false and effete and old. The one nature found itself in a new world, and set itself to discover the new ways for the new duties that were given it. The other nature, full of the false pride of blood, set itself to reproduce in a new world the institutions and the spirit of the old, to build anew the structure of the feudalism which had been corrupt in its own day, and which had been left far behind by the advancing conscience and needs of the progressing race. The one nature magnified labor, the other nature depreciated and despised it. The one honored the laborer, and the other scorned him. The one was simple and direct; the other, complex, full of sophistries and self-excuses. The one was free to look all that claimed to be truth in the face, and separate the error from the truth that might be in it; the other did not dare to investigate, because its own established pride and systems were dearer to it than the truth itself, and so even truth went about in it doing the work of error. The one was ready to state broad principles, of the brotherhood of man, the universal fatherhood and justice of God, however imperfectly it might realize them in practice; the other denied even the principles, and so dug deep and laid below its special sins the broad foundation of a consistent, acknowl-edged sinfulness. In a word, one nature was full of the influences of Freedom, the other nature was full of the influences of Slavery.

In general, these two regions of our national life were separated by a geographical boundary. One was the spirit of the North, the other was the spirit of the South. But the Southern nature was by no means all a Southern thing. There it had an organized, established form, a certain definite, established institution about which it clustered. Here, lacking advantage, it lived in less expressive ways and so lived more weakly. There, there was the horrible sacrament of slavery, the out-ward and visible sign round which the inward and spiritual temper gathered and kept itself alive. But who doubts that among us the spirit of slavery lived and thrived? Its formal existence had been swept away from one State after another, partly on conscientious, partly on eco-nomical grounds, but its spirit was here, in every sympathy that North winds carried to the listening ear of the Southern slaveholder, and in every oppression of the weak by the strong, every proud assumption of idleness over labor which echoed the music of Southern life back to us. Here in our midst lived that worse and falser nature, side by side with the true and better nature which God meant should be the nature of Americans, and of which he was shaping out the type and champion in his chosen David of the sheepfold.

Here then we have the two. The history of our country for many years is the history of how these two elements of American life approached collision. They wrought their separate reactions on each other. Men debate and quarrel even now about the rise of Northern Abolitionism, about whether the Northern Abolitionists were right or wrong, whether they did harm or good. How vain the quarrel is! It was inevitable. It was inevitable in the nature of things that two such natures living here together should be set violently against each other. It is inevitable, till man be far more unfeeling and untrue to his convictions than he has always been, that a great wrong asserting itself vehemently should arouse to no less vehement assertion the opposing right. The only wonder is that there was not more of it. The only wonder is that so few were swept away to take by an impulse they could not resist their stand of hatred to the wicked institution. The only wonder is, that only one brave, reckless man came forth to cast himself, almost single-handed, with a hopeless hope, against the proud power that he hated, and trust to the influence of a soul marching on into the history of his countrymen to stir them to a vindication of the truth he loved. At any rate, whether the Abolitionists were wrong or right, there grew up about their violence, as there always will about the extremism of extreme reformers, a great mass of feeling, catching their spirit and asserting it firmly, though in more moderate degrees and methods. About the nucleus of Abolitionism grew up a great American Anti-Slavery determination, which at last gathered strength enough to take its stand to insist upon the checking and limiting the extension of the power of slavery, and to put the type-man, whom God had been preparing for the task, before the world, to do the work on which it had resolved. Then came discontent, secession, treason. The two American natures, long advancing to encounter, met at last, and a whole country, yet trembling with the shock, bears witness how terrible the meeting was.

Thus I have tried briefly to trace out the gradual course by which God brought the character which He designed to be the controlling character of this new world into distinct collision with the hostile character which it was to destroy and absorb, and set it in the person of its type-man in the seat of highest power. The character formed under the discipline of Freedom and the character formed under the discipline of Slavery developed all their difference and met in hostile conflict when this war began. Notice, it was not only in what he did and was towards the slave, it was in all he did and was everywhere that we accept Mr. Lincoln's character as the true result of our free life and institutions. Nowhere else could have come forth that genuine love of the people, which in him no one could suspect of being either the cheap flattery of the demagogue or the abstract philanthropy of the philosopher, which made our President, while he lived, the center of a great household land, and when he died so cruelly, made every humblest household thrill with a sense of personal bereavement which the death of rulers is not apt to bring. Nowhere else than out of the life of freedom could have come that personal unselfishness and generosity which made so gracious a part of this good man's character. How many soldiers feel yet the pressure of a strong hand that clasped theirs once as they lay sick and weak in the dreary hospital! How many ears will never lose the thrill of some kind word he spoke—he who could speak so kindly to promise a kindness that always matched his word! How often he surprised the land with a clemency which made even those who questioned his policy love him the more for what they called his weakness,—seeing how the man in whom God had most embodied the discipline of Freedom not only could not be a slave, but could not be a tyrant! In the heartiness of his mirth and his enjoyment of simple joys; in the directness and shrewdness of perception which constituted his wit; in the untired, undiscouraged faith in human nature which he always kept; and perhaps above all in the plainness and quiet, unostentatious earnestness and independence of his religious life, in his humble love and trust of God—in all it was a character such as only Freedom knows how to make.

Now it was in this character, rather than in any mere political position, that the fitness of Mr. Lincoln to stand forth in the struggle of the two American natures really lay. We are told that he did not come to the Presidential chair pledged to the abolition of Slavery. When will we learn that with all true men it is not what they intend to do, but it is what the qualities of their natures bind them to do, that determines their career! The President came to his power full of the blood, strong in the strength of Freedom. He came there free, and hating slavery. He came there, leaving on record words like these spoken three years before and never contradicted. He had said, "A house divided against itself cannot stand. I believe this Government cannot endure permanently, half slave and half free. I do not expect the Union to be dissolved; I do not expect the house to fall; but I expect it will cease to be divided. It will become all one thing or all the other." When the question came, he knew which thing he meant that it should be. His whole nature settled that question for him. Such a man must always live as he used to say he lived (and was blamed for saying it), "controlled by events, not controlling them."[1] And with a reverent and clear mind, to be controlled by events means to be controlled by God. For such a man there was no hesitation when God brought him up face to face with Slavery and put the sword into his hand and said, "Strike it down dead." He was a willing servant then. If ever the face of a man writing solemn words glowed with a solemn joy, it must have been the face of Abraham Lincoln, as he bent over the page where the Emancipation Proclamation of 1863 was growing into shape, and giving manhood and freedom as he wrote it to hundreds of thousands of his fellow-men. Here was a work in which his whole nature could rejoice. Here was an act that crowned the whole culture of his life. All the past, the free boyhood in the woods, the free youth upon the farm, the free manhood in the honorable citizen's employments—all his freedom gathered and completed itself in this. And as the swarthy multitudes came in, ragged, and tired, and hungry, and ignorant, but free forever from anything but the memorial scars of the fetters and the whip, singing rude songs in which the new triumph of freedom struggled and heaved below the sad melody that had been shaped for bondage; as in their camps and hovels there grew up to their half-superstitious eyes the image of a great Father almost more than man, to whom they owed their freedom,—were they not half right? For it was not to one man, driven by stress of policy, or swept off by a whim of pity, that the noble act was due. It was to the American nature, long kept by God in his own intentions till his time should come, at last emerging into sight and power, and

---

1. Paraphrase from a letter to Albert G. Hodges, Apr. 4, 1864.

bound up and embodied in this best and most American of all Americans, to whom we and those poor frightened slaves at last might look up together and love to call him, with one voice, our Father.

Thus, we have seen something of what the character of Mr. Lincoln was, and how it issued in the life he lived. It remains for us to see how it resulted also in the terrible death which has laid his murdered body here in our town among lamenting multitudes today. It is not a hard question, though it is sad to answer. We saw the two natures, the nature of Slavery and the nature of Freedom, at last set against each other, come at last to open war. Both fought, fought long, fought bravely; but each, as was perfectly natural, fought with the tools and in the ways which its own character had made familiar to it. The character of Slavery was brutal, barbarous, and treacherous; and so the whole history of the slave power during the war has been full of ways of warfare brutal, barbarous, and treacherous, beyond anything that men bred in freedom could have been driven to by the most hateful passions. It is not to be marveled at. It is not to be set down as the special sin of the war. It goes back beyond that. It is the sin of the system. It is the barbarism of Slavery. When Slavery went to war to save its life, what wonder if its barbarism grew barbarous a hundred-fold!

One would be attempting a task which once was almost hopeless, but which now is only needless, if he set himself to convince a Northern congregation that Slavery was a barbarian institution. It would be hardly more necessary to try to prove how its barbarism has shown itself during this war. The same spirit which was blind to the wickedness of breaking sacred ties, of separating man and wife, of beating women till they dropped down dead, of organizing licentiousness and sin into commercial systems, of forbidding knowledge and protecting itself with ignorance, of putting on its arms and riding out to steal a State at the beleaguered ballotbox away from freedom—in one word (for its simplest definition is its worst dishonor), the spirit that gave man the ownership in man in time of peace, has found out yet more terrible barbarisms for the time of war. It has hewed and burned the bodies of the dead. It has starved and mutilated its helpless prisoners. It has dealt by truth, not as men will in time of excitement, lightly and with frequent violations, but with a cool, and deliberate, and systematic contempt. It has sent its agents into Northern towns to fire peaceful hotels where hundreds of peaceful men and women slept. It has undermined the prisons where its victims starved, and made all ready to blow with one blast their wretched life away. It has delighted in the lowest and basest scurrility even on the highest and most honorable lips. It has corrupted the graciousness of women and killed out the truth of men.

I do not count up the terrible catalogue because I like to, nor because I wish to stir your hearts to passion. Even now, you and I have no right to indulge in personal hatred to the men who did these things. But we are not doing right by ourselves, by the President that we have lost, or by God who had a purpose in our losing him, unless we know thoroughly that it was this same spirit which we have seen to be a tyrant in peace and a savage in war, that has crowned itself with the working of this final woe. It was the conflict of the two American natures, the false and the true. It was Slavery and Freedom that met in their two representatives, the assassin and the President; and the victim of the last desperate struggle of the dying Slavery lies dead to-day in Independence Hall.

Solemnly, in the sight of God, I charge this murder where it belongs, on Slavery. I dare not stand here in His sight, and before Him or you speak doubtful and double-meaning words of vague repentance, as if we had killed our President. We have sins enough, but we have not done this sin, save as by weak concessions and timid compromises we have let the spirit of Slavery grow strong and ripe for such a deed. In the barbarism of Slavery the foul act and its foul method had their birth. By all the goodness that there was in him; by all the love we had for him (and who shall tell how great it was?) by all the sorrow that has burdened down this desolate and dreadful week,— I charge this murder where it belongs, on Slavery. I bid you to remember where the charge belongs, to write it on the door-posts of your mourning houses, to teach it to your wondering children, to give it to the history of these times, that all times to come may hate and dread the sin that killed our noblest President.

If ever anything were clear, this is the clearest. Is there the man alive who thinks that Abraham Lincoln was shot just for himself; that it was that one man for whom the plot was laid? The gentlest, kindest, most indulgent man that ever ruled a State! The man who knew not how to speak a word of harshness or how to make a foe! Was it he for whom the murderer lurked with a mere private hate? It was not he, but what he stood for. It was Law and Liberty, it was Government and Freedom, against which the hate gathered and the treacherous shot was fired. And I know not how the crime of him who shoots at Law and Liberty in the crowded glare of a great theater differs from theirs who have leveled their aim at the same great beings from behind a thousand ambuscades and on a hundred battle-fields of this long war. Every general in the field, and every false citizen in our midst at home, who has plotted and labored to destroy the lives of the soldiers of the Republic, is brother to him who did this deed. The American nature, the American truths, of which our President was the anointed and supreme embodiment, have been embodied in multitudes of heroes who marched unknown and fell unnoticed in our ranks. For them, just as for him, character decreed a life and a death. The blood of all of them I charge on the same head. Slavery armed with Treason was their murderer.

Men point out to us the absurdity and folly of this awful crime. Again and again we hear men say, "It was the worst thing for themselves they could have done. They have shot a representative man, and the cause he represented grows stronger and sterner by his death. Can it be that so wise a devil was so foolish here? Must it not have been the act of one poor madman, born and nursed in his own reckless brain?" My friends, let us understand this matter. It was a foolish act. Its folly was only equaled by its wickedness. It was a foolish act. But when did sin begin to be wise? When did wickedness learn wisdom? When did the fool stop saying in his heart, "There is no God," and acting godlessly in the absurdity of his impiety? The cause that Abraham Lincoln died for shall grow stronger by his death,—stronger and sterner. Stronger to set its pillars deep into the structure of our nation's life; sterner to execute the justice of the Lord upon his enemies. Stronger to spread its arms and grasp our whole land into freedom; sterner to sweep the last poor ghost of Slavery out of our haunted homes. But while we feel the folly of this act, let not its folly hide its wickedness. It was the wickedness of Slavery putting on a foolishness for which its wickedness and that alone is responsible, that robbed the nation of a President and the people of a father. And remember this, that the folly of the Slave power in striking the representative of Freedom, and thinking that thereby it killed Freedom itself, is only a folly that we shall echo if we dare to think that in punishing the representatives of Slavery who did this deed, we are putting Slavery to death. Dispersing armies and hanging traitors, imperatively as justice and necessity may demand them both, are not killing the spirit out of which they sprang. The traitor must die because he has committed treason. The murderer must die because he has committed murder. Slavery must die, because out of it, and it alone, came forth the treason of the traitor and the murder of the murderer. Do not say that it is dead. It is not, while its essential spirit lives. While one man counts another man his born inferior for the color of his skin, while both in North and South prejudices and practices, which the law cannot touch, but which God hates, keep alive in our people's hearts the spirit of the old iniquity, it is not dead. The new American nature must supplant the old. We must grow like our President, in his truth, his independence, his religion, and his wide humanity. Then the character by which he died shall be in us, and by it we shall live. Then peace shall come that knows no war, and a law that knows no treason; and full of his spirit a grateful land shall gather round his grave, and in the daily psalm of prosperous and righteous living, thank God forever for his life and death.

So let him lie here in our midst to-day, and let our people go and bend with solemn thoughtfulness and look upon his face and read the lessons of his burial. As he paused here on his journey from the Western home and told us what by the help of God he meant to do, so let him pause upon his way back to his Western grave and tell us with a silence more eloquent than words how bravely, how truly, by the strength of God, he did it. God brought him up as he brought David up from the sheep-fold, to feed Jacob, his people, and Israel, his inheritance. He came up in earnestness and faith, and he goes back in triumph. As he pauses here today, and from his cold lips bids us bear witness how he has met the duty that was laid on him, what can we say out of our full hearts but this—"He fed them with a faithful and true heart, and ruled them prudently with all his power." The *Shepherd of the People!* that old name that the best rulers ever craved. What ruler ever won it like this dead President of ours? He fed us faithfully and truly. He fed us with counsel when we were in doubt, with inspiration when we sometimes faltered, with caution when we would be rash, with calm, clear, trustful cheerfulness through many an hour when our hearts were dark. He fed hungry souls all over the country with sympathy and consolation. He spread before the whole land feasts of great duty and devotion and patriotism, on which the land grew strong. He fed us with solemn, solid truths. He taught us the sacredness of government, the wickedness of treason. He made our souls glad and vigorous with the love of liberty that was in his. He showed us how to love truth and yet be charitable—how to hate wrong and all oppression and yet not treasure one personal injury or insult. He fed *all* his people, from the highest to the lowest, from the most privileged down to the most enslaved. Best of all, he fed us with a reverent and genuine religion. He spread before us the love and fear of God just in that shape in which we need them most, and out of his faithful service of a higher Master who of us has not taken and eaten and grown strong? "He fed them with a faithful and true heart." Yes, till the last. For at the last, behold him standing with hand reached out to feed the South with mercy and the North with charity, and the whole land with peace, when the Lord who had sent him called him and his work was done!

He stood once on the battle-field of our own State, and said of the brave men who had saved it words as noble as any countryman of ours ever spoke. Let us stand in the country he has saved, and which is to be his grave and monument, and say of Abraham Lincoln what he said of the soldiers who had died at Gettysburg. He stood there with their graves before him, and these are the words he said:—

> "We cannot dedicate, we cannot consecrate, we cannot hallow this ground. The brave men who struggled here have consecrated it far beyond our power to add or detract. The world will little note nor long remember what we say here, but it can never forget what they did here. It is for us the living rather to be dedicated to the unfinished work which they who fought here have thus far so nobly advanced. It is rather for us to be here dedicated to the great task remaining before us, that from these honored dead we take increased devotion to that cause for which they gave the last full measure of devotion; that we here highly resolve that these dead shall not have died in vain; and this nation, under God, shall have a new birth of freedom, and that government of the people, by the people, and for the people, shall not perish from the earth."

May God make us worthy of the memory of Abraham Lincoln.

How Shall the Nation Show Its Sorrow?

UNION SQUARE
NEW YORK CITY, NEW YORK
APRIL 25, 1865

On the fourth day of the journey, the body of Lincoln arrived in New York City, a place that had not always welcomed the Illinoisan with enthusiasm. But now times were different. The New Yorkers resolved that no place would surpass their city in its display of grief. Lloyd Lewis said the city "put on the biggest show of its career, a hippodrome of sorrow, much of it pure ostentation."[1] Accompanied by a long solemn procession, witnessed by thousands along the route, the hearse carried the dead president to the rotunda of the city hall for public viewing. The following day the cortege resumed its westward journey toward Albany.

A great meeting attended by 2,000 was held in Union Square to express the public sorrow.[2] George Bancroft, a historian, was invited to deliver the principal address. The committee made an excellent choice in Bancroft, who had written his *History of the United States,* served as United States secretary of navy, established the Naval Academy at Annapolis, and had been the U.S. minister to Great Britain. Furthermore, after the issuance of the Emancipation Proclamation he had supported the Lincoln administration. Nevertheless, Richard Nelson Current has observed that "in retrospect," the selection of Bancroft, a lifelong Democrat and early critic of Lincoln, "was certainly less than perfect" to deliver a eulogy of Lincoln.[3]

Within a comparatively short time the historian delivered a second eulogy on Lincoln. Following the New York address, the United States Congress drafted Bancroft to commemorate Lincoln before a joint session on February 12, 1866. In this formal second address, Bancroft became expansive in his placing of Lincoln in the context of democratic movement and in the long struggle to abolish slavery beginning with the ancient Greeks. The orator became ponderous

62

and long-winded in an attempt to present a panorama worthy of Lincoln. Later it was published in an impressive memorial volume,[4] though many historians, including Current, thought that "among official eulogies of American public figures," the Bancroft speech of 1866, "must surely be one of the least eulogistic on record."[5]

In many ways the less pretentious New York speech was a better oration than the congressional dissertation. Having little time to prepare and under the spell of the fearful tragedy and the anxieties over the installation of the new president, Bancroft was more timely in what he had to say, though he violated the eulogistic context in many places.

Bancroft made his New York memorial more a tribute to the successful completion of the war and the abolition of slavery than a eulogy of Abraham Lincoln. The historian seemed almost reluctant to discuss the personal qualities of the president. Instead of giving any value judgments, he suggested that "those who come after us will decide how much of the wonderful results of his public career" were "due to his own good common sense, his shrewd sagacity, readiness of wit, quick interpretation of the public mind; . . . how much to the American people, who, . . . inspired him with their wisdom and energy; and how much the overruling laws of the moral world, by which the selfishness of evil is made to defeat itself." Unlike those eulogists who made Lincoln a symbol of freedom and democracy, Bancroft expressed little commendation of Lincoln's virtues or greatness. Instead the historian showed his eagerness to use public grief as a means to assure "the march of Providence."

Bancroft was concerned about how the nation would adjust to the new administration of Andrew Johnson. He knew that some New Yorkers, not so long before, had vigorously opposed Lincoln and his policies and that the peace Democrats, Copperheads, opponents of the draft, some business interests, and sore-headed Lincoln critics hoped that the new Republican administration would fail.

In response to opponents of Lincoln, Bancroft amplified the theme that "grief must take the character of action, and breathe itself forth in the assertion of the policy to which he fell a sacrifice." Bancroft included an extensive legal justification of the Emancipation Proclamation and abolition, concluding "the proclamation of freedom shall stand as a reality"; and "no one can turn back or stay the march of

Providence." He met head-on mutterings about the capabilities of the new president and urged vigorous support. In an unusual apocalyptic appeal, the orator concluded, "To that Union Abraham Lincoln has fallen a martyr. His death . . . binds it more closely and more firmly than ever. The blow aimed at him was aimed . . . not at the citizen of Illinois, but at the man who, as President, . . . stood as the representative of every man in the United States. . . . His enduring memory will assist during countless ages to bind the States together, and to incite to the love of our one undivided, indivisible country." Adroitly in his peroration the historian shifted attention away from Lincoln as man to Lincoln as representative of the "whole people." Making the "blow" a strike against the Union, he turned the martyrdom of the "citizen of Illinois" into an appeal for reconciliation.

1. Lloyd Lewis, *Myths after Lincoln* (New York: Harcourt, Brace, 1941), 119.
2. *New York Times,* Apr. 26, 1865.
3. Richard Nelson Current, *Speaking of Abraham Lincoln* (Urbana: University of Illinois Press, 1983), 173.
4. *Memorial Addresses before the Two Houses of Congress on the Life and Character of Abraham Lincoln, James A. Garfield, William McKinley* (Washington, D.C.: Government Printing Office, 1903).
5. Current, *Speaking of Abraham Lincoln,* 184.

The speech is reprinted from John Gilmary Shea, ed., *The Lincoln Memorial: A Record of the Life, Assassination, and Obsequies of the Martyred President* (New York: Bunce and Huntington, 1865), 199–204. The address was also published in full in the *New York Times,* Apr. 26, 1865, p. 8.

Our grief and horror at the crime which has clothed the continent in mourning find no adequate expression in words and no relief in tears. The President of the United States of America has fallen by the hands of an assassin. Neither the office with which he was invested by the approved choice of a mighty people, nor the most simple-hearted kindliness of nature, could save him from the fiendish passions of relentless fanaticism. The wailings of the millions attend his remains as they are borne in solemn procession over our great rivers, along the sea-side, beyond the mountains, across the prairie, to their final resting place in the valley of the Mississippi. The echoes of his funeral knell vibrate through the world, and the friends of freedom of every tongue and in every clime are his mourners. Too few days have passed away since Abraham Lincoln stood in the flush of vigorous manhood to permit any attempt at an analysis of his character or an exposition of his career. We find it hard to believe that his large eyes, which in their softness and beauty expressed nothing but benevolence and gentleness, are closed in death; we almost look for the pleasant smile that brought out more vividly the earnest cast of his features, which were serious even to sadness. A few years ago he was a village attorney, engaged in the support of a rising family, unknown to fame, scarcely named beyond his neighborhood; his administration made him the most conspicuous man in his country, and drew on him first the astonished gaze, and then the respect and admiration of the world. Those who come after us will decide how much of the wonderful results of his public career is due to his own good common sense, his shrewd sagacity, readiness of wit, quick interpretation of the public mind; his rare combination of fixedness and pliancy; his steady tendency of purpose; how much to the American people, who, as he walked with them side by side, inspired him with their wisdom and energy; and how much the overruling laws of the moral world, by which the selfishness of evil is made to defeat itself. But after every allowance, it will remain that members of the government which preceded his administration opened the gates to treason, and he closed them; that when he went to Washington the ground on which he trod shook under his feet, and he left the republic on a solid

65

foundation; that traitors had seized public forts and arsenals, and he recovered them for the United States, to whom they belonged; that the capital which he found the abode of slaves, is now only the home of the free; that the boundless public domain which was grasped at, and, in a great measure, held for the diffusion of slavery, is now irrevocably devoted to freedom; that then men talked a jargon of a balance of power in a republic between Slave States and Free States, and now the foolish words are blown away forever by the breath of Maryland, Missouri, and Tennessee; that a terrible cloud of political heresy rose from the abyss threatening to hide the light of the sun, and under its darkness a rebellion was rising to undefinable proportions. Now the atmosphere is purer than ever before, and the insurrection is vanishing away; the country is cast into another mould, and the gigantic system of wrong which had been the work of more than two centuries, is dashed down, we hope forever. And as to himself personally: he was then scoffed at by the proud as unfit for his station, and now against the usage of later years, and in spite of numerous competitors, he was the unbiassed and the undoubted choice of the American people for a second term of service. Through all the mad business of treason he retained the sweetness of a most placable disposition; and the slaughter of myriads of the best on the battle-field and the more terrible destruction of our men in captivity by the slow torture of exposure and starvation, had never been able to provoke him into harboring one vengeful feeling or one purpose of cruelty.

How shall the nation most completely show its sorrow at Mr. Lincoln's death? How shall it best honor his memory? There can be but one answer. He was struck down when he was highest in its service, and in strict conformity of duty was engaged in carrying out principles affecting its life, its good name, and its relations to the cause of freedom and the progress of mankind. Grief must take the character of action, and breathe itself forth in the assertion of the policy to which he fell a sacrifice. The standard which he held in his hand must be uplifted again, higher and more firmly than before, and must be carried on to triumph. Above every thing else, his proclamation of the first day of January, 1863, declaring throughout the parts of the country in rebellion the freedom of all persons who had been held as slaves, must be affirmed and maintained. Events, as they rolled onward, have removed every doubt of the legality and binding force of that proclamation. The country and the rebel government have each laid claim to the public service of the slave, and yet but one of the two can have a rightful claim to such service. That rightful claim belongs to the United States, because every one born on their soil, with the few exceptions of the children of travelers and transcient residents, owes them a primary allegiance. Every one so born has been counted among those represented in Congress; every slave has ever been represented in Congress—imperfectly and wrongly it may be—but still he has been counted and represented. The slave born on our soil always owed allegiance to the general government. It may in time past have been a qualified allegiance, manifested through his master, as the allegiance of a ward through its guardian, or of an infant through its parent. But when the master became false to his allegiance the slave stood face to face with his country, and his allegiance, which may before have been a qualified one, became direct and immediate. His chains fell off, and he stood at once in the presence of the nation, bound, like the rest of us, to its public defence. Mr. Lincoln's proclamation did but take notice of the already existing right of the bondman to freedom. The treason of the master made it a public crime for the slave to continue his obedience; the treason of a State set free the collective bondmen of that State. This doctrine is supported by the analogy of precedents. In the times of feudalism the treason of the lord of the manor deprived him of his serfs; the spurious feudalism that existed among us differs in many respects from the feudalism of the middle ages; but so far the precedent runs parallel with the present case; for treason the master then, for treason the master now, loses his slaves. In the middle ages the sovereign appointed another lord over the serfs and the land which they cultivated; in our day the sovereign makes them masters of their own persons, lords over themselves.

It has been said that we are at war, and that emancipation is not a belligerent right. The objection disappears before analysis. In a war between independent powers the invading foreigner invites to his standard all who will give him aid, whether bond or free, and he rewards them according to his ability and his pleasure with gifts or freedom; but when at peace he withdraws from the invaded country he must take his aiders and comforters with him; or if he leaves them behind, where he has no court to enforce his decrees, he can give them no security, unless it be by the stipulations of a treaty. In a civil war it is altogether different. There, when rebellion is crushed, the old government is restored, and its courts resume their jurisdiction. So it is with us; the United States have courts of their own that must punish the guilt of treason, and vindicate the freedom of persons whom the fact of rebellion has set free. Nor may it be said that because slavery existed in most of the States when the Union was formed, it cannot rightfully be interfered with now. A change has taken place, such as Madison foresaw, and for which he pointed out the remedy. The constitution of States had been transformed before the plotters of treason carried them away into rebellion. When the Federal constitution was formed general emancipation was thought to be near, and everywhere the respective legislatures had authority, in the exercise of their ordinary functions, to do away with slavery; since that time the attempt has been made in what are called slave States to make the condition of slavery perpetual; and events have proved, with the clearness of demonstation, that a constitution which seeks to continue a caste of hereditary bondmen through endless generations is inconsistent with the existence of republican institutions. So, then, the new President and the people of the United States must insist that the proclamation of freedom shall stand as a reality; and, moreover, the people must never cease to insist that the constitution shall be so amended as utterly to prohibit slavery on any part of our soil forevermore.

Alas! that a State in our vicinity should withhold its assent to this last beneficent measure; its refusal was an encouragement to our enemies equal to the gain of a pitched battle, and delays the only hopeful method of pacification. The removal of the cause of the rebellion is not only demanded by justice; it is the policy of mercy, making room for a wider clemency; it is the part of order against a chaos of controversy; its success brings with it true reconcilement, a lasting peace, a continuous growth of confidence through an assimilation of the social condition. Here is the fitting expression of the mourning of to-day.

And let no lover of his country say that this warning is uncalled for. The cry is delusive, that slavery is dead. Even now it is nerving itself for a fresh struggle for continuance. The last winds from the South waft to us the sad intelligence that a man, who had surrounded himself with the glory of the most brilliant and most varied achievements, who but a week ago was named with affectionate pride among the greatest benefactors of his country and the ablest generals of all time, has usurped more than the whole power of the executive, and under the name of peace has revived slavery and given security and political power to traitors from the Chesapeake to the Rio Grande. Why could he not remember the dying advice of Washington—never to draw the sword but for self-defence or the rights of his country; and, when drawn, never to sheath it till its work should be accomplished? And yet from this bad act, which the people with one united voice condemn, no great evil will follow save the shadow on his own fame. The individual, even in the greatness of military glory, sinks into insignificance before the resistless movements in the history of man. No one can turn back or stay the march of Providence.

No sentiment of despair may mix with our sorrow. We owe it to the memory of the dead, we owe it to the cause of popular liberty throughout the world, that the sudden crime which has taken the life of the President of the United States shall not produce the least impediment in the smooth course of public affairs. This great city, in the midst of unexampled emblems of deeply seated grief, has sustained itself with composure and magnanimity. It has nobly done its part in guarding against the derangement of business or the slightest shock to public credit. The enemies of the Republic put it to the severest trial; but the voice of faction has not been heard; doubt and despondency have been unknown. In serene majesty the country rises in the beauty and strength and hope of youth, and proves to the world the quiet energy and the durability of institutions growing out of the reason and affections of the people. Heaven has willed it that the United States shall live. The nations of the earth cannot spare them. All the worn out aristocracies of Europe saw in the spurious feudalism of slaveholding their strongest outpost, and banded themselves together with the deadly enemies of our national life. If the Old World will discuss the respective advantages of oligarchy or equality; of the union of church and state, or the rightful freedom of religion; of land accessible to the many, or of land monopolized by an ever decreasing number of the few—the United States must live to control the decision by their quiet and unobtrusive example. It has often and truly been observed that the trust and affection of the masses gathers naturally round an individual; if the inquiry is made whether the man so trusted and beloved shall elicit from the reason of the people enduring institutions of their own, or shall sequester political power for a superintending dynasty, the United States must live to solve the problem. If a question is raised on the respective merits of Timoleon or Julius Caesar, of Washington or Napoleon, the United States must be there to call to mind that there were twelve Caesars, most of them the opprobrium of the human race, and to contrast with them the line of American Presidents.

The duty of the hour is incomplete, our mourning is insincere, if while we express unwavering trust in the great principles that underlie our government, we do not also give our support to the man to whom the people have entrusted its administration. Andrew Johnson is now, by the Constitution, the President of the United States, and he stands before the world as the most conspicuous representative of the industrial classes. Left an orphan at four years old, poverty and toil were his steps to honor. His youth was not passed in the halls of colleges; nevertheless he has received a thorough political education in statesmanship in the school of the people, and by long experience of public life. A village functionary; member successively of each branch of the Tennessee Legislature, hearing with a thrill of joy the words, "The Union, it must be preserved"; a representative in Congress for successive years; Governor of the great State of Tennessee, approved as its Governor by re-election; he was at the opening of the rebellion a senator from that State in Congress. Then at the Capitol, when senators, unrebuked by the government, sent word by telegram to seize forts and arsenals, he alone from that Southern region told them what the government did not dare to tell them—that they were traitors, and deserved the punishment of treason. Undismayed by a perpetual purpose of public enemies to take his life, bearing up against the still greater trial of the persecution of his wife and children, in due time he went back to his State, determined to restore it to the Union, or die with the American flag for his winding sheet. And now, at the call of the United States, he has returned to Washington as a conqueror, with Tennessee as a free State for his trophy. It remains for him to consummate the vindication of the Union.

To that Union Abraham Lincoln has fallen a martyr. His death, which was meant to sever it beyond repair, binds it more closely and more firmly than ever. The blow aimed at him was aimed, not at the native of Kentucky, not at the citizen of Illinois, but at the man who, as President, in the executive branch of the government, stood as the representative of every man in the United States. The object of the crime was the life of the whole people, and it wounds the affections of the whole people. From Maine to the southwest boundary on the Pacific it makes us one. The country may have needed an imperishable grief to touch its inmost feeling. The grave that receives the remains of Lincoln receives the martyr to the Union; the monument which will rise over his body will bear witness to the Union; his enduring memory will assist during countless ages to bind the States together, and to incite to the love of our one undivided, indivisible country. Peace to the ashes of our departed friend, the friend of his country and his race. Happy was his life, for he was the restorer of the Republic; he was happy in his death, for the manner of his end will plead forever for the Union of the States and the freedom of man.

Under the Permissive Hand of God

OAK RIDGE CEMETERY
SPRINGFIELD, ILLINOIS
MAY 4, 1865

The thirteen-day pilgrimage of 1,654 miles of the funeral train's journey finally ended at Springfield on May 3. Following the display of the body in the Illinois Hall of the House of Representatives, the temporary interment was held the next day at Oak Ridge Cemetery with Bishop Matthew Simpson of the Methodist Episcopal Church as the speaker. It was ironic that the bishop, who not long before had aggressively badgered the president about the appointments of Methodists to prominent positions and had become somewhat of a problem to Lincoln, should now present the final benediction.[1] In the earlier service at the White House on April 19, at which Phineus D. Gurley had preached, Simpson had prayed. Now at "the open mouth" of the vault, dropping "the tears of sorrow around the ashes of the mighty dead," the preacher knew that he faced a weary audience, drained emotionally by the long eighteen-day wait for Lincoln's return and by the flood of remorse that had filled the newspapers. What had often sincerely been intended appeared excessive, effusive, and questionable. With good reason, one authority declared that the extended funeral procession "had become half circus, half heartbreak."[2] Striving to capture the tragic grandeur of the Lincoln scenario, Simpson became expansive in his long tribute. At some places he almost seemed to make the dead president secondary to recounting historical details, many of which must have been thoroughly familiar to Lincoln's friends and neighbors.[3]

Though not a great speech, the Simpson eulogy reflected the prevailing sentiment and near hysteria of the sad occasion. After the long introduction in which he presented the details of the slow-moving cortege from Washington, Simpson interpreted the deep sadness that had fallen over "a weeping nation." He thought that their

72

bewilderment had resulted from the sudden shock that came from moving from elation over the end of the tragic war to dismay over the assassination. In one of his best passages, he lamented: "All that feeling which had been gathering for four years in the form of excitement, grief, horror, and joy, turned into one wail of woe; a sadness inexpressible, an anguish unutterable."

The heart of his explanation of the public grief centered on the loss of "the man himself," who "by the hand of God . . . was especially singled out to guide our Government in these troublous times." Throughout his eulogy Simpson asserted his belief in predestination and the Western influence upon Lincoln's physical, mental, and moral stature. Much like Emerson and Brooks, Simpson saw Lincoln as a Western man: "His home was in the growing West, the heart of the Republic, and, invigorated by the wind which swept over its prairies, he learned lessons of self-reliance, which sustained him in seasons of adversity."

Simpson praised Lincoln's greatness for bringing the war to a successful conclusion and particularly in the issuance of the Emancipation: "The great act of the mighty chieftain . . . is that of giving freedom to a race. . . . When other events shall have been forgotten . . . this act shall still be conspicuous on the pages of history; and we are thankful that God gave to Abraham Lincoln the decision and wisdom and grace to issue that proclamation." When he discussed Lincoln as a "good man," the bishop dared to venture into the troublesome areas of Lincoln's religious and marital life. Although he admitted that he could not speak "definitely" about "his religious experience," Simpson asserted that Lincoln "believed in Christ" and that in "his domestic life" he "was a devoted husband and father." Why in Springfield did Simpson choose to assert such strong opinions about what later became most controversial? It may well have been that he was attempting to stop what was to be common gossip in Springfield and a favorite subject of William Herndon.

Simpson turned to the "fearful lesson" to be learned from tragedy. Suddenly the good bishop became a Radical Republican and delivered what he called his "painful duty," advocating that rebel leaders "be brought to speedy and to certain punishment." With little Christian compassion and none of the understanding of Lincoln, the speaker advocated strong punishment for the Confederates, "a felon's death" for rebel officers, and "forgiveness" for the "deluded masses." Stern and unrelenting, he suggested, "Men may attempt to compromise and to restore these traitors and murderers to society again, but the American people will rise in their majesty and sweep all such compromises and compromisers away, and shall declare that there shall be no peace to rebels."

Like the other ministers, Simpson emphasized: "let us resolve to carry forward the policy which he so nobly began." Simpson suggested his belief in predestination when he remarked that in the struggle on behalf of "human freedom" and "republics... all over this world" Lincoln "fell under the permissive hand of God" and did the "work for which God had sent him."

1. Mark E. Neely, Jr., *The Abraham Lincoln Encyclopedia* (New York: McGraw-Hill, 1982), 121–22, 277–78.

2. Lloyd Lewis, *Myths after Lincoln* (New York: Harcourt, 1941), 124.

3. *New York Times,* May 5, 1865; Chicago *Tribune,* May 6, 1865.

The speech is reprinted from *The Assassination and History of the Conspiracy,* with a foreword by Roy P. Basler (New York: Hobbs, Dorman, 1965), 125–42.

Fellow-citizens of Illinois and of many parts of our entire Union, near the Capital of this large and growing State of Illinois: In the midst of this beautiful grove, and at the open mouth of this vault, which has just received the remains of our fallen chieftain, we gather to pay a tribute of respect and to drop the tears of sorrow around the ashes of the mighty dead. A little more than four years ago, from his plain, quiet home in yonder city, he started, receiving the parting words of the concourse of friends who gathered around him, and in the midst of the dropping of the gentle shower, he told of the pangs of parting from the place where his children had been born, and his home had been made pleasant by early recollections; and as he left, he made an earnest request, in the hearing of some who are present at this meeting, that, as he was about to enter upon the responsibilities which he believed to be greater than any which had fallen upon any man since the days of Washington, the people would offer up prayers that God would aid and sustain him in the work which they had given him to do. His company left our quiet city, but as it went, snares were in waiting for the Chief Magistrate. Scarcely did he escape the dangers of the way, or the hands of the assassin as he neared Washington, and I believe he escaped only through the vigilance of officers and the prayers of his people, so that the blow was suspended for more than four years, which was at last permitted, through the providence of God, to fall. How different the occasion which witnessed his departure from that which witnessed his return! You expected to take him by the hand, to feel the warm grasp which you had felt in other days, and to see the tall form walking among you which you had delighted to honor in years past. But he was never permitted to return until he came with lips mute and silent, the frame encoffined, and a weeping nation followed as his mourners.

Such a scene as his return to you, was never witnessed among the events of history. There have been great processions of mourners. There was one for the Patriarch Jacob, which came up from Egypt, and the Egyptians wondered at the evidences of reverence and filial affection which came from the hearts of the Israelites. There was mourning when Moses fell upon the heights of Pisgah, and vanished from human view. There have been mournings in the kingdoms of the earth, when Kings and Princes have fallen; but never was there in the history of man such mourning as that which has accompanied this funeral procession, and has gathered around the mortal remains of him who was our loved one, and who now sleeps among us.

If we glance at the procession which followed him, we see how the nation stood aghast! Tears filled the eyes of manly, sun-burnt faces; strong men, as they clasped the hands of their friends, were unable to find vent for their grief in words. Women and children caught up the tidings as they ran through the land, and were melted into tears. The nation stood still, and men left their plows in the field and asked what the end should be. The hum of manufactories ceased, and the sound of the hammer was not heard. Busy merchants closed their doors, and in the Exchange gold passed no more from hand to hand. Though three weeks have passed, the nation has scarcely breathed easily yet. A mournful silence is abroad upon the land. Nor is this mourning confined to any class, or to any district of country. Men of all political parties, and of all religious creeds, have united in paying this mournful tribute. The Archbishop of the Roman Catholic Church, in New York, and a Protestant Minister, walked side by side in the sad procession, and a Jewish Rabbi performed a part of the solemn services.

There are gathered around this tomb the representatives of the army and navy, Senators, Judges, Governors, and officers of all the branches of the Government. Here, too, are all members of civic professions, with men and women from the humblest as well the highest occupations. Here and there, too, are tears as sincere and warm as any that drop, which come from the eyes of those whose kindred and whose race have been freed from their chains by him whom they mourn as their deliverer. Far more have gazed on the face of the departed than ever looked upon the face of any other departed man. More races have looked on the procession for 1,600 miles or more, by night and by day, by sunlight, dawn, twilight, and by torchlight, than ever before watched the progress of a procession.

We ask, why this wonderful mourning, this great procession? I answer, first, a part of the interest has arisen from the times in which we live, and in which he, that has fallen, was a principal actor. It is a principle of our nature that feeling once excited, readily leave the object by which they are excited for some other object, which may, for the time being, take possession of the mind. Another principle is, that the deepest affections of our hearts gather around some human form, in which are embodied the living thoughts and ideas of the passing ages. If we look, then, at the times we see an age of excitement. For four years the popular heart has been stirred to its utmost depths. War had come upon us, devouring families, separating nearest and dearest friends, a war, the extent and magnitude of which no one could estimate; a war in which the blood of brethren was shed by a brother's hand. A call for soldiers was made by this voice now hushed, and all over this land, from hill and mountain, from plain and valley, there sprung up hundreds of thousands of bold hearts, ready to go forth and save our national Union.

The feeling of excitement was transferred next into a feeling of deep grief, because of the danger in which our country was placed. Many said, "Is it possible to save our nation?" Some in our country, and nearly all the leading men in other countries, declared it to be impossible to maintain the Union, and many an honest and patriotic heart was deeply pained with apprehensions of common ruin; and many in grief, and almost in despair, anxiously inquired, "What shall the end of these things be?" In addition to this, wives had given their husbands, mothers their sons, the pride and joy of their hearts. They saw them put on the uniform—they saw them take the martial step, and they tried to hide their deep feeling of sadness. Many dear ones stepped upon the battle-field never to return again, and there was mourning in every mansion and in every cabin in our broad land.

Then came a feeling of deeper sadness, as the story came of prisoners tortured to death or starved, through the mandates of those who are called the representatives of chivalry, or who claim to be honorable ones of the earth; and as we read the stories of frames attenuated and reduced to mere skeletons, our grief turned partly into horror and partly into a cry for vengeance. Then this feeling was changed to one of joy. There came signs of the end of this rebellion. We followed the cue of our glorious Generals. We saw our army under the command of the brave officer who is guiding this procession, climb up the hights of Lookout Mountain and drive the rebels from their strongholds. Another brave General swept through Georgia, South and North Carolina, and drove the combined armies of the rebels before him, while the honored Lieutenant-General held Lee and his followers in a death-grasp.

Then the tidings came that Richmond was evacuated and that Lee had surrendered. The bells rang merrily all over the land. The booming of cannon was heard, illuminations and torchlight processions manifested the general joy, and families were looking for the speedy return of their loved ones from the field of battle. Just in the wildest joy, in one hour, nay, in one moment the tidings thrilled throughout the land that Abraham Lincoln, the best of Presidents, had perished by the hands of an assassin, and then all that feeling which had been gathering for four years in the form of excitement, grief, horror, and joy, turned into one wail of woe; a sadness inexpressible, an anguish unutterable; but it was not the times, merely, which caused the mourning. The mode of his death must be taken into the account. Had he died on a bed of sickness, with kind friends around him; had the sweat of death been wiped from his brow by gentle hands while he was yet conscious; could he have had power to speak words of affection to his stricken widow; words of comfort to us, like those which we heard in parting, and at Washington, in his inaugural, which shall now be immortal; but it would have softened or assuaged something of the grief—there might at least have been preparation for the event. But no moment of warning was given to him or to us. He was stricken down, too, when his hopes for the end of the rebellion were bright, and the prospect of a joyous life was before him.

There was a Cabinet meeting that day, said to have been the most cheerful and happy of any held since the beginning of the rebellion. After this meeting he talked with his friends, and spoke of the four years of tempest; of the storm being over; and of the four years of pleasure and joy now awaiting him, as the weight of care or anguish would be taken from his mind, and he could have happy days with his family again. In the midst of his anticipations, he left his house never to return alive. The evening was Good Friday—the saddest day in the whole calendar for the Christian church, henceforth, in this country to be made sadder, if possible, by the memory of the nation's loss; and so filled with grief was every Christian heart, that even all the joyous thought of Easter Sunday failed to move the crushing sorrow, under which the true worshipper bowed in the house of God.

But the great cause of this mourning is to be found in the man himself. Mr. Lincoln was no ordinary man, and I believe the conviction has been growing on the nation's mind, as it certainly has been on my own, especially in the last years of his administration, that, by the hand of God, he was especially singled out to guide our Government in these troublous times, and, it seems to me, that the hand of God may be traced in many of the events connected with his history.

First, then, I recognize this in the physical education which he received, and which prepared him for enduring herculean labor, in the toils of his boyhood and the labors of his manhood, God was giving him an iron frame. Next to this was his identification with the heart of the great people, understanding their feelings, because he was one of them, and connected with them in their movements and life. His education was simple; a few months spent in a school-house, which gave him the elements of education. He read a few books, but mastered all he read. Bunyan's Pilgrim's Progress, fables, and the Life of Washington, were his favorites. In these we recognize the works which gave the bias to his character, and which partly molded his style. His early life, with its varied struggles, joined him indissolubly to the working masses, and no elevation in society diminished his respect for the sons of toil. He knew what it was to fell the tall trees of the forest, and to stem the current of the hard Mississippi. His home was in the growing West, the heart of the Republic, and, invigorated by the wind which swept over its prairies, he learned lessons of self-reliance, which sustained him in seasons of adversity. His genius was soon recognized, as true genius always will be, and he was placed in the Legislature of his State. Already acquainted with the principles of law, he devoted his thoughts to matters of public interest, and soon began to be looked upon as the coming statesman.

As early as 1849 he presented resolutions in the Legislature, asking for emancipation in the District of Columbia, while, with but rare exceptions, the whole popular mind of his State was opposed to the measure. From that hour he was a steady and uniform friend of humanity, and was preparing for the conflict of later years.

You ask me on what mental characteristics his greatness rested. I answer, on a quick and ready perception of facts; on a memory unusually tenacious and retentive; and on a logical turn of mind, which followed sternly and unwaveringly every link in the chain of thought, on any subject which he was called on to investigate. I think there have been minds more broad in their character, more comprehensive in their scope; but I doubt if ever there has been a man who could follow step by step, with logical power, the points which he desired to illustrate. He gained this power by a close study of geometry, and by a determination to persevere in the truth in its relations and simplicity.

It is said of him that in childhood, when he had any difficulty in listening to a conversation to ascertain what people meant, if he tried to rest, he could not sleep until he tried to understand the precise points intended, and when understood, to convey them in a clearer manner to those who did not. Who that has read his messages fails to perceive the directness and the simplicity of his style; and this very trait, which was scoffed at and derided by opponents, is now recognized as one of the strong points of that mighty mind which has so powerfully influenced the destiny of this nation, and which shall for ages to come influence the destiny of humanity.

It is not, however, chiefly by his mental faculties that he gained such control over mankind. His moral power gave him pre-eminence. The convictions of men that Abraham Lincoln was an honest man, led them to yield to his guidance. As has been said of Mr. [Richard] Cobden, whom he greatly respected, he made every man feel a better sense of himself—a recognizement of individuality—a self-relying power. They saw in him a man whom they believed would do what was right, regardless of all consequences. It was the moral feeling which gave him the greatest hold on the people, and made his utterances almost oracular.

When the nation was angered by the perfidy of foreign nations in allowing privateers to be fitted out, he uttered the significant expression, "One war at a time," and it stilled the national heart. When his own friends were divided as to what steps should be taken as to slavery, that simple utterance, "I will save the Union, if I can, with slavery; but if not slavery must perish; for the Union must be preserved"—became the rallying word.[1] Men felt the struggle was for the Union, and all other questions must be subsidiary. But after all, by the acts of a man shall his fame be perpetuated. Much praise is due to the men who aided him. He called able counselors around him, and able Generals

---

1. Paraphrase of a letter to Horace Greeley, Aug. 22, 1862.

into the field—men who have borne the sword as bravely as ever any human arm has borne it. He had the aid of prayerful and thoughtful men every-where, but under his own guiding hands the movements of our land have been conducted. Turn toward the different departments. We had an unorganized militia, a mere skeleton army, yet, under his care, that army has been enlarged into a force which, for skill, intelligence, efficiency and bravery, surpasses any which the world has ever seen. Before its veterans, the face of even the renowned veterans of Napoleon shall pale. And the mothers and sisters on these hill-sides, and all over the land, shall take to their arms again braver men than ever fought in European wars. The reason is obvious. Money, or a desire for fame collected those armies, or they were rallied to sustain favorite thrones or dynasties; but the armies he called into being fought for liberty, for the Union, and for the right of self-government; and many of them felt that the battles they won were for humanity every-where and for all time; for I believe that God has not suffered this terrible rebellion to come upon our land merely for a chastise-ment to us, or a lesson to our age. There are moments which involve in themselves eternities. There are instants which seem to contain germs which shall develop and bloom forever. Such a moment came in the tide of time, to our land, when a question must be settled—the power of affecting all the earth. The contest was for human freedom, not for this Republic merely; not for the Union simply, but to decide whether the people, as a people, in their entire majesty, were destined to be the Government, or whether they were to be subject to tyrants or autocrats, or to class rule of any kind.

This is the great question for which we have been fighting, and its decision is at hand; and the result of the contest will affect the ages to come. If successful, republics will spread, in spite of monarchs, all over this earth.

I turn from the army to the navy. What was it when the war commenced? Now we have our ships of war at home and abroad to guard privateers in foreign sympathizing ports, as well as to care for every part of our own coast. They have taken forts that military men said could not be taken; and a brave Admiral, for the first time in the world's history, lashes himself to the mast, there to remain as long as he had a particle of skill or strength to watch over his ship while it engaged in the perilous contest of taking the strong forts of the enemy.

Then, again, I turn to the Treasury Department. Where should the money come from? Wise men predicted ruin; but our national credit has been maintained and our currency is safer to-day than it ever was before. Not only so, but through our national bonds, if properly used, we shall have a permanent basis for currency, and an investment so desirable for capitalists of other nations, that under the laws of trade, I believe the center of exchange will be transferred from England to the United States.

But the great act of the mighty chieftain, on which his fame shall rest long after his frame shall molder away, is that of giving freedom to a race. We have all been taught to revere the sacred characters. We have thought of Moses, of his power, and the prominence he gave to the moral law, and how his name now towers high among the names in heaven, and how he delivered three millions of his kindred out of bondage; and yet we may assert that Abraham Lincoln, by his proclamation, liberated more enslaved people than ever Moses set free, and those not of his kindred or of his race. Such a power or such an opportunity has seldom been given to man. When other events shall have been forgotten; when the world shall become a net-work of republics; when every throne shall have been swept from the face of the earth; when literature shall enlighten all minds; when the claims of humanity shall be recognized everywhere, this act shall still be conspicuous on the pages of history; and we are thankful that God gave to Abraham Lincoln the decision and wisdom and grace to issue that proclamation, which stands high above all other papers which have been penned by uninspired men.

Abraham Lincoln was a good man; he was known as an honest, temperate, forgiving man; a just man; a man of a noble heart in every way. As to his religious experience, I cannot speak definitely, because I was not privileged to know much of his private sentiments. My acquaintance with him did not give me the opportunity to hear him speak on those topics. This I know, however, he read the Bible frequently, loved it for its great truths, and profound teachings; and he tried to be guided by its precepts. He believed in Christ, the Saviour of sinners, and I think he was sincerely trying to bring his life into the principles of revealed religion. Certainly, if there ever was a man who illustrated some of the principles of pure religion, that man was our departed President. Look over all his speeches; listen to his utterances. He never spoke unkindly of any man; even the rebels received no words of anger from him; and the last day illustrated, in a remarkable manner, his forgiving disposition. A dispatch was received that afternoon, that Thompson and Tucker were trying to make their escape through Maine, and it was proposed to arrest them. Mr. Lincoln, however, preferred, rather to let them quietly escape. He was seeking to save the very men who had been plotting his destruction, and this morning we read a proclamation offering $25,000 for the arrest of these men, as aiders and abettors of assassination. So that in his expiring acts he was saying, "Father, forgive them; they know not what they do."

To the address of a large religious body he replied; "Thanks be unto God, who, in our national trials, giveth us the churches" [response to Methodists, May 14, 1864]. To a minister who said "he hoped the Lord was on our side," he replied that it gave him no concern whether the Lord was on our side or not, "for" he added "I know the Lord is always on the side of right"; and with deep feeling added, "but God is my witness that it is my constant anxiety and prayer that both myself and this nation should be on the Lord's side."

As a rule, I doubt if any President has ever shown such a trust in God, or in public documents so frequently referred to Divine aid. Often did he remark to friends and to delegations that his hope for our success rested in his conviction that God would bless our efforts, because we were trying to do right.

In his domestic life he was exceedingly kind and affectionate. He was a devoted husband and father. During his Presidential term he lost his second son, Willie. To an officer of the army he said not long since: "Do you ever find yourself talking with the dead?" and added—"Since Willie's death, I catch myself every day involuntarily talking with him as if he were with me."

On his widow, who is unable to be here, I need only invoke the blessing of Almighty God, that she may be comforted and sustained. For his son, who has witnessed the exercises of this hour, all that I can desire is that the mantle of his father may fall upon him.

Let us pause a moment on the lesson of the hour before we part. This man, though he fell by an assassin, still fell under the permissive hand of God. He had some wise purpose in allowing him so to fall. What more could he have desired of life to himself? Were not his honors full? There was no office to which he could aspire. The popular heart clung around him as around no other man. The nations of the world had learned to honor our Chief Magistrate. If rumors of a desired alliance with England be true, Napoleon trembled when he heard of the fall of Richmond, and asked what nation would join him to protect him against our Government.

Besides, the guidance of such a man, his fame, was full; his work was done, and he sealed his glory by becoming the nation's great martyr for liberty.

He appears to have had a strange presentiment early in his political life that some day he would be President. You see it indicated in 1839. Of the slave power he said: "Broken by it I too may be; bow to it I never will. The probability that we may fail in this struggle, ought not to deter us from the support of a cause which we deem to be just. It shall not deter me. If ever I feel the soul within me elevate and expand to those dimensions not wholly unworthy of its Almighty architect, it is when I contemplate the cause of my country. Deserted by all the world beside, and standing up boldly and alone, and hurling defiance at her victorious oppressors; here, without contemplating consequences, before high heaved and in the face of the world, I swear eternal fidelity to the just cause, as I deem it, of the land of my life, my liberty, and my love."[2] And yet secretly he said to more than one, "I never shall live out the four years of my term. When the rebellion is crushed, my work is done." So it was. He lived to see the last battle fought, and to dictate a dispatch from the home of Jefferson Davis; lived till the power of the rebellion was broken, and then, having done the work for which God had sent him, angels, I trust, were sent to shield him from one moment of pain or suffering, and to bear him from this world to that high and glorious realm where the patriot and the good shall live forever.

His example teaches young men that every position of eminence is open before the diligent and the worthy, to the active men of the country. His example urges the country to trust in God and do right.

Standing as we do to-day, by his coffin and sepulcher, let us resolve

2. From Joseph H. Barrett, *Life of Abraham Lincoln* (New York: Moore, Wilstoch, and Baldwin, 1865), 833–34; origin doubtful.

to carry forward the policy which he so nobly began. Let us do right to all men. Let us vow, in the sight of Heaven, eradicate every vestige of human slavery; to give every human being his true position before God and man; to crush every form of rebellion, and to stand by the flag which God has given us. How joyful that it floated over a part of every State before Mr. Lincoln's career was ended.

How singular that, to the fact of the assassin's heel being caught in the folds of the flag, we are probably indebted for his capture. The flag and the traitor must ever be enemies.

Traitors will probably suffer by the change of rulers, for one of sterner mold, and who himself has deeply suffered from the rebellion, now wields the sword of justice.

Our country, too, is stronger for the trial. A republic was declared by monarchists too weak to endure a civil war. Yet we have crushed the most gigantic rebellion in history, and have grown in strength and population every year of the struggle. We have passed through the ordeal of a popular election, while swords and bayonets were in the field, and have come out unharmed.

And now in an hour of excitement, with a large minority having preferred another man for President, the bullet of the assassin has laid our President prostrate. Has there been a mutiny? Has any rival proposed his claims? Out of an army of near a million, no officer or soldier uttered one note of dissent; and in an hour or two after Mr. Lincoln's death, another leader, with constitutional powers, occupied his chair, and the Government moved forward without a single jar. The world will learn that republics are the strongest governments on earth.

To the ambitious there is this fearful lesson: Of the four candidates for Presidential honors in 1860, two of them, Douglas and Lincoln, once competitors—but now sleeping patriots—rest from their labors; Bell perished in poverty and misery, as a traitor might perish, and Breckinridge is a frightened fugitive, with the brand of traitor on his brow.

And now, my friends, in the words of the departed, "With malice toward none"; free from all feeling of personal vengeance, yet believing the sword must not be borne in vain, let us go forward, even in painful duty. Let every man who was a Senator, or Representative in Congress, and who aided in beginning this rebellion, and thus led to the slaughter of our sons and daughters, be brought to speedy and to certain punishment. Let every officer educated at public expense, and who, having been advanced to position has perjured himself, and has turned his sword against the vitals of his country, be doomed to a felon's death. This, I believe, is the will of the American people. Men may attempt to compromise and to restore these traitors and murderers to society again, but the American people will rise in their majesty and sweep all such compromises and compromisers away, and shall declare that there shall be no peace to rebels.

But to the deluded masses we shall extend arms of forgiveness. We will take them to our hearts. We will walk with them side by side, as we go forward to work out a glorious destiny. The time will come when, in the beautiful words of him whose lips are now forever sealed, "the mystic cords of memory, which stretch from every battle-field and from every patriot's grave shall yield a sweeter music when touched by the angels of our better nature."

PART TWO

Emancipation Celebrated

When he visited Richmond, Virginia, after its surrender, Abraham Lincoln was greeted by worshipful blacks who cheered and bowed on their knees to the man whom they looked upon as their savior.[1] The contrite chief executive responded, "Don't kneel to me. . . . You must kneel to God only, and thank him for the liberty you will hereafter enjoy. I am but God's humble instrument."[2]

Some freed slaves commenced to deify Lincoln from the moment of his signing of the Emancipation Proclamation. No act of his administration aroused such enthusiasm and praise as this proclamation, called "potentially the most revolutionary document in U.S. history since the Declaration of Independence."[3] Many liberals here and abroad, including abolitionists, Radical Republicans, freed slaves, and defenders of liberty regard this act as the high mark of Lincoln's career. This proclamation made them soon forget his slowness to act on emancipation, his hesitancy to authorize the use of black troops, and his revocation of General John C. Fremont's early emancipation in Missouri. Nevertheless, the proclamation was a bitter pill for Southerners and Northern conservatives to take, even his closer personal friends. Because of the proclamation, liberal thinkers now present Lincoln as the great apostle of freedom. Mark Neely, Jr., summed up all the reactions: "The Proclamation was the most important and most controversial executive document of Abraham Lincoln's Presidency."[4]

1. William H. Crook, "Lincoln's Last Days," *Harper's Magazine* 115 (Sept. 1905), 521.

2. David D. Porter, *Incidents and Anecdotes of the Civil War* (New York: Appleton, 1885), 293 ff; as quoted in Paul M. Angle, *The Lincoln Reader* (New Brunswick, N.J.: Rutgers University Press, 1947), 507–12.

3. Thomas H. Johnson, *Oxford Companion to American History* (New York: Oxford University Press, 1966), 272.

4. Mark E. Neely, Jr., *The Abraham Lincoln Encyclopedia* (New York: McGraw-Hill, 1982), 103–5.

Expression of Gratitude for Freedom

UNVEILING OF THE FREEDMEN'S MONUMENT
LINCOLN PARK, WASHINGTON, D.C.
APRIL 14, 1876

Greatly distressed by the assassination, Charlotte Scott, a poor ex-slave of Marietta, Ohio, said to her employer, " 'The colored people have lost their best friend on earth! Mr. Lincoln was our best friend and I will give five dollars of my wages toward erecting a monument in his memory.' " That small token was the beginning of the efforts of freed slaves to express in a concrete way their gratitude to Lincoln. They finally raised $17,000, which paid for the Freedmen's Monument, dedicated on April 14, 1876, in Lincoln Park, Washington, D.C. Through the offices of the Western Sanitary Commission, Thomas Ball, a versatile artist, was persuaded in 1869 to undertake the creation of the monument.

The artist showed President Lincoln standing over a kneeling black, who was looking upward in gratitude. Although no longer popular, especially with blacks, in its time it was symbolic in its period, origin, form, and dedication. To achieve "historical accuracy," Ball chose as a model for the kneeling slave, "a living man" who was "the last slave [Archer Alexander] in Missouri taken up under the fugitive slave law." Even more symbolic was the impressive presentation ceremony, attended by President Ulysses S. Grant, members of his cabinet, justices of the Supreme Court, members of Congress, and other notables.[1]

The former slave and well-known orator was an excellent choice to make the formal presentation. He had been a personal friend of the president, having visited with him several times. Lincoln had intervened when the police attempted to prevent Douglass from attending the inaugural reception in 1865. The president went to the door, greeted Douglass, and led him into the room, saying " 'Here comes my friend Douglass.' " Later Douglass remembered, "In all my interviews with Mr. Lincoln I was impressed with his entire freedom from popular prejudice against the colored race. He was the first great man that I talked with in the United States freely, who in no single instance reminded me of the difference between himself and myself, of the difference of color, and I thought that all the more remarkable because he came from a state where there were black laws."[2]

The recognition that the administration gave the presentation added dignity to the occasion. Congress had authorized the erection of the monument in Lincoln Park, a mile east of the Capitol, and appropriated $3,000 for the pedestal to hold the statue.[3] Nevertheless, the assembling of whites and blacks on more or less equal terms in 1876 created for many a provocative meeting. Sensitive to current sentiments and prejudices, Douglass observed: "Harmless, beautiful, proper, and praiseworthy as this demonstration is, I cannot forget that no such demonstration would have been tolerated here twenty years ago." In addressing his listeners, he chose to speak to the whites as *you* and the blacks as *we.* He said, "you are the children of Abraham Lincoln. We are at best only his step-children; children by adoption, children by force of circumstances and necessity." Just as adroitly he worked around the touchy point of blacks honoring Lincoln: "To you it especially belongs to sound his praise, to preserve and perpetuate his memory.... Instead of supplanting you at this altar, we would exhort you to build high his monuments.... But while in the abundance of your wealth, and in the fulness of your just and patriotic devotion ... we entreat you to despise not the humble offering we this day unveil to view."

In his presentation, Douglass had at least four goals: to congratulate the freed slaves upon the completion of the monument ("we have done a good work for our race to-day"), "to express ... our [ex-slaves] grateful sense of the vast, high, and pre-eminent services rendered to ourselves ... by Abraham Lincoln," and to honor "the exalted character and great works of ... the first martyr President." More subtle and indirect was his fourth goal: to foster the respect of the administration for the gratitude, goodwill, and good efforts of freed slaves.

This eulogy is unlike other speeches in this collection because the speaker dared to cite negative aspects of Lincoln's administration prior to the issuance of the proclamation. The contrast may have heightened Douglass's final appraisal for many listeners, but his frankness might have embarrassed the administration, which was trying to forget Lincoln's earlier positions.

1. *Oration by Frederick Douglass Delivered on the Occasion of the Unveiling of the Freedmen's Monument in Memory of Abraham Lincoln in Lincoln Park, Washington, D.C., April 14, 1876* (Washington, D.C.: Gibson Brothers, 1876). Deposited in the Illinois State Historical Library, Springfield, Ill. See appendix, 17–20.

2. Richard N. Current, *The Lincoln Nobody Knows* (New York: Hill and Wang, 1958), 234–35.

3. *Oration by Frederick Douglass,* 19; F. Lauriston Bullard, *Lincoln in Marble and Bronze* (New Brunswick, N.J.: Rutgers University Press, 1952), 64–70.

The speech is reprinted from *Oration by Frederick Douglass Delivered on the Occasion of the Unveiling of the Freedmen's Monument in Memory of Abraham Lincoln in Lincoln Park, Washington, D.C., April 14, 1876* (Washington, D.C.: Gibson Brothers, 1876). Deposited in the Illinois State Historical Library, Springfield, Ill.

F*riends and Fellow Citizens:* I warmly congratulate you upon the highly interesting object which has caused you to assemble in such numbers and spirit as you have to-day. This occasion is in some respects remarkable. Wise and thoughtful men of our race, who shall come after us, and study the lesson of our history in the United States; who shall survey the long and dreary spaces over which we have travelled; who shall count the links in the great chain of events by which we have reached our present position, will make a note of this occasion; they will think of it and speak of it with a sense of manly pride and complacency.

I congratulate you, also, upon the very favorable circumstances in which we meet to-day. They are high, inspiring, and uncommon. They lend grace, glory, and significance to the object for which we have met. Nowhere else in this great country, with its uncounted towns and cities, unlimited wealth, and immeasurable territory extending from sea to sea, could conditions be found more favorable to the success of this occasion than here.

We stand to-day at the national centre to perform something like a national act—an act which is to go into history; and we are here where every pulsation of the national heart can be heard, felt, and reciprocated. A thousand wires, fed with thought and winged with lightning, put us in instantaneous communication with the loyal and true men all over this country.

Few facts could better illustrate the vast and wonderful change which has taken place in our condition as a people than the fact of our assembling here for the purpose we have to-day. Harmless, beautiful, proper, and praiseworthy as this demonstration is, I cannot forget that no such demonstration would have been tolerated here twenty years ago. The spirit of slavery and barbarism, which still lingers to blight and destroy in some dark and distant parts of our country, would have made our assembling here the signal and excuse for opening upon us all the flood-gates of wrath and violence. That we are here in peace to-day is a compliment and a credit to American civilization, and a prophecy of still greater national enlightenment and progress in the future. I refer to the past not in malice, for this is no day for malice;

but simply to place more distinctly in front the gratifying and glorious change which has come both to our white fellow-citizens and ourselves, and to congratulate all upon the contrast between now and then; the new dispensation of freedom with its thousand blessings to both races, and the old dispensation of slavery with its ten thousand evils to both races—white and black. In view, then, of the past, the present, and the future, with the long and dark history of our bondage behind us, and with liberty, progress, and enlightenment before us, I again congratulate you upon this auspicious day and hour.

Friends and fellow-citizens, the story of our presence here is soon and easily told. We are here in the District of Columbia, here in the city of Washington, the most luminous point of American territory; a city recently transformed and made beautiful in its body and in its spirit; we are here in the place where the ablest and best men of the country are sent to devise the policy, enact the laws, and shape the destiny of the Republic; we are here, with the stately pillars and majestic dome of the Capitol of the nation looking down upon us; we are here, with the broad earth freshly adorned with the foliage and flowers of spring for our church, and all races, colors, and conditions of men for our congregation—in a word, we are here to express, as best we may, by appropriate forms and ceremonies, our grateful sense of the vast, high, and pre-eminent services rendered to ourselves, to our race, to our country, and to the whole world by Abraham Lincoln.

The sentiment that brings us here to-day is one of the noblest that can stir and thrill the human heart. It has crowned and made glorious the high places of all civilized nations with the grandest and most enduring works of art, designed to illustrate the characters and per-petuate the memories of great public men. It is the sentiment which from year to year adorns with fragrant and beautiful flowers the graves of our loyal, brave, and patriotic soldiers who fell in defence of the Union and liberty. It is the sentiment of gratitude and appreciation, which often, in presence of many who hear me, has filled yonder heights of Arlington with the eloquence of eulogy and the sublime enthusiasm of poetry and song; a sentiment which can never die while the Republic lives.

For the first time in the history of our people, and in the history of the whole American people, we join in this high worship, and march conspicuously in the line of this time-honored custom. First things are always interesting, and this is one of our first things. It is the first time that, in this form and manner, we have sought to do honor to an American great man, however deserving and illustrious. I commend the fact to notice; let it be told in every part of the Republic; let men of all parties and opinions hear it; let those who despise us, not less than those who respect us, know that now and here, in the spirit of liberty, loyalty, and gratitude, let it be known everywhere, and by everybody who takes an interest in human progress and in the amelioration of the condition of mankind, that, in the presence and with the approval of the members of the American House of Representatives, reflecting the general sentiment of the country; that in the presence of that august body, the American Senate, representing the highest intelligence and the calmest judgment of the country; in presence of the Supreme Court and Chief-Justice of the United States, to whose decisions we all patriotically bow; in the presence and under the steady eye of the honored and trusted President of the United States, with the members of his wise and patriotic Cabinet, we, the colored people, newly emancipated and rejoicing in our blood-bought freedom, near the close of the first century in the life of this Republic, have now and here unveiled, set apart, and dedicated a monument of enduring granite and bronze, in every line, feature, and figure of which the men of this generation may read, and those of after-coming generations may read, something of the exalted character and great works of Abraham Lincoln, the first martyr President of the United States.

Fellow-citizens, in what we have said and done to-day, and in what we may say and do hereafter, we disclaim everything like arrogance and assumption. We claim for ourselves no superior devotion to the character, history, and memory of the illustrious name whose monument we have here dedicated to-day. We fully comprehend the relation of Abraham Lincoln both to ourselves and to the white people of the United States. Truth is proper and beautiful at all times and in all places, and it is never more proper and beautiful in any case than when speaking of a great public man whose example is likely to be commended for honor and imitation long after his departure to the solemn shades, the silent continents of eternity. It must be admitted, truth compels me to admit, even here in the presence of the monument we have erected to his memory, Abraham Lincoln was not, in the fullest sense of the word, either our man or our model. In his interests, in his associations, in his habits of thought, and in his prejudices, he was a white man.

He was pre-eminently the white man's President, entirely devoted to the welfare of white men. He was ready and willing at any time during the first years of his administration to deny, postpone, and sacrifice the rights of humanity in the colored people to promote the welfare of the white people of this country. In all his education and feeling he was an American of the Americans. He came into the Presidential chair upon one principle alone, namely, opposition to the extension of slavery. His arguments in furtherance of this policy had their motive and mainspring in his patriotic devotion to the interests of his own race. To protect, defend, and perpetuate slavery in the States where it existed Abraham Lincoln was not less ready than any other President to draw the sword of the nation. He was ready to execute all the supposed constitutional guarantees of the United States Constitution in favor of the slave system anywhere inside the slave States. He was willing to pursue, recapture, and send back the fugitive slave to his master, and to suppress a slave rising for liberty, though his guilty master were already in arms against the Government. The race to which we belong were not the special objects of his consideration. Knowing this, I concede to you, my white fellow-citizens, a pre-eminence in this worship at once full and supreme. First, midst, and last, you and yours were the objects of his deepest affection and his most earnest solicitude. You are the children of Abraham Lincoln. We are at best only his step-children; children by adoption, children by force of circumstances and necessity. To you it especially belongs to sound his praises, to preserve and perpetuate his memory, to multiply his statues, to hang his pictures high upon your walls, and commend his example, for to you he was a great and glorious friend and benefactor. Instead of supplanting you at this altar, we would exhort you to build high his monuments; let them be of the most costly material, of the most cunning workmanship; let their forms be symmetrical, beautiful, and perfect; let their bases be upon solid rocks, and their summits lean against the unchanging blue, overhanging sky, and let them endure forever! But while in the abundance of your wealth, and in the fulness of your just and patriotic devotion, you do all this, we entreat you to despise not the humble offering we this day unveil to view; for while Abraham Lincoln saved for you a country, he delivered us from a bondage, according to Jefferson, one hour of which was worse than ages of the oppression your fathers rose in rebellion to oppose.

Fellow-citizens, ours is no new-born zeal and devotion—merely a thing of this moment. The name of Abraham Lincoln was near and dear to our hearts in the darkest and most perilous hours of the Republic. We were no more ashamed of him when shrouded in clouds of darkness, of doubt, and defeat than when we saw him crowned with victory, honor, and glory. Our faith in him was often taxed and strained to the uttermost, but it never failed. When he tarried long in the mountain; when he strangely told us that we were the cause of the war; when he still more strangely told us to leave the land in which we were born; when he refused to employ our arms in defence of the Union; when, after accepting our services as colored soldiers, he refused to retaliate our murder and torture as colored prisoners; when he told us he would save the Union if he could with slavery; when he revoked the Proclamation of Emancipation of General Frémont; when he refused to remove the popular commander of the Army of the Potomac, in the days of its inaction and defeat, who was more zealous in his efforts to protect slavery than to suppress rebellion; when we saw all this, and more, we were at times grieved, stunned, and greatly bewildered; but our hearts believed while they ached and bled. Nor was this, even at that time, a blind and unreasoning superstition. Despite the mist and haze that surrounded him; despite the tumult, the hurry, and confusion of the hour, we were able to take a comprehensive view of Abraham Lincoln, and to make reasonable allowance for the circumstances of his position. We saw him, measured him, and estimated him; not by stray utterances to injudicious and tedious delegations, who often tried his patience; not by isolated facts torn from their connection; not by any partial and imperfect glimpses, caught at inopportune moments; but by a broad survey, in the light of the stern logic of great events, and in view of that divinity which shapes our ends, rough hew them how we will, we came to the conclusion that the hour and the man of our redemption had somehow met in the person of Abraham Lincoln. It mattered little to us what language he might employ on special occasions; it mattered little to us, when we fully knew him, whether he was swift or slow in his movements; it was enough for us that Abraham Lincoln was at the head of a great movement, and was in living and earnest sympathy with that movement, which, in the nature of things, must go on until slavery should be utterly and forever abolished in the United States.

When, therefore, it shall be asked what we have to do with the memory of Abraham Lincoln, or what Abraham Lincoln had to do with us, the answer is ready, full, and complete. Though he loved Caesar less than Rome, though the Union was more to him than our freedom or our future, under his wise and beneficent rule we saw ourselves gradually lifted from the depths of slavery to the heights of liberty and manhood; under his wise and beneficent rule, and by measures approved and vigorously pressed by him, we saw that the handwriting of ages, in the form of prejudice and proscription, was rapidly fading away from the face of our whole country; under his rule, and in due time, about as soon after all as the country could tolerate the strange spectacle, we saw our brave sons and brothers laying off the rags of bondage, and being clothed all over in the blue uniforms of the soldiers of the United States; under his rule we saw two hundred thousand of our dark and dusky people responding to the call of Abraham Lincoln, and with muskets on their shoulders, and eagles on their buttons, timing their high footsteps to liberty and union under the national flag; under his rule we saw the independence of the black republic of Hayti, the special object of slaveholding aversion and horror, fully recognized, and her minister, a colored gentleman, duly received here in the city of Washington; under his rule we saw the internal slave-trade, which so long disgraced the nation, abolished, and slavery abolished in the District of Columbia; under his rule we saw for the first time the law enforced against the foreign slave-trade, and the first slave-trader hanged like any other pirate or murderer; under his rule, assisted by the greatest captain of our age, and his inspiration, we saw the Confederate States, based upon the idea that our race must be slaves, and slaves forever, battered to pieces and scattered to the four winds; under his rule, and in the fullness of time, we saw Abraham Lincoln, after giving the slave-holders three months' grace in which to save their hateful slave system, penning the immortal paper, which, though special in its language, was general in its principles and effect, making slavery forever impossible in the United States. Though we waited long, we saw all this and more.

Can any colored man, or any white man friendly to the freedom of all men, ever forget the night which followed the first day of January, 1863, when the world was to see if Abraham Lincoln would prove to be as good as his word? I shall never forget that memorable night, when in a distant city I waited and watched at a public meeting, with three thousand others not less anxious than myself, for the word of deliverance which we have heard read to-day. Nor shall I ever forget the outburst of joy and thanksgiving that rent the air when the lightning brought to us the emancipation proclamation. In that happy hour we forgot all delay, and forgot all tardiness, forgot that the President had bribed the rebels to lay down their arms by a promise to withhold the bolt which would smite the slave-system with destruction; and we were thenceforward willing to allow the President all the latitude of time, phraseology, and every honorable device that statesmanship might require for the achievement of a great and beneficent measure of liberty and progress.

Fellow-citizens, there is little necessity on this occasion to speak at length and critically of this great and good man, and of his high mission in the world. That ground has been fully occupied and completely covered both here and elsewhere. The whole field of fact and fancy has been gleaned and garnered. Any man can say things that are true of Abraham Lincoln, but no man can say anything that is new of Abraham Lincoln. His personal traits and public acts are better known to the American people than are those of any other man of his age. He was a mystery to no man who saw him and heard him. Though high in position, the humblest could approach him and feel at home in his presence. Though deep, he was transparent; though strong, he was gentle; though decided and pronounced in his convictions, he was tolerant towards those who differed from him, and patient under reproaches. Even those who only knew him through his public utterances obtained a tolerably clear idea of his character and his personality. The image of the man went out with his words, and those who read them, knew him.

I have said that President Lincoln was a white man, and shared the prejudices common to his countrymen towards the colored race. Looking back to his times and to the condition of his country, we are compelled to admit that this unfriendly feeling on his part may be safely set down as one element of his wonderful success in organizing

98

the loyal American people for the tremendous conflict before them, and bringing them safely through that conflict. His great mission was to accomplish two things: first, to save his country from dismemberment and ruin; and second, to free his country from the great crime of slavery. To do one or the other, or both, he must have the earnest sympathy and the powerful co-operation of his loyal fellow-countrymen. Without this primary and essential condition to success his efforts must have been vain and utterly fruitless. Had he put the abolition of slavery before the salvation of the Union, he would have inevitably driven from him a powerful class of the American people and rendered resistance to rebellion impossible. Viewed from the genuine abolition ground, Mr. Lincoln seemed tardy, cold, dull, and indifferent; but measuring him by the sentiment of his country, a sentiment he was bound as a statesman to consult, he was swift, zealous, radical, and determined.

Though Mr. Lincoln shared the prejudices of his white fellow-countrymen against the negro, it is hardly necessary to say that in his heart of hearts he loathed and hated slavery. The man who could say, "Fondly do we hope, fervently do we pray, that this mighty scourge of war shall soon pass away, yet if God wills it continue till all the wealth piled by two hundred years of bondage shall have been wasted, and each drop of blood drawn by the lash shall have been paid for by one drawn by the sword, the judgments of the Lord are true and righteous altogether," gives all needed proof of his feeling on the subject of slavery. He was willing, while the South was loyal, that it should have its pound of flesh, because he thought that it was so nominated in the bond; but farther than this no earthly power could make him go.

Fellow-citizens, whatever else in this world may be partial, unjust, and uncertain, time, time! is impartial, just, and certain in its action. In the realm of mind, as well as in the realm of matter, it is a great worker, and often works wonders. The honest and comprehensive statesman, clearly discerning the needs of his country, and earnestly endeavoring to do his whole duty, though covered and blistered with reproaches, may safely leave his course to the silent judgment of time. Few great public men have ever been the victims of fiercer denunciation than Abraham Lincoln was during his administration. He was often wounded in the house of his friends. Reproaches came thick and fast upon him from within and from without, and from opposite quarters. He was assailed by Abolitionists; he was assailed by slave-holders; he was assailed by the men who were for peace at any price; he was assailed by those who were for a more vigorous prosecution of the war; he was assailed for not making the war an abolition war; and he was most bitterly assailed for making the war an abolition war.

But now behold the change: the judgment of the present hour, that taking him for all in all, measuring the tremendous magnitude of the work before him, considering the necessary means to ends, and surveying the end from the beginning, infinite wisdom has seldom sent any man into the world better fitted for his mission than Abraham Lincoln. His birth, his training, and his natural endowments, both mental and physical, were strongly in his favor. Born and reared among the lowly, a stranger to wealth and luxury, compelled to grapple single handed with the flintiest hardships of life, from tender youth to sturdy manhood, he grew strong in the manly and heroic qualities demanded by the great mission to which he was called by the votes of his countrymen. The hard condition of his early life, which would have depressed and broken down weaker men, only gave greater life, vigor, and buoyancy to the heroic spirit of Abraham Lincoln. He was ready for any kind and any quality of work. What other young men dreaded in the shape of toil, he took hold of with the utmost cheerfulness.

> A spade, a rake, a hoe,
>   A pick-axe, or a bill;
> A hook to reap, a scythe to mow,
>   A flail, or what you will.

All day long he could split heavy rails in the woods, and half the night long he could study his English Grammar by the uncertain flare and glare of the light made by a pine-knot. He was at home on the land with his axe, with his maul, with gluts, and his wedges; and he was equally at home on water, with his oars, with his poles, with his planks, and with his boat-hooks. And whether in his flat-boat on the Mississippi river, or at the fireside of his frontier cabin, he was a man of work. A son of toil himself, he was linked in brotherly sympathy with the sons of toil in every loyal part of the Republic. This very fact gave him tremendous power with the American people, and materially contributed not only to selecting him to the Presidency, but in sustaining his administration of the Government.

Upon his inauguration as President of the United States, an office, even where assumed under the most favorable conditions, fitted to tax and strain the largest abilities, Abraham Lincoln was met by a tremendous crisis. He was called upon not merely to administer the Government, but to decide, in the face of terrible odds, the fate of the Republic.

A formidable rebellion rose in his path before him; the Union was already practically dissolved; his country was torn and rent asunder at the centre. Hostile armies were already organized against the Republic, armed with the munitions of war which the Republic had provided for its own defence. The tremendous question for him to decide was whether his country should survive the crisis and flourish, or be dismembered and perish. His predecessor in office had already decided the question in favor of national dismemberment, by denying to it the right of self-defence and self-preservation—a right which belongs to the meanest insect.

Happily for the country, happily for you and for me, the judgment of James Buchanan, the patrician, was not the judgment of Abraham Lincoln, the plebeian. He brought his strong common sense, sharpened in the school of adversity, to bear upon the question. He did not hesitate, he did not doubt, he did not falter; but at once resolved that at whatever peril, at whatever cost, the union of the States should be preserved. A patriot himself, his faith was strong and unwavering in the patriotism of his countrymen. Timid men said before Mr. Lincoln's inauguration, that we had seen the last President of the United States. A voice in influential quarters said "Let the Union slide." Some said that a Union maintained by the sword was worthless. Others said a rebellion of 8,000,000 cannot be suppressed; but in the midst of all this tumult and timidity, and against all this, Abraham Lincoln was clear in his duty, and had an oath in heaven. He calmly and bravely heard the voice of doubt and fear all around him; but he had an oath in heaven, and there was not power enough on the earth to make this honest boatman, back-woodsman, and broad-handed splitter of rails evade or violate that sacred oath. He had not been schooled in the ethics of slavery; his plain life had favored his love of truth. He had not been taught that treason and perjury were the proof of honor and honesty. His moral training was against his saying one thing when he meant another. The trust which Abraham Lincoln had in himself and in the people was surprising and grand, but it was also enlightened and well founded. He knew the American people better than they knew themselves, and his truth was based upon this knowledge.

Fellow-citizens, the fourteenth day of April, 1865, of which this is the eleventh anniversary, is now and will ever remain a memorable day in the annals of this Republic. It was on the evening of this day, while a fierce and sanguinary rebellion was in the last stages of its desolating power; while its armies were broken and scattered before the invincible armies of Grant and Sherman; while a great nation, torn and rent by war, was already beginning to raise to the skies loud anthems of joy at the dawn of peace, it was startled, amazed, and overwhelmed by the crowning crime of slavery—the assassination of Abraham Lincoln. It was a new crime, a pure act of malice. No purpose of the rebellion was to be served by it. It was the simple gratification of a hell-black spirit of revenge. But it has done good after all. It has filled the country with a deeper abhorrence of slavery and a deeper love for the great liberator.

Had Abraham Lincoln died from any of the numerous ills to which flesh is heir; had he reached that good old age of which his vigorous constitution and his temperate habits gave promise; had he been permitted to see the end of his great work; had the solemn curtain of death come down but gradually—we should still have been smitten with a heavy grief, and treasured his name lovingly. But dying as he did die, by the red hand of violence, killed, assassinated, taken off without warning, not because of personal hate—for no man who knew Abraham Lincoln could hate him—but because of his fidelity to union and liberty, he is doubly dear to us, and his memory will be precious forever.

Fellow-citizens, I end, as I began, with congratulations. We have done a good work for our race to-day. In doing honor to the memory of our friend and liberator, we have been doing highest honors to ourselves and those who come after us; we have been fastening ourselves to a name and fame imperishable and immortal; we have also been defending ourselves from a blighting scandal. When now it shall be said that the colored man is soulless, that he has no appreciation of benefits or benefactors; when the foul reproach of ingratitude is hurled at us, and it is attempted to scourge us beyond the range of human brotherhood, we may calmly point to the monument we have this day erected to the memory of Abraham Lincoln.

JAMES A. GARFIELD

The Scene in the Silent and Pathetic Language of Art

JOINT SESSION OF CONGRESS
WASHINGTON, D.C.
FEBRUARY 12, 1878

The Francis B. Carpenter painting *The First Reading of the Emancipation Proclamation of President Lincoln* was formally presented to the United States government on February 12, 1878, at a joint session of Congress. In addition to the senators and representatives, the audience included relatives of Lincoln, members of the war cabinet, the donor, Elizabeth Thompson, with her escort, and the artist.

The room was made more awe-inspiring because the lifesize painting (fourteen feet six inches long and nine feet high), draped with an American flag, was displayed behind the presiding officer's desk. It memorialized what many considered the most significant accomplishment of Lincoln's four years and symbolized for many the end of human slavery and the beginning of freedom. Caught up in the patriotic fervor, Thompson, concerned that the great masterpiece might disappear, purchased it from the artist for $25,000.

No other historical American painting had such an unusual beginning. The painter gained the privilege of painting it in the State Dining Room of the White House from February through July of 1864. Actually residing at the White House, Carpenter had more or less free access to those included in his composition, observed the presidential activities, and talked frequently with Lincoln and the cabinet members. Further, the painter persuaded the principals to pose for photographs taken at Brady's studio. These pictures enabled the artist to achieve greater realism.

The composition in its final arrangement was not posed, but became "a curious mingling of fact and allegory" from Carpenter's imagination. Lincoln and the seven cabinet members appear as the painter fanta-

103

sized the historical day in September of 1862. While the painter worked, Lincoln followed his progress and gave his blessings to the interpretation. Lincoln supposedly told Carpenter, "'I believe I am about as glad over the success of the work as you are.'"[1]

As a by-product of the six-month project, Carpenter published *Six Months at the White House with Abraham Lincoln: The Story of a Picture* that ran through sixteen editions. It became an important source of intimate details about Lincoln's life in the White House. In 1866 Alexander Hay Ritchie made a steel engraving of the painting (twenty-one by thirty-two inches), prints of which were revered in thousands of homes.[2]

After its formal presentation in August of 1864, thousands viewed Carpenter's masterpiece in the rotunda of the Capitol, and later in Boston, Chicago, Milwaukee, New York, Pittsburgh (where it was at the time of the assassination), and other eastern and western cities. Presently, the painting hangs in the Old Senate Chamber in the Capitol.

In her letter of presentation, Elizabeth Thompson gave vital information about the painting and expressed her sentiments:

> To the Senate and House of Representatives in Congress Assembled.
> Your petitioner most respectfully represents as follows:—
> The Proclamation of Emancipation by President Lincoln was one of the great historic events of the century.—scarcely second in importance to any in our national annals. The historical painting celebrating this act, executed under the direct supervision of President Lincoln at the Executive mansion in 1864, has become widely known through engraved copies which may be seen hanging upon the walls of thousands of homes throughout the land. The public press has from time to time given expression to the popular desire that this painting, associated as it is with the memory of the lamented Lincoln, should be preserved among the other historic art-works of the national Capitol. . . .
> Your petitioner ventures the hope that, should her gift meet the approval of Congress, an hour may be designated, on Lincoln's birthday, February 12, to receive the painting.
> Elizabeth Thompson
> New York, January 9, 1878[3]

At the formal presentation to the United States, James A. Garfield, representative from Ohio at the time, and Alexander H. Stephens, former vice-president of the Confederacy and at the time representative from Georgia, gave commemorative addresses. Speaking in front of the painting, Garfield made the official acceptance and used the depicted scene as a visual aid to reinforce his remarks about the evolution of the proclamation. Speaking of the figures in the painting, Garfield gave passing praise to Seward, Chase, and Stanton, and then turned eloquent about Abraham Lincoln, whose birthday had been sixty-nine years before.

Showing awareness about "great and honest differences of opinion," the speaker suggested that the listeners were "too near the great events of which this act formed so conspicuous a part, to understand its deep significance." Garfield included three long quotations, which were inserted in his presentation: Lincoln's speech at Independence Hall in 1861, Lincoln's reply to Greeley, and the Chase account of Lincoln's presentation of the proclamation on September 22, 1863. Through this quoted matter, Garfield added realism to the event commemorated.

However, in his survey of the painting Garfield clearly set forth the importance of keeping alive a vivid memory of the episode, hence his little details were manifestations of the growing legend. For this reason the Garfield eulogy is not important for its rhetorical excellence, but as an instance of the intensification of the Lincoln myth.

Following the Garfield speech, the former vice-president of the Confederacy, now an old man in a wheelchair, rolled to the front and delivered an extemporaneous, thirty-minute speech. His appearance stirred more interest than that of the former Union general who would be president.[4] Stephens's correspondence indicated that the artist and the donor had wanted the old Georgian to make the formal speech of acceptance. Carpenter had written Stephens, "It is believed . . . that the speech you will make will produce the most profound impression and the most beneficial results."[5] Though he recognized that the ceremony provided a remarkable opportunity for a statement about reconciliation, Stephens first declined, citing poor health as an excuse, but perhaps he knew that he would face stern censure from many unreconstructed rebels. Nevertheless, when Garfield concluded Stephens was ready. He began, "there is but little left to say in the performance of the part assigned me in the programme arranged for this august occasion." He affirmed that he "knew Mr. Lincoln well [and] . . . was as intimate with him as with any other man of that Congress except one Robert Toombs." He called Lincoln "warmhearted . . . generous . . . 'with malice toward none, with charity for all.' "⁶

In harmony with the spirit of the occasion, the former rebel conceded that the Emancipation Proclamation was "one of the greatest epochs in our days" and confirmed that the South had responded favorably to "the changed condition of their status [blacks], though it was the leading cause of the late terrible conflict of arms between the States, yet I think I may venture to affirm there is not one within the circle of my acquaintance, or in the whole Southern country, who would wish to see the relation restored." Before closing, he rationalized the Southern position about freeing the slaves and concluded with an appeal for good relations between the North and the South.

1. *Lincoln Lore*, 1482 (Aug. 1961), and 1483 (Sept. 1961). Francis B. Carpenter, *Six Months at the White House: The Story of a Picture* (New York: Hurd and Houghton, 1866), 343.

2. Mark E. Neely, Jr., *The Abraham Lincoln Encyclopedia* (New York: McGraw-Hill, 1982), 47–48.

3. *Congressional Record*, 45th Cong., 2d sess., 1878. Vol. 7, pt. 1, 968–71.

4. Ibid.

5. Stephen Robert Guempel, *A Rhetorical Analysis of Selected Ceremonial Speeches of Alexander H. Stephens, 1875-1883* (M.A. thesis, Louisiana State University, 1975), 127–56. I am much indebted to my former student Guempel for his insights.

6. *New York Times*, Feb. 13, 1878; *Congressional Record*, 970–71.

The speech is reprinted from *Congressional Record*, 45th Cong., 2d sess., 1878. Vol. 7, pt. 1, 968–71.

M*r. President:* By the order of the Senate and the House, and on behalf of the donor, Mrs. Elizabeth Thompson, it is made my pleasant duty to deliver to Congress the painting which is now unveiled. It is the patriotic gift of an American woman whose years have been devoted to gentle and generous charities, and to the instruction and elevation of the laboring poor.

Believing that the perpetuity and glory of her country depend upon the dignity of labor and the equal freedom of all its people, she has come to the Capitol, to place in the perpetual custody of the nation, as the symbol of her faith, the representation of that great act which proclaimed 'liberty throughout all the land unto all the inhabitants thereof.'

Inspired by the same sentiment, the representatives of the nation have opened the doors of this Chamber to receive at her hands the sacred trust. In coming hither, these living representatives have passed under the dome and through that beautiful and venerable hall which, on another occasion, I have ventured to call the third House of American representatives, that silent assembly whose members have received their high credentials at the impartial hand of history. Year by year, we see the circle of its immortal membership enlarging; year by year, we see the elect of their country, in eloquent silence, taking their places in this American pantheon, bringing within its sacred precincts the wealth of those immortal memories which made their lives illustrious; and year by year, that august assembly is teaching deeper and grander lessons to those who serve in these more ephemeral Houses of Congress.

Among the paintings, hitherto assigned to places within the Capitol, are two which mark events forever memorable in the history of mankind; thrice memorable in the history of America.

The first is the painting by [John] Vanderlyn, which represents, though with inadequate force, the great discovery which gave to the civilized world a new hemisphere.

The second, by [John] Trumbull, represents that great Declaration which banished forever from our shores the crown and scepter of imperial power, and proposed to found a new nation upon the broad and enduring basis of liberty.

To-day, we place upon our walls this votive tablet, which commemorates the third great act in the history of America—the fulfillment of the promises of the Declaration.

Concerning the causes which led to that act, the motives which inspired it, the necessities which compelled it, and the consequences which followed and are yet to follow it, there have been, there are, and still will be great and honest differences of opinion. Perhaps we are yet too near the great events of which this act formed so conspicuous a part, to understand its deep significance and to foresee its far-off consequences.

The lesson of history is rarely learned by the actors themselves, especially when they read it by the fierce and dusky light of war, or amid the deeper shadows of those sorrows which war brings to both. But the unanimous voice of this House in favor of accepting the gift, and the impressive scenes we here witness, bear eloquent testimony to the transcendent importance of the event portrayed on yonder canvas.

Let us pause to consider the actors in that scene. In force of character, in thoroughness and breadth of culture, in experience of public affairs, and in national reputation, the Cabinet that sat around that council-board has had no superior, perhaps no equal, in our history. [William H.] Seward, the finished scholar, the consummate orator, the great leader of the Senate, had come to crown his career with those achievements which placed him in the first rank of modern diplomatists. [Salmon P.] Chase, with a culture and a frame of massive grandeur, stood as the rock and pillar of the public credit, the noble embodiment of the public faith. [Edwin M.] Stanton was there, a very Titan of strength, the great-organizer of victory. Eminent lawyers, men of business, leaders of States and leaders of men completed the group.

But the man who presided over that council, who inspired and guided its deliberations, was a character so unique that he stood alone, without a model in history or a parallel among men. Born on this day, sixty-nine years ago, to an inheritance of extremest poverty; surrounded by the rude forces of the wilderness; wholly unaided by parents; only one year in any school; never, for a day, master of his own time, until he reached his majority; making his way to the profession of law by the hardest and roughest road; yet by force of

108

unconquerable will and persistent, patient work, he attained a fore-most place in his profession.

> And, moving up from high to higher,
> Became, on fortune's crowning slope,
> The pillar of a people's hope,
>   The center of a world's desire.
>   [Tennyson, *In Memoriam*, sec. 64]

At first, it was the prevailing belief that he would be only the nomi-nal head of his administration; that its policy would be directed by the eminent statesmen he had called to his council. How erroneous this opinion was, may be seen from a single incident:

Among the earliest, most difficult, and most delicate duties of his administration, was the adjustment of our relations with Great Britain. Serious complications, even hostilities, were apprehended. On the 21st of May, 1861, the Secretary of State [Seward] presented to the Presi-dent his draught of a letter of instructions to Minister [Charles Francis] Adams, in which the position of the United States and the attitude of Great Britain were set forth with the clearness and force, which long experience and great ability had placed at the command of the secretary.

Upon almost every page of that original draught are erasures, addi-tions and marginal notes, in the hand-writing of Abraham Lincoln, which exhibit a sagacity, a breadth of wisdom, and a comprehension of the whole subject, impossible to be found except in a man of the very first order. And these modifications of a great State paper were made by a man who, but three months before, had entered, for the first time, the wide theatre of executive action.[1]

Gifted with an insight and a foresight which the ancients would have called divinition, he saw, in the midst of darkness and obscurity, the logic of events, and forecasted the result. From the first, in his own quaint, original way, without ostentation or offense to his asso-ciates, he was pilot and commander of his administration. He was one of the few great rulers whose wisdom increased with his power, and whose spirit grew gentler and tenderer as his triumphs were multiplied.

---

1. Revised statement of Seward to Adams, May 31, 1861.

This was the man, and those his associates, who look down upon us from the canvas.

The present is not a fitting occasion to examine, with any completeness, the causes that led to the proclamation of emancipation; but the peculiar relation of that act to the character of Abraham Lincoln cannot be understood, without considering one remarkable fact in his history.

His earlier years were passed in a region remote from the centers of political thought, and without access to the great world of books. But the few books that came within his reach, he devoured with the divine hunger of genius. One paper, above all others, led him captive, and filled his spirit with the majesty of its truth and the sublimity of its eloquence. It was the Declaration of American Independence—the liberty and equality of all men. Long before his fame had become national, he said:

> That is the electric cord in the Declaration, that links the hearts of patriotic and liberty-loving men together, and that will link such hearts as long as the love of liberty exists in the minds of men throughout the world. [speech, Chicago, July 10, 1858]

That truth runs, like a thread of gold, through the whole web of his political life. It was the spearpoint of his logic, in his debates with Douglas. It was the inspiring theme of his remarkable speech at the Cooper Institute, which gave him the nomination to the presidency. It filled him with reverent awe when, on his way to the capital, to enter the shadows of the terrible conflict then impending, he uttered, in Carpenter's Hall, at Philadelphia, these remarkable words, which were prophecy then, but are history now:

> I have never had a feeling, politically, that did not spring from the sentiments embodied in the Declaration of Independence. I have often pondered over the dangers which were incurred by the men who assembled here and framed and adopted that Declaration. I have pondered over the toils that were endured by the officers and soldiers of the army who achieved that independence. I have often inquired of myself what great principle or idea it was that kept this confederacy so long together. It was not the mere matter of the separation of the colonies from the mother land, but that sentiment in the Declaration of Independence, which gave liberty, not alone to the people of this country, but, I hope, to the world, for all

future time. It was that which gave promise that, in due time, the weight would be lifted from the shoulders of all men. This is the sentiment embodied in the Declaration of Independence. Now, my friends, can this country be saved on that basis? If it can, I shall consider myself one of the happiest men in the world if I can help to save it. If it cannot be saved upon that principle, it will be truly awful. But if this country cannot be saved without giving up that principle, I was about to say, *I would rather be assassinated on this spot than surrender it.* [speech, Feb. 22, 1861]

Deep and strong was his devotion to liberty; yet deeper and stronger still was his devotion to the union, for he believed that without the union, permanent liberty for either race on this continent would be impossible. And because of this belief, he was reluctant, perhaps more reluctant than most of his associates, to strike slavery with the sword. For many months, the passionate appeals of millions of his associates seemed not to move him. He listened to all the phases of the discussion, and stated, in language clearer and stronger than any opponent had used, the dangers, the difficulties and the possible futility of the act.

In reference to its practical wisdom, Congress, the Cabinet and the country were divided. Several of his generals had proclaimed the freedom of slaves within the limits of their commands. The President revoked their proclamations. His first Secretary of War had inserted a paragraph in his annual report, advocating a similar policy. The President suppressed it.

On the 19th of August, 1862, Horace Greeley published a letter, addressed to the President, entitled 'The Prayer of Twenty Millions,' in which he said:

> On the face of this wide earth, Mr. President, there is not one disinterested, determined, intelligent champion of the union cause who does not feel that all attempts to put down the rebellion, and at the same time uphold its inciting cause, are preposterous and futile.

To this the President responded in that ever-memorable dispatch of August 22, in which he said:

> If there be those who would not save the union unless they could at the same time save slavery, I do not agree with them.
> If there be those who would not save the union unless they could at the same time destroy slavery, I do not agree with them.

My paramount object is to save the union, and not either to save or destroy slavery.

If I could save the union without freeing any slave, I would do it, if I could save it by freeing all the slaves, I would do it; and if I could do it by freeing some and leaving others alone, I would also do that.

What I do about slavery and the colored race, I do because I believe it helps to save the union; and what I forbear, I forbear because I do not believe it helps to save the union. I shall do less whenever I believe that what I am doing hurts the cause; and I shall do more whenever I believe doing more will help the cause.

Thus, against all importunities on the one hand, and remonstrances on the other, he took the mighty question to his own heart, and, during the long months of that terrible battle-summer, wrestled with it alone.

But at length, he realized the saving truth, that great, unsettled questions have no pity for the repose of nations.

On the 22d of September, he summoned his Cabinet to announce his conclusion. It was my good fortune, on that same day, and a few hours after the meeting, to hear, from the lips of one who participated, the story of the scene.

As the chiefs of the executive departments came in one by one, they found the President reading a favorite chapter from a popular humorist. He was lightening the weight of the great burden which rested upon his spirit. He finished the chapter, reading it aloud. And here I quote from the published journal of the late chief-justice, an entry, written immediately after the meeting, and bearing unmistakable evidence that it is almost a literal transcript of Lincoln's words:

> The President then took a graver tone, and said: "Gentlemen, I have, as you are aware, thought a great deal about the relation of this war to slavery; and you all remember that, several weeks ago, I read to you an order I had prepared upon the subject, which, on account of objections made by some of you, was not issued. Ever since then, my mind has been much occupied with this subject, and I have thought all along that the time for acting upon it might probably come. I think the time has come now. I wish it was a better time. I wish that we were in a better condition. The action of the army against the rebels has not been quite what I should have best liked, but they have been driven out of Maryland, and Pennsylvania is no longer in danger of invasion.

When the rebel army was at Frederick, I determined, as soon as it should be driven out of Maryland, to issue a proclamation of emancipation, such as I thought most likely to be useful. I said nothing to any one, but I made a promise to myself and (hesitating a little) to my Maker. The rebel army is now driven out, and I am going to fulfill that promise. I have got you together to hear what I have written down. I do not wish your advice about the main matter, for that I have determined for myself. This I say, without intending anything but respect for any one of you. But I already know the views of each upon this question. They have been heretofore expressed, and I have considered them as thoroughly and carefully as I can. What I have written is that which my reflections have determined me to say. If there is anything in the expressions I use, or in any minor matter which any one of you think had best be changed, I shall be glad to receive your suggestions. One other observation I will make. I know very well that many others might, in this matter as in others, do better than I can; and if I was satisfied that the public confidence was more fully possessed by any one of them than by me, and knew of any constitutional way in which he could be put in my place, he should have it. I would gladly yield to him. But though I believe I have not so much of the confidence of the people as I had some time since, I do not know that, all things considered, any other person has more; and, however this may be, there is no way in which I can have any other man put where I am. I am here; I must do the best I can, and bear the responsibility of taking the course which I feel I ought to take."

The President then proceeded to read his Emancipation Proclamation, making remarks on the several parts as he went on, and showing that he had fully considered the subject in all the lights under which it had been presented to him.[2]

The proclamation was amended in a few matters of detail. It was signed and published that day. The world knows the rest, and will not forget it till 'the last syllable of recorded time.'

In the painting before us, the artist has chosen the moment when the reading of the proclamation was finished, and the Secretary of State was offering his first suggestion. I profess no skill in the subtle mysteries of art criticism. I can only say of a painting, what the

2. J. W. Schuckers, *Life and Public Services of Salmon Portland Chase* (New York: Appleton, 1874), 453–54.

painting says to me. I know not what this may say to others; but to me, it tells the whole story of the scene, in the silent and pathetic language of art.

We value the Trumbull picture of the Declaration,—that promise and prophecy of which this act was the fulfillment,—because many of its portraits were taken from actual life. This picture is a faithful reproduction, not only of the scene, but its accessories. It was painted at the executive mansion, under the eye of Mr. Lincoln, who sat with the artist during many days of genial companionship, and aided him in arranging the many details of the picture.

The severely plain chamber, not now used for cabinet councils; the plain marble mantel, with the portrait of a hero president above it; the council-table, at which Jackson and his successor had presided; the old-fashioned chairs; the books and maps; the captured sword, with its pathetic history;—all are there, as they were, in fact, fifteen years ago. But what is of more consequence, the portraits are true to the life. Mr. Seward said of the painting, 'It is a vivid representation of the scene, with portraits of rare fidelity'; and so said all his associates.

Without this painting, the scene could not even now be reproduced. The room has been remodeled; its furniture is gone; and death has been sitting in that council, calling the roll of its members in quick succession. Yesterday, he added another name to his fatal list; and to-day, he has left upon the earth but a single witness of the signing of the proclamation of emancipation.

With reverence and patriotic love, the artist accomplished his work; with patriotic love and reverent faith, the donor presents it to the nation. In the spirit of both, let the re-united nation receive it and cherish it forever.

PART THREE

The Republican Celebrations

When memories of the assassination commenced to fade and reconciliation between the North and South became popular, many persons became eager to assert their personal connections with Lincoln and to declare their enthusiasms for his programs. They made Lincoln the symbol of the American ideal of freedom, epitomized in the phrase "all men are created equal," but sometimes they also exploited the Lincoln memory to promote selfish causes. At the annual gatherings around festive boards at elegant hotels they met to hear distinguished personalities ignite fires for the mythical hero. Hence, the Lincoln myth became a most appealing persuasive symbol to stir Lincolnites, particularly Republicans.

Immediately after the assassination, Radical Republicans exploited the memory of the assassination for their party purposes. To win several elections, they accused Democrats of being responsible for the tragedy and waved the bloody shirt. Hence, Lincoln's birthday soon became an opportune time for the faithful to gather at Republican clubs, such as the Union League Club of New York City, the Marquette Club of Chicago, and the Republican Club of the City of New York, to renew and recharge Republican enthusiasms. Annually from 1887 through 1927, the Republican Club of the City of New York, later the National Republican Club, enlisted prominent speakers to honor Lincoln at their banquets. They preserved sixty-eight of these resulting orations in two published volumes.[1]

1. James P. Foster, "Permanent Republican Clubs," *North American Review* 146 (Mar. 1888): 17–18; David Donald, *Lincoln Reconsidered,* 2d ed., enlarged (New York: Random, 1961), 8–12; Lloyd Lewis, *Myths after Lincoln* (New York: Harcourt, Brace, 1941), 105–30.

Savior of the Nation

ANNUAL BANQUET OF THE REPUBLICAN CLUB
OF THE CITY OF NEW YORK
NEW YORK, NEW YORK
FEBRUARY 12, 1890

For their fourth banquet the Republican Club of the City of New York asked Shelby M. Cullom, the Illinois senator from Springfield who was a former governor and U.S. representative, to speak about his friend.[1] The old Illinoisan, along with Joseph G. Cannon, both personal acquaintances of Lincoln, still served in Congress and were frequently asked to reflect about their memories of him. Cullom could truthfully brag that "the name of Lincoln" had been "a household word" in his family and that he had known the Illinois lawyer as a practicing attorney, campaigner, opponent of Stephen A. Douglas, and the president. Slipping readily into the role of an eyewitness, Cullom recalled the exciting days in rural Illinois and wartime Washington. Unable to avoid superlatives such as "great-hearted patriot," "the savior of the Union," and "never... a nobler man," Cullom gained rhetorical power by personally reflecting on what he had actually heard and seen, but he contributed little new information. Almost forgetting his theme for a moment, the old senator slipped into the second person, speaking directly to Lincoln: "You fought a good fight. You finished your work. The world is better for your having lived in it, and it will call you blessed as long as the love of liberty shall dwell in the soul of humanity." This apocalyptic interpretation became the basis for his analysis, and he drew a direct parallel to Christ. Cullom said that Lincoln "died with a martyr's crown of glory upon his brow."

In his conclusion, Cullom revealed that his primary purpose in reviving Lincoln's memory was to rally his Republican colleagues and to urge that "the fight must go on" for "honest elections," defeat of "merciless monopolists," and the breakup of trusts. He suggested that

116

the battle should continue "until the mission of the Republican party, founded by Lincoln . . . shall have been fully accomplished." The old warrior could not have been more explicit had he been speaking at the hustings in rural Illinois.

1. *New York Times,* Feb. 13, 1890; New York *Tribune,* Feb. 13, 1890.

The speech has been reprinted from *Addresses Delivered at the Lincoln Dinners of Republican Club of the City of New York in Response to the Toast: Abraham Lincoln, 1887–1909* (New York: Republican Club of the City of New York, 1909), 37–46.

M *r. President and Gentlemen of the Republican Club of the City of New York:* I esteem it a great honor to be present on this occasion, and a still greater honor to be called upon to respond to the announcement just made by your president.

How true the utterance of the matchless Shakespeare of the Old World when applied to immortal Lincoln of the New! "The elements were so mixed in him, that Nature might stand up and say to all the world, 'This is a man' " [Julius Caesar, 5.5. 73–75]. His life was gentle, pure, noble, and courageous; and from his early manhood all who knew him were ready to say of him, "This is a man." The name of Lincoln, Mr. President and gentlemen, has been to me as a household word from my very earliest recollection. He was the friend of my father in my early boyhood, and I am proud to believe that he was my friend for many years before his death. I knew him somewhat in the sacred circle of his family. I knew him in the ordinary walks of life. I knew him as a practising lawyer at the bar. I knew him at the hustings as a public speaker and debater. I knew him as President of the United States, in that period in our history when men's souls were tried, and when the life of our nation seemed to be suspended as by a thread. In the home circle he was gentle, affectionate, and true. In the ordinary walks of life he was plain, simple, and generous; a perfect type, so far as men can be, of all that makes a worthy citizen of a great Republic. At the bar he was conscientious, fair, powerful, and he seldom failed to gain his cause against the most able legal antagonists.

On the platform of debate he had few, if any, equals in this or any other country.

Mr. President, the world has had few such men as Abraham Lincoln. He was of gentle nature, great in heart, in head, and in deed. As a political leader he was actuated in his movements by strong convictions of duty, and had great power in convincing people of the righteousness of his cause. No man could stand in his presence and hear him without feeling sure of the honesty of his purposes and declarations, or of the strength of his arguments in behalf of whatever cause he championed. I have heard him often. I heard several of the famous debates between him and the great Douglas. I heard his great speech in which he uttered, I may say, that immortal declaration, that a house divided against itself cannot stand. It must be all one thing or the other; and I do not believe that an address was ever delivered in this country that produced a more profound and lasting impression upon the minds of the people of the country than this.

As Chief Magistrate of the nation, he was wise and prudent. He lived to witness that foul blot of slavery, which gave the lie to the Declaration of Independence, swept away. He was the savior of the Union and the liberator by his own hand of four millions of slaves.

Great-hearted patriot, and martyr to the cause of union and liberty, how we honor your name and your memory to-night! You fought a good fight. You finished your work. The world is better for your having lived in it, and it will call you blessed as long as the love of liberty shall dwell in the soul of humanity, which will be as long as time shall last upon the earth.

Mr. President, if I may be allowed to say it, Abraham Lincoln was given to the nation by Illinois. It seems to me but yesterday that I felt the warm grasp of his hand, and saw him leave his home at the capital of his state, where I have the honor of residing, to enter upon a larger field of usefulness at the capital of the nation, where he won immortality and died with a martyr's crown of glory upon his brow.

Never was a nobler man born of woman, and never throbbed a purer heart in human breast. The distinguished of the Old World, proud of their claims of long descent, may sneer at his humble birth; but, in my estimation, he was one of the greatest of men.

I do not know, fellow-citizens, but you may think me too partial toward that great man; but I have read his speeches, have seen him in the common walks of life, walked with him, as my friend here said, upon the streets, heard him talked about ever since I was ten years old, and I have deliberately come to the conclusion that no man has ever existed on the American continent superior to Abraham Lincoln.

By his consummate statesmanship he saved the republic from the evils of anarchy, and with self-denying patriotism refused to assume almost regal power when it was within his reach. He educated public opinion until it became ready to endorse what he knew to be right, and what wise statesmanship demanded at his hands.

Fellow-citizens, if you will think of his career as Chief Magistrate of the nation in that period of national peril, you will agree with me that his course and wisdom were such as to lead the people, and teach them as though he taught them not, and then he did what the country was ready to have done.

While Abraham Lincoln had not the advantages of a scholastic education, yet he fully appreciated and understood the beautiful in sentiment and diction, and no man has uttered more elegant language and tender words, touching the hearts of humanity, than he. To me his utterances were both powerful and elegant, and I would rather be the author of that great paper by which he gave freedom to four millions of slaves than be the author of the poems of Homer or the plays of Shakespeare. He was the savior of the Union, but though he did live to see the power of the Rebellion broken, he did not live to see the authority of the Union established in all the rebellious States. He was permitted to go up into Mount Nebo and to catch a glimpse of the promised land of the restored Union, but his weary feet were not allowed to cross the border that separated it from the wilderness of Civil War. In the very moment of victory he was robbed of life by the cruel hand of a traitorous assassin, and his body was brought back amid the lamentations of a whole nation—even his foes giving to his merit the meed of tears—to find its last resting place in the soil of Illinois. As I gazed for the last time upon his face on the solemn occasion, sad and gentle in death as it had been in life, I thanked God that the good that he had done would live after him and give his name in honor to story and to song.

It is said that the story of every human life, if rightly told, may be a useful lesson to those who survive. There are none whose lives teach to Americans or to the world a grander or more profitable lesson than the life of Abraham Lincoln. The study of his life leads to private and public virtue; to correct ideas of our relations to each other; and to moral courage to stand by our convictions.

Lincoln was a child of Providence, raised up in a period in our history when there was need of such a man. A pioneer raised in a cabin, laboring with his hands, acquainted with the woods and fields, he communed with nature in all its beauty and grandeur as it voiced itself to the quiet man of destiny. He was a martyr to the cause of union and liberty, a noble victim to duty.

To repeat the sentiment embodied in the announcement of the President, "The fight must go on," and I am glad to the very bottom of my heart that I have the honor of standing in the presence of a great assembly of intelligent, earnest Republicans, who will join in that sentiment when I say that the fight must go on [in several letters, Nov. 1858]. "The cause of liberty must not be surrendered at the end of one or even one hundred defeats" [to Henry Asbury, Nov. 19, 1858]. Such words uttered by Lincoln, gave evidence of his convictions to duty. "Yes," said he, "I will speak for freedom against slavery so long as the Constitution of our country guarantees free speech; until everywhere in this broad land the sun shall shine, the wind shall blow, and the rain shall fall upon no man who goes forth to unrequited toil."[1]

Mr. President and gentlemen, the fight must go on in favor of liberty and justice to the people of all classes, colors, and conditions in our country until every man in all this broad land shall stand equal before the law, in civil and political rights, equal in fact and equal in law, with no system of intimidation at elections, or fraudulent counting when the polls are closed.

The fight must go on, and no surrender at the end of one or one hundred defeats, until honest elections are secured everywhere in this country.

The fight must go on until merciless monopolists are subordinated, and the interests of the great body of the people are carefully regarded.

The fight must go on until trusts and combinations, prompted by greed and inordinate avarice, shall be broken up.

The fight must go on until the mission of the Republican party, founded by Lincoln and his compeers, shall have been fully accomplished in the destruction of all barriers to perfect equality in the civil and political rights of all the people of the country.

Gentlemen, how glorious the results of the great culminating struggle in which Lincoln was the mighty leader on the side of liberty! Did you ever reflect upon the consequences of a divided Union? Thanks to Lincoln, the great leader; and to that wise statesman, William H. Seward of New York, another great leader of the Republican party; and to my distinguished friend—and I am proud to have him here in your presence to-night—the gallant pathfinder and hero of the late war, General Fremont; and to Grant, that silent man; and to Sherman;

---

1. Paraphrase from J. G. Holland, *Life of Abraham Lincoln* (Springfield, Mass.: G. Bill, 1866), 150.

and to Sheridan and Thomas; and to Hancock, the gallant leader; and to my dearest friend of latter days, the gallant John A. Logan; and to the great army of patriots whom they and others commanded in the struggle for national life, the dissolution of the Union was not accomplished.

How we are blessed as a nation! No standing army worth the name. No royal dynasty in this country. Fellow-citizens, in a little while every nation on the American continent, I trust, will be in full sympathy with each other, from the frozen regions of the North to the lower peninsula of the South. The people sovereign. No danger from foreign foe. Surrounded by the two oceans, the lakes, and the gulf. What an opportunity to build up the greatest nation the world ever saw!

A career of unprecedented glory awaits this nation. Slavery gone. Secession banished, I trust for all time. No gloomy clouds to obscure the light. "[Let] the mystic chords of memory . . . swell the chorus of the Union, when again touched, as surely they will be, by the better angels of our nature," and let us as citizens study and imitate the life and character of Lincoln, in its devotion to liberty, in the hope that the great principle for which Lincoln lived and died shall preserve this country as the purest and best country on the face of the globe [First Inaugural Address, Mar. 4, 1861].

The Outline of the Greatness
of His Gigantic Figure

ANNUAL BANQUET OF THE REPUBLICAN
CLUB OF THE CITY OF NEW YORK
WALDORF–ASTORIA HOTEL
FEBRUARY 13, 1905

The Nineteenth Annual Dinner of the Republican Club of the City of New York became a huge spectacle, lavishly staged to honor the principal guest, President Theodore Roosevelt. The large banquet audience of 1,300, including 225 women, filled the banquet hall and the neighboring rooms. The *New York Times* reported that it was the largest such gathering in the history of the city. The featured speaker was, of course, the president, who sermonized in his usual way for forty-five minutes, largely upon race relations. He attracted headlines with his remark, "You here are Republicans only secondarily—You are Americans first.[1]

Jonathan P. Dolliver, senator from Iowa, spoke after Roosevelt. The Iowan, an energetic Republican from the post-war generation, knew Lincoln only through the recollections of others and hearsay.[2] To make clear his source, Dolliver suggested that he had relied upon Nicolay and Hay's *Abraham Lincoln: A History*. Vigorous in his senate leadership, Dolliver at this time was known as a powerful speaker for the GOP regulars.[3]

Dolliver built his eulogy around a narration of details, running from Lincoln's boyhood to his death. Making his plan and emphasis clear, he said, "we find ourselves laying down the *narrative* [italics added] which records them [events], with a strange feeling . . . that may be . . . we are not reading about a man . . . but about some mysterious personality, in the hands of the higher Powers, with a supernatural commission to help and to bless the human race." This reference to the mystery of the Lincoln power had become a significant theme for

123

the Lincoln mythmakers. Eulogists frequently implied that Lincoln was godsent.

Showing more finesse than Cullom had fifteen years before, Dolliver effectively used comparison and contrast. In the first half of the speech, he followed a four-step progression in developing four claims: stating the commonly held claim, denying it, supporting with details of denial, and producing counternarrative detail to demonstrate that Lincoln in action exceeded the claim. The schema may be diagrammed as follows: [*Claim*] "Some have told us that he was a great lawyer"; [*Denial*] "He was nothing of the sort"; [*Support of negative claim*] "But he practiced law without a library"; [*Counternarrative detail*] "The notion . . . was slowly forming in his mind, that he held a brief, with Power of Attorney from on High, for the unnumbered millions of his fellow men and was only loitering around the county seats of Illinois until the case came on for trial."

In his narrative Dolliver considered four additional claims: "Some tell us that he was a great orator"; "He has been described as a great statesman"; "There are some . . . who make of Lincoln an exceptional military genius"; "The whole world now knows his stature. But while he lived hardly anybody was able to take his measure."

In the final part of the eulogy, Dolliver enlarged upon the mystery of the man: "It took his countrymen the full four years to find Abraham Lincoln out." The speaker then amplified Lincoln's political ideal that centered around "All men are created equal."

> All his life there had dwelt in his recollection a little sentence from an historic document which had been carelessly passed along from one Fourth of July celebration to another, "All men are created equal. . . ." He knew that the hand which wrote that sentence was guided by a wisdom somewhat higher than the front porch of a slave plantation in Virginia; that first principles overshadow time and place; and that when men take their lives in their hands to lay the foundations of free nations, they must speak the truth lest the heavens fall. With a sublime faith, shared within the limits of their light by millions, he believed that sentence.

In the process of amplifying Lincoln's virtues, Dolliver slipped into his running account familiar glimpses of the Illinois lawyer in action:

124

He cracked his jokes about the office stove in country taverns, where he spoke to everybody by his first name

The log cabin student, learning to read and write by the light of the kitchen fire in the woods of Indiana

The awkward farm hand of the Sangamon who covered his bare feet in the fresh dirt which his plow had turned up . . . while he sat down at the end of the furrow to rest his team

The country lawyer who rode on horseback from county to county, with nothing in his saddlebags except a clean shirt and the code of Illinois to try his cases

By the light of the camp fires of victorious armies they learned to see the outline of his gigantic figure

In the speech three basic themes emerge: first, Lincoln had, divine guidance. Second, Lincoln had the goal to establish a government that assured freedom to all Americans regardless of color. Third, Lincoln stood as a symbol of unity in that "the ministry of his life was to all parties; to all peoples; to all ages."

The Dolliver speech showed a greater concentration upon eulogizing Lincoln than had many of the others delivered to the Republican Club. In spite of what the promoters may have sought, the Iowan avoided crass partisanship. Nevertheless, in his last sentence he acknowledged that "the Republican party stands pledged to make it ["a square deal"] good, and to keep it good for all men and for all time to come." Of course, Dolliver had said what was political—particularly with President Roosevelt seated at the head table. But for the most part Dolliver had confined his development to eulogy.

1. *New York Times,* Feb. 14, 1905.

2. Gordon F. Hostettler, "Jonathan Prentiss Dolliver: The Formative Years," *Iowa Journal of History* 49 (Jan. 1951): 23–50. Also see the Hostettler Ph.d. diss., "The Oratorical Career of Jonathan Prentiss Dolliver" (State University of Iowa, 1947).

3. Dolliver heard Cullom speak in 1890; *New York Times,* Feb. 13, 1890.

The speech is reprinted from *Addresses Delivered at the Lincoln Dinners of the Republican Club of the City of New York, in Response to the Toast: Abraham Lincoln, 1887–1909* (New York: Republican Club of the City of New York, 1909), 229–41.

M r. *President, Ladies and Gentlemen:* It has been a good many years, fourteen, I think, since I had the opportunity of joining this club, and one would think that the lapse of that time would be enough to get a man out of the habit of making after-dinner speeches unless he had become, like my friend, Secretary [Elihu] Root, and others here, hopelessly addicted to it.

The first thing that strikes me is that a good many people have joined this club since I did, and the next thing, that you have had the wisdom to invite your wives here to see that you get home all right.

It is a circumstance of unusual interest that the President is here; not counting it beneath our highest official dignity to mingle freely with his political associates, in the party organization of which he is a member, and to add the inspiration of his eloquent counsel to their celebration of the birthday of the first great Republican leader. For, while the memory of Abraham Lincoln is too great to be claimed by a political party, too great to belong to a single nation, too great to be absorbed in the renown of one century, yet there is a sense so sacred that it barely admits of the suggestion in which his name is our peculiar possession, the most precious thing in our Republican inheritance. The ministry of his life was to all parties; to all peoples; to all ages. But to the children of the old Republican homestead has been confided, under the bonds of an especial obligation, the care of his fame and the keeping of his faith.

Within less than half a century this man, once despised, once derided, once distrusted and maligned, has been transfigured, in the light of universal history, so that all men and all generations of men may see him and make out if possible the manner of man he was. His life in this world was not long, less than three score years; only ten of them visible above the dead level of affairs. Yet into that brief space events were crowded, so stupendous in their ultimate significance, that we find ourselves laying down the narrative which records them, with a strange feeling coming over us, that may be after all we are not reading about a man at all, but about some mysterious personality, in the hands of the higher Powers, with a supernatural commission to help and to bless the human race. Our book shelves were filling up so fast with apocryphal literature of the Civil War that if it had not been for the loving labors of the two men, John Hay and John G. Nicolay, who knew him best, and have gathered up the fragments of his life, so that nothing has been lost, we would have had by this time only a blurred and doubtful picture of his retiring and unpretentious character.

Some have told us that he was a great lawyer. He was nothing of the sort. It is true that he grasped without apparent effort the principles of the common law, and his faculties were so normal and complete that he did not need a commentary, nor a copy of the Madison papers, thumb-marked by the doubts and fears of three generations, to make him sure that the men who made the Constitution were building for eternity. But he practiced law without a library, and all who were acquainted with him testify that in a law suit he was of no account, unless he knew the right was on his side. It was against his intellectual and his moral grain to accept Lord Bacon's cynical suggestion that there is no way of knowing whether a cause be good or bad till the jury had brought in its verdict.

The familiar judicial circuit around Springfield, where he cracked his jokes about the office stove in country taverns, where he spoke to everybody by his first name and everybody liked to hear him talk, did much for him in every way; but the noble profession, so ably represented about this board, will bear me witness that an attorney who gives his advice away for nothing, who does not have the foresight to ask for a retainer, and usually lacks the business talent to collect his fee, whatever other merits he may have, is not cut out by nature for a lawyer. I have talked with many of the oldtime members of the bar at which he used to practice law, thinking all the while of other things, and from what they say I cannot help believing that the notion even then was slowly forming in his mind, that he held a brief, with Power of Attorney from on High, for the unnumbered millions of his fellow men and was only loitering around the county seats of Illinois until the case came on for trial.

Some tell us that he was a great orator. If that is so, the standards of the schools, ancient and modern, must be thrown away. Perhaps they ought to be; and when they are this curious circuit-rider of the law; who refreshed his companions with wit and argument from the well of English undefiled; this champion of civil liberty, confuting Douglas with a remorseless logic, cast in phrases rich with the homely wisdom

127

of proverbial literature; this advocate of the people, head and shoulders above his brethren, stating their case before the bar of history, in sentences so simple that a child can follow them; surely such a one cannot be left out of the company of the masters who have added something to the conquests of the mother tongue. He was dissatisfied with his modest address at Gettysburg, read awkwardly from poorly written manuscript; and thought Edward Everett's oration was the best he had ever heard, but Mr. Everett himself discerned without a minute for reflection, that the little scrap of crumpled paper which the President held in his unsteady hand that day would be treasured from generation to generation after his own laborious deliverance had been forgotten. The old school of oratory and the new met on that rude platform among the graves under the trees, and congratulated each other. They have not met very often since, for both of them have been pushed aside to make room for the essayists, the declaimers, the statisticians, and other enterprising pedlars of intellectual wares, who have descended like a swarm on all human deliberations.

He has been described as a great statesman. If by that you mean that he was trained in the administrative mechanism of the government, or that he was wiser than his day in the creed of the party in whose fellowship he passed his earlier years, there is little evidence of that at all; the most that can be said is that he clung to the fortunes of the old Whig leadership through evil, as well as good report, and that he stumped the county and afterwards the State; but the speeches which he made, neither he nor anybody else regarded it important to preserve. His platform from the first was brief and to the point. "I am in favor of a national bank. I am in favor of the internal improvement system, and a high protective tariff."[1] But while for half his life he followed Henry Clay, like a lover more than a disciple, yet when that popular hero died and Lincoln was selected to make a memorial address in the old State House, he dismissed the principles of his party creed without a word, and reserved his tribute for the love of liberty and the devotion of the Union which shone even to the end, in that superb career.

To speak of Lincoln as a statesman, whatever adjectives you use, opens no secret of his biography and rather seems to me to belittle the

---

1. Speech, Pappsville, Ill., July 1832; unverified.

epic grandeur of the drama in which he moved. Of course he was a statesman; exactly so, Saul of Tarsus, setting out from Damascus, became a famous traveller, and Christopher Columbus, inheriting a taste for the sea, became a mariner of high repute.

There are some who have given a study, more or less profound, to the official records of the rebellion who make of Lincoln an exceptional military genius, skilful in the management of armies and prepared better even than his generals to give direction to their movements. I doubt this very much. He was driven into the war department by the exigency of the times, and if he towered above the ill-fitting uniforms, which made their way, through one influence and another, to positions of brief command during the first campaigns of the Civil War, it is not very high praise after all. One thing, however, he must be given credit for; he perceived the size of the undertaking which he had in hand, and he kept looking until his eyes were weary for the man who could grasp the whole field and get out of the Army what he knew was in it. It broke his heart to see its efforts scattered and thrown away by quarrels among its officers, endless in number, and unintelligible for the most part to the outside world. When he passed the command of the Army of the Potomac over to General Hooker, he did it in terms of reprimand and admonition, which read like a father's last warning to a wayward son. He told him that he had wronged his country and done a gross injustice to a brother officer. Recalling Hooker's insubordinate suggestion that the Army and the Government both needed a dictator, he reminded him that "only those generals who gain successes can set up dictators," and added, with a humor as grim as death, "what I now ask of you is military success, and I will risk the dictatorship" [letter to Joseph Hooker, Jan. 26, 1863]. If the General did not tear up his commission when he read that letter it was because he was brave enough to bear the severity of the naked truth.

All this time he had his eye upon a man in the West, who had been doing an extensive business down in Tennessee, "a copious worker and fighter, but a very meagre writer," as he afterwards described him in a telegram to Burnside. He had watched him with attentive interest, noticing particularly that his plans always squared with the event; that he never regretted to report; and after Vicksburg fell and the tide of invasion had been rolled back from the borders of Maryland and

Pennsylvania, he wrote two letters, one to General Meade, calling him to a stern account for not following up his victory, and one to General Grant directing him to report to Washington for duty. The letter to General Meade, now resting peacefully in Nicolay's collection of the writings of Lincoln, all the fires of its wrath long since gone out, was never sent. But General Grant got his. And from that day there were no more military orders from the White House, no exhortations to advance, no despatches to move upon the enemy's works. He still had his own ideas how the job ought to be done, but he did not even ask the General to tell him his. He left it all to him. And as the plan of the great Captain unfolded, he sent to his headquarters this exultant message:

"I begin to see it. You will succeed. God bless you all.
                    "A. Lincoln." [to U.S. Grant, June 15, 1864]

And so these two, each adding something to the other's fame, go down to history together; God's blessing falling like a benediction upon the memory of both.

The whole world now knows his stature. But while he lived hardly anybody was able to take his measure. The foremost statesman of his Cabinet, after pestering him for a month with contradictory pieces of advice, placed before him a memorandum, grotesque in its assumption of superior wisdom, which ended with an accommodating proposal to take the responsibilities of the administration off his hands. After the battle of Bull Run even so incorruptible a patriot as Edwin M. Stanton, known in after years as the organizer of victory, wrote to James Buchanan, then living near the Capital in the quiet of his country seat at Wheatland, these words of mockery and contempt:

"The imbecility of the administration culminated in that catastrophe; and irretrievable misfortune and national disgrace never to be forgotten are to be added to the ruin of peaceful pursuits and national bankruptcy as the result of Lincoln's 'running the machine' for five full months."

From the sanctum of the old Tribune, where for a generation Horace Greeley had dominated the opinions of the people as no American editor has done before or since his day, came a confidential letter, a maudlin mixture of enterprise and despair; a despair which, after seven sleepless nights, had given up the fight; an enterprise which sought for inside information of the inevitable hour of the surrender near at hand. "You are not considered a great man," said Mr. Greeley for the President's eye alone.

Who is this, sitting all night long on a lounge in the public offices of the White House, listening, with the comments of a quaint humor, to privates and officers and scared Congressmen and citizens, who poured across the Long Bridge from the first battlefield of the rebellion to tell their tale of woe to the only man in Washington who had sense enough left to appreciate it, or patience enough left to listen to it? Is it the log cabin student, learning to read and write by the light of the kitchen fire in the woods of Indiana? It is he. Can it be the adventurous voyager of the Mississippi, who gets ideas of lifting vessels over riffles while he worked his frail craft clear of obstructions in the stream; and ideas broad as the free skies, of helping nations out of barbarism as he traced the divine image in the faces of men and women chained together, under the hammer, in the slavemarket at New Orleans? It is he. Can it be the awkward farm hand of the Sangamon who covered his bare feet in the fresh dirt which his plow had turned up to keep them from getting sunburned, while he sat down at the end of the furrow to rest his team and to regale himself with a few more pages of worn volumes borrowed from the neighbors? It is he. Can it be the country lawyer who rode on horseback from county to county, with nothing in his saddlebags except a clean shirt and the code of Illinois to try his cases and to air his views in the cheerful company which always gathered about the court house? It is he. Is it the daring debater, blazing out for a moment with the momentous warning "A house divided against itself cannot stand," then falling back within the defenses of the Constitution, that the cause of liberty, hindered already by the folly of its friends, might not make itself an outlaw in the land? It is he. Is it the weary traveller who begged the prayers of anxious neighbors as he set out for the last time from home, and talked in language sad and mystical of One who could go with him, and remain with them and be everywhere for good? It is he.

They said he laughed in a weird way that night on the sofa in the public offices of the White House, and they told funny tales about how he looked, and the comic papers of London and New York portrayed him in brutal pictures of his big hands; hands that were

131

about to be stretched out to save the civilization of the world; and his overgrown feet; feet that for four torn and bleeding years were not too weary in the service of mankind. They said that his clothes did not fit him; that he stretched his long legs in ungainly postures; that he was common and uncouth in his appearance. Some said that this being a backwoodsman was becoming a rather questionable recommendation for a President of the United States; and they recalled with satisfaction the grace of courtly manners brought home from St. James'. Little did they dream that the rude cabin yonder on the edge of the hill country of Kentucky was about to be transformed by the tender imagination of the people into a mansion more stately than the White House; more royal than all the palaces of the earth; it did not shelter the childhood of a king, but there is one thing in this world more royal than a king—it is a man.

They said he jested and acted unconcernedly as he looked at people through eyes that moved slowly from one to another in the crowd. They did not know him; or they might have seen that he was not looking at the crowd at all; that his immortal spirit was girding for its ordeal. And if he laughed, it may be that he heard cheerful voices from above; for had he not read somewhere that He that sitteth in the heavens sometimes looks down with laughter and derision upon the impotent plans of men to turn aside the everlasting purposes of God?

It took his countrymen the full four years to find Abraham Lincoln out. By the light of the camp fires of victorious armies they learned to see the outline of his gigantic figure, to assess the integrity of his character, to comprehend the majesty of his conscience; and when at last they looked upon his care-worn face as the nation reverently bore his body to the grave, through their tears they saw him exalted above all thrones in the affection of the human race.

We have been accustomed to think of the Civil War as an affair of armies, for we come of a fighting stock and the military instinct in us needs little cultivation or none at all. But it requires no very deep insight into the hidden things of history to see that the real conflict was not between armed forces, was not on battlefields, nor under the walls of besieged cities; and that fact makes Abraham Lincoln greater than all his generals, greater than all his admirals, greater than all the armies and all the navies that responded to his proclamation. He stands apart because he bore the ark of the covenant. He was making

132

not his own fight, not merely the fight of his own country, or of the passing generation. The stars in their courses had enlisted with him; he had a treaty, never submitted to the Senate, which made him the ally of the Lord of Hosts, with infinite reinforcements at his call. The battle he was waging was not in the fallen timber about the old church at Shiloh; nor in the Wilderness of Virginia; he contended not alone with an insurrection of the slave power; he was hand to hand with a rebellion ancient as selfishness and greed which in all centuries has denied the rights of man, made of human governments a pestilent succession of despotisms and turned the history of our race into a dull recital of crimes and failures and misfortunes. Thus he was caught up like Ezekiel, prophet of Israel, and brought to the East gate of the Lord's house; and when he heard it said unto him, "Son of Man, these are the men who devise mischief," he knew what the vision meant; for he understood better than any man who ever lived what this endless struggle of humanity is, and how far the nation of America had fallen away from its duty and its opportunity.

All his life there had dwelt in his recollection a little sentence from an historic document which had been carelessly passed along from one Fourth of July celebration to another, "All men are created equal." To him the words sounded like an answer to a question propounded by the oldest of the Hebrew sages, "If I despise the cause of my man servant, or my maid servant, when he contendeth with me, what shall I do when God riseth up? Did not He that made me make him?"–a strategic question that had to be answered aright before democracy or any other form of civil liberty could make headway in the world [Job 31:13–15]. All men are created equal. He knew that the hand which wrote that sentence was guided by a wisdom somewhat higher than the front porch of a slave plantation in Virginia; that first principles overshadow time and place; and that when men take their lives in their hands to lay the foundations of free nations, they must speak the truth lest the heavens fall. With a sublime faith, shared within the limits of their light by millions, he believed that sentence. He had tested the depth of it till his plummet touched the foundation of the earth. From his youth that simple saying had been ringing in his ears, "All men are created equal." It was the answer of the Eighteenth Century of Christ, to all the dim millenniums that were before Him; yet he had heard it ridiculed, narrowed down to nothing and explained

133

away. He understood the meaning of the words and came to their defence.

Brushing away the wretched sophistries of partisan expediency, he rescued the handwriting of Thomas Jefferson from obloquy and contempt. "I think," he said, "that the authors of that notable instrument intended to include all men. But they did not intend to declare all men equal in all respects. They did not mean to say that all were equal in color, size, intellect, moral development, or social capacity. They defined, with tolerable distinctness, in what respects they did consider all men created equal—equal, with certain inalienable rights among which are life, liberty and the pursuit of happiness. This they said and this they meant. They did not mean to assert the obvious untruth that all men were then actually enjoying that equality, nor [yet] that they were about to confer it immediately upon them. In fact they had no power to confer such a boon. They meant simply to declare the right, so that the enforcement of it should follow as fast as circumstances would permit. They meant to set up a standard maxim for free society, which should be familiar to all and revered by all; constantly looked to, constantly labored for, and even though never perfectly attained, constantly approximated; thereby constantly spreading and deepening its influence and augmenting the value and happiness of life to all people, of all colors, everywhere" [Springfield, Ill., June 26, 1857]. That was the message of Abraham Lincoln to the nations of America. And as if to make it certain, that it was no mere flourish of a joint debate, he turned aside on his triumphal journey to the Capital, just before he took the oath of office, to repeat the sacred precepts of the Declaration in the hall at Philadelphia, where our fathers first spoke them, and to add his pledge to theirs that he would defend them with his life.

Here is the summit, the spiritual height, from which he was able to forecast the doom of all tyrannies, the end of all slaveries, the unconditional surrender of all the strongholds of injustice and avarice and oppression; this is the mountain top from which he sent down these inspiring words of good cheer and hope: "This essentially is a people's contest; on the side of the Union, a struggle to maintain in the world that form and substance of government, the leading object of which is to elevate the condition of men, to lift artificial weights from shoulders; to clear the path[s] of laudable pursuit for all, and to afford all an unfettered start and a fair chance in the race of life" [message to Congress, July 4, 1861]. No American, North or South, regrets that this war for the Union ended as it did—"that we are not enemies, but friends" [First Inaugural Address, Mar. 4, 1861]. Nor can I help believing that the words which he has spoken here to-night have brought the President of the United States [Theodore Roosevelt] nearer to our brethren beyond the line, once so real, now happily so imaginary, which formerly divided and estranged our people. Thanks be unto God, we are one nation and even in our partisan traditions we share in the heritage of a common faith in the institutions founded by our fathers. As Democrats we repeat the words "equal rights to all and special privileges to none." As Republicans we answer, "an unfettered start and a fair chance in the race of life." The doctrine is the same, nor is the day as far off as some may think when the people, without regard to the divisions of their political opinions, shall treasure in thankful hearts, the blunt and fearless platform of Theodore Roosevelt, "A square deal for every man, no less, no more." The doctrine is the same, and if it is not true there is no foundation for institutions such as ours. But the doctrine is forever true, and by the memory of Abraham Lincoln the Republican party stands pledged to make it good, and to keep it good for all men and for all time to come.

PART FOUR

The Commemoration of Lincoln's Birth

The one hundredth anniversary of the birthday of Abraham Lincoln inspired a nationwide celebration of the man and his achievements. The time was right. In the forty-four years since the assassination the mythmakers had taken over the Lincoln image; old war wounds had healed; acceptable Lincoln biographies had been published; the states were reunited; prominent Southerners now participated in responsible positions in the federal government. In fact, Lincoln had been elevated to a symbol of unity for all citizens.

In numerous communities Lincoln centennial memorial committees of distinguished citizens were put in charge of planning celebrations to honor his birth. By a joint resolution in 1907, the Illinois state legislature directed the governor to plan a fitting ceremony for Springfield. The mayor of Chicago formed the Committee of One Hundred for the same purpose. The state of Kentucky made plans to focus on Lincoln's birthplace in Hodgenville. The principal cities in many states joined in the nationwide commemoration.[1]

Magazines such as *Century* had already published dozens of recollections and interpretations of Lincoln, coming from numerous persons, some with only the slightest Lincoln connection. John G. Nicolay and John Hay had produced *Abraham Lincoln: A History,* advertised as the official biography. Americans who had been dissatisfied with the biographical efforts of Ward Lamon and William Herndon now took pleasure in the mythical Lincoln that his two former private secretaries recounted.

Under the editorship of Nathan William MacChesney, the Chicago committee went a step further than other groups and published a memorial volume of speeches to "give permanent form to many masterly tributes to Lincoln by noted men . . . [to] preserve . . . the remarkable spirit of the occasion." MacChesney reported that he had hundreds of speeches and over sixty thousand clippings from which to make his selection for his volume *Abraham Lincoln: The Tribute of a Century, 1809–1909.* He preserved fifty-five orations, including those from Bloomington; Chicago; the Illinois Supreme Court; Peoria; Springfield; Cincinnati; Boston; Denver; Hodgenville; New York City; Cornell University; Rochester, New York; Madison and Janesville, Wisconsin; Washington, D.C.; Philadelphia; Pittsburgh; Manchester, England; Berlin; Paris; and Rome.

Eulogies from the extravaganza came from many notable figures including Lyman Abbott, William J. Bryan, Shelby M. Cullom, Joseph H. Choate, Chauncey M. Depew, Charles Evans Hughes, Henry Cabot Lodge, Theodore Roosevelt, Adlai E. Stevenson, Booker T. Washington, and Woodrow Wilson. It is doubtful whether this flood of oratory about a single man, coming from such an array of foremost speakers, has ever been matched on any other occasion, before or since.[2]

1. "The Lincoln Centennial," *Colliers Weekly* 42 (Feb. 13, 1909): 12–13; "The Lincoln Centennial Celebration," *Review of Reviews* 39 (Feb. 1909): 172–75.

2. Nathan William MacChesney, *Abraham Lincoln: The Tribute of a Century, 1809–1909* (Chicago: McClung, 1910); Shelby M. Cullom, *Fifty Years of Public Service: Personal Recollections,* 2d ed. (Chicago: McClung, 1911), 428–31.

Lincoln as an Orator

STATE ARSENAL
SPRINGFIELD, ILLINOIS
FEBRUARY 12, 1909

The citizens of Lincoln's hometown of Springfield, Illinois, conducted a day-long celebration to honor the one hundredth birthday of its most famous resident. In the morning a pilgrimage of notable visitors was escorted to the Lincoln home, the courthouse where Lincoln had practiced, his office building, the Presbyterian Church where he had rented a pew for Mary, and the tomb at Oak Ridge Park. In the afternoon eight thousand convened at the tabernacle to hear William J. Bryan, Jonathan P. Dolliver, British Ambassador James Bryce, and French Ambassador Jean A. A. J. Jusserand. In the evening at the main event, a banquet at the state arsenal, the same speakers addressed an audience of seven hundred, which included the governor, other state officials, and representatives from other groups.[1]

The invitation to a famous Democrat to eulogize a Republican may have jarred some Lincoln admirers. Seldom, if ever, had a prominent Democrat been called upon to speak about Lincoln. One exception had been Henry W. Watterson, editor of the Louisville *Courier Journal,* who had delivered a Lincoln lecture many times. But Bryan, who had just vigorously opposed William Howard Taft for the presidency, was a bête noire to Republican stalwarts. The program planners had probably included Bryan as a complement to Republican Jonathan Dolliver. Surmising this strategy, Bryan sought to sidestep what Dolliver might wish to say and what might stir the ire of Republican Lincolnites.

It seemed entirely fitting to invite a native of Salem, Illinois, and a widely known speaker to comment on Lincoln as an orator. Of course Bryan's own ethos and gift for eloquence added significantly to his remarks about Lincoln.[2] By concentrating upon Lincoln's "merits as a public speaker," Bryan avoided a rehash of familiar appeals and moral platitudes so prevalent in many Lincoln eulogies. He therefore focused

139

on "the *means* [italics added] employed . . . to bring before the public the ideas which attracted attention." Reports of Lincoln's stumping had made the Springfield lawyer a folk hero in the Illinois towns where he had campaigned, and Illinoisans thought well of Bryan for placing Lincoln in the company of Demosthenes and Cicero. He knew that a premium was placed upon being well-informed, earnest, a master of statement, brevity, not speaking "over the heads of his hearers," simplicity, and frequent citations of the Bible.

1. Nathan William MacChesney, *Abraham Lincoln: The Tribute of a Century, 1809–1909* (Chicago: McClung, 1910), 183–85; "The Lincoln Centennial Celebration," *Review of Reviews* 39 (Feb. 1909): 172–75.

2. Donald K. Springen, "William Jennings Bryan," in *American Orators of the Twentieth Century,* ed. Bernard K. Duffy and Halford R. Ryan (Westport, Conn.: Greenwood, 1987), 31–38.

The speech is reprinted from *Lincoln Centennial: Addresses Delivered at the Memorial Exercises Held at Springfield, Illinois, February 19, 1909* (Springfield: Illinois Centennial Commission, 1909), 114–31.

Lincoln's fame as a statesman and as the Nation's Chief Executive during its most crucial period has so overshadowed his fame as an orator that his merits as a public speaker have not been sufficiently emphasized. When it is remembered that his nomination was directly due to the prominence which he won upon the stump; that in a remarkable series of debates he held his own against one of the most brilliant orators America has produced; and that to his speeches, more than to the arguments of any other one man, or, in fact, of all other public men combined, was due the success of his party—when all these facts are borne in mind, it will appear plain, even to the casual observer, that too little attention has been given to the extraordinary power which he exercised as a speaker. That his nomination was due to the effect that his speeches produced, cannot be disputed. When he began his fight against slavery in 1858, he was but little known outside of the counties in which he attended court. It is true that he had been a member of Congress some years before, but that time he was not stirred by any great emotion connected with the discussion of any important theme, and he made but little impression upon national politics. The threatened extension of slavery, however, aroused him, and with a cause which justified his best efforts, he threw his whole soul into the fight. The debates with Douglas have never had a parallel in this, or, so far as history shows, in any other country.

In engaging in this contest with Douglas, he met a foeman worthy of his steel, for Douglas had gained a deserved reputation as a great debater, and recognized that his future depended upon the success with which he met the attacks of Lincoln. On one side, an institution supported by history and tradition; and on the other, a growing sentiment against the holding of a human being in bondage—these presented a supreme issue. Douglas won the senatorial seat for which the two at that time had contested, but Lincoln won a larger victory—he helped to mold the sentiment that was dividing parties and rearranging the political map of the country. When the debates were concluded, every one recognized him as the leader of the cause which he had espoused, and it was a recognition of this leadership which he had secured through his public speeches that enabled him, a western man, to be nominated over the eastern candidates—not only a western man, but a man lacking in book learning and the polish of the schools. No other American President has ever so clearly owed his elevation to his oratory. Washington, Jefferson, and Jackson, the Presidents usually mentioned in connection with him, were all poor speakers.

In analyzing Lincoln's characteristics as a speaker, one is impressed with the completeness of his equipment. He possessed the two things that are absolutely essential to effective speaking—namely, information and earnestness. If one can be called eloquent who knows what he is talking about and means what he says—and I know of no better definition—Lincoln's speeches were eloquent. He was thoroughly informed upon the subject; he was prepared to meet his opponent upon the general proposition discussed, and upon any deductions which could be drawn from it. There was no unexplored field into which his adversary could lead him; he had carefully examined every foot of the ground, and was not afraid of pitfall or ambush, and what was equally important, he spoke from his own heart to the hearts of those who listened. While the printed page cannot fully reproduce the impressions made by a voice trembling with emotion or tender with pathos one cannot read the reports of the debates without feeling that Lincoln regarded the subject as far transcending the ambitions of the personal interests of the debaters. It was of little moment, he said, whether they voted him or Judge Douglas up or down, but it was tremendously important that the question should be decided rightly. His reputation may have suffered in the opinion of some, because he made them think so deeply upon what he said that they, for the moment, forgot him altogether, and yet, is this not the very perfection of speech? It is the purpose of the orator to persuade, and to do this he presents, not himself, but his subjects. Someone, in describing the difference between Demosthenes and Cicero, said that "When Cicero spoke, people said, 'How well Cicero speaks'; but when Demosthenes spoke, they said, 'Let us go against Philip!' " In proportion as one can forget himself and become wholly absorbed in the cause which he is presenting does he measure up to the requirements of oratory.

In addition to the two essentials, Lincoln possessed what may be called the secondary aids to oratory. He was a master of statement. Few have equalled him in the ability to strip a truth of surplus verbiage and present it in its naked strength. In the Declaration of

142

Independence we read that there are certain self-evident truths, which are therein enumerated. If I were going to amend the proposition, I would say that all truth is self-evident. Not that any truth will be universally accepted, for not all are in a position or in an attitude to accept any given truth. In the interpretation of the parable of the sower, we are told that "the cares of this world and the deceitfulness of riches choke the truth," and it must be acknowledged that every truth has these or other difficulties to contend with [Matt. 13:22]. But a truth may be so clearly stated that it will commend itself to anyone who has not some special reason for rejecting it.

No one has more clearly stated the fundamental objections to slavery than Lincoln stated them, and he had a great advantage over his opponent in being able to state those objections frankly, for Judge Douglas neither denounced nor defended slavery as an institution—his plan embodied a compromise, and he could not discuss slavery upon its merits without alienating either the slave owner or the abolitionist.

"Brevity is the soul of wit," and a part of Lincoln's reputation for wit lies in his ability to condense a great deal into a few words. He was epigrammatic. A molder of thought is not necessarily an originator of the thought molded. Just as lead molded into the form of bullets has its effectiveness increased, so thought may have its propagating power enormously increased by being molded into a form that the eye catches and the memory holds. Lincoln was the spokesman of his party—he gave felicitous expression to the thoughts of his followers.

His Gettysburg speech is not surpassed, if equalled, in beauty, simplicity, force, and appropriateness by any speech of the same length of any language. It is the world's model of eloquence, elegance, and condensation. He might safely rest his reputation as an orator on that speech alone.

He was apt in illustration—no one more so. A simple story or simile drawn from everyday life flashed before his hearers the argument that he wanted to present. He did not speak over the heads of his hearers, and yet his language was never commonplace. There is strength in simplicity, and Lincoln's style was simplicity itself.

He understood the power of the interrogatory, for some of his most powerful arguments were condensed into questions. Of all those who discussed the evils of separation and the advantages to be derived from the preservation of the Union, no one ever put the matter more forcibly than Lincoln did when, referring to the possibility of war and the certainty of peace sometime, even if the Union was divided, he called attention to the fact that the same question would have to be dealt with, and then asked, "Can enemies [aliens] make treaties easier than friends can make laws? [First Inaugural Address, Mar. 4, 1861].

He made frequent use of Bible language and of illustrations drawn from Holy Writ. It is said that when he was preparing his Springfield speech of 1858, he spent hours trying to find language that would express the idea that dominated his entire career—namely, that a republic could not permanently endure half free and half slave, and that finally a Bible passage flashed through his mind and he exclaimed, "I have found it! 'A house divided against itself cannot stand.'" And probably no other Bible passage ever exerted as much influence as this one in the settlement of a great controversy.

I have enumerated some, not all—but the more important—of his characteristics as an orator, and on this day I venture for the moment to turn the thoughts of this audience away from the great work that he accomplished as a patriot, away from his achievements in the line of statecraft, to the means employed by him to bring before the public the ideas which attracted attention to him. His power as a public speaker was the foundation of his success, and while it is obscured by the superstructure that was reared upon it, it cannot be entirely overlooked as the returning anniversary of his birth calls increasing attention to the widening influence of his work. With no military career to dazzle the eye or excite the imagination; with no public service to make his name familiar to the reading public, his elevation to the presidency would have been impossible without his oratory. The eloquence of Demosthenes and Cicero were no more necessary to their work, and Lincoln deserved to have his name written on the scroll with theirs.

Celebrating Lincoln

COOPER INSTITUTE
NEW YORK, NEW YORK
FEBRUARY 12, 1909

The New York City commemoration of the one hundredth birthday of Lincoln became a day-long, city-wide celebration. The centenary day opened at 8:00 A.M. with a multigun salute from the National Guard and Naval Militia batteries, the battleships in the harbor, and all the forts of the harbor. Precisely at noon the students at the 561 public schools heard a reading of the Gettysburg Address; in the afternoon speakers participated in exercises at the forty-six district schools. The Lincoln Centenary Committee issued two hundred thousand finely illustrated pamphlets concerning the life of Lincoln, which were distributed among the school pupils.

In the evening, public meetings were held at Carnegie Hall, the College of the City of New York, and the fourteen armories of the National Guard scattered over the city. At the American Museum of National History, William Webster Ellsworth of *Century* delivered an illustrated lecture entitled "Abraham Lincoln: Boy and Man." Booker T. Washington addressed a banquet of the Republican Club of the City of New York at the Waldorf-Astoria.

In the afternoon a great central meeting assembled at Cooper Institute to commemorate Lincoln's speech of February 27, 1860. As chairman of the Lincoln Centenary Committee appointed by the mayor, Joseph H. Choate, former ambassador to Great Britain and prominent attorney, briefly reflected on memories of what he had personally heard spoken forty-nine years before.[1] He blended into his account of Lincoln's address vivid impressions of the speaking of "this rude son of the people."

> His fame as a powerful speaker had come out of the West.
> When he spoke he was transfigured before us.

145

For an hour and more he held his audience in the hollow of his hand.

The grand simplicities of the Bible, with which he was so familiar, were distinctly his.

In his narrative sequence Choate emphasized the apocalypse, saying that Lincoln "had come as a stranger, departed with the laurels of a great triumph." In a closing paragraph Choate pointed to the catastrophic event: "We saw him again for the last time in this city, borne in his coffin through the draped streets." In a final step in the apocalyptic progression the speaker lauded Lincoln as the "saviour and redeemer to save it [the country] from self-destruction, and to redeem it from the cancer of slavery." Of course in a climax he said that Lincoln and George Washington "had done the most to promote liberty, justice, civilization, and peace." The atmosphere of the historical auditorium and Choate's personal testimony helped the listeners fantasize how Lincoln had "spoken with all the fire of his aroused and inspired conscience, with a full outpouring of his love of justice and liberty."

The speech is reprinted from Nathan William MacChesney, *Abraham Lincoln: The Tribute of a Century, 1809–1909* (Chicago: McClung, 1910), 275–80.

Just forty-nine years ago, in this very month of February, on this very spot, before just such an audience as this, which filled this historic hall to overflowing, I first saw Abraham Lincoln, and heard him deliver that thrilling address which led to his nomination at Chicago three months afterwards and to his triumphant election in November. The impression of that scene and of that speech can never be effaced from my memory.

After his great success in the West, which had excited the keenest expectation, he came to New York to make a political address—as he had supposed at Plymouth Church in Brooklyn, and it was only when he left his hotel that he found he was coming to Cooper Institute. He appeared in every sense of the word like one of the plain people, among whom he always loved to be counted.

At first sight there was nothing impressive or imposing about him. Nothing but his great stature singled him out from the crowd. His clothes hung awkwardly on his gaunt and giant frame. His face was of a dark pallor, without a tinge of color. His seamed and rugged features bore the furrows of hardship and struggle. His deep-set eyes looked sad and anxious. His countenance in repose gave little evidence of that brain-power which had raised him from the lowest to the highest station among his countrymen. As he spoke to me before the meeting opened, he seemed ill at ease, with that sort of apprehension that a young man might feel before facing a new and strange audience whose critical disposition he dreaded. Here were assembled all the noted men of his party—all the learned and cultured men of the city, editors, clergymen, statesmen, lawyers, merchants, critics. They were all most curious to hear him. His fame as a powerful speaker had come out of the West.

When Mr. Bryant presented him on this platform, a vast sea of eager, upturned faces greeted him, full of intense curiosity to see what this rude son of the people was like. He was equal to the occasion. When he spoke he was transfigured before us. His eye kindled, his voice rang, his face shone and seemed to light up the whole assembly as by an electric flash. For an hour and more he held his audience in the hollow of his hand. His style of speech and manner of delivery

147

were severely simple. The grand simplicities of the Bible, with which he was so familiar, were distinctly his. With no attempt at ornament or rhetoric, without pretence or parade, he spoke straight to the point. It was marvellous to see how this untutored man, by mere self-discipline and the chastening of his own spirit, had outgrown all meretricious arts and had found his own way to the grandeur and the strength of absolute simplicity.

He spoke upon the theme which he had mastered so thoroughly. He demonstrated with irresistible force, the power and the duty of the Federal Government to exclude slavery from the Territories. In the kindliest spirit he protested against the threat of the Southern States to destroy the Union if a Republican President were elected. He closed with an appeal to his audience, spoken with all the fire of his aroused and inspired conscience, with a full outpouring of his love of justice and liberty, to maintain their political purpose on that lofty issue of right and wrong which alone could justify it, and not to be intimidated from their high resolve and sacred duty, by any threats of destruction to the government or of ruin to themselves. He concluded with that telling sentence which drove the whole argument home to all our hearts, "Let us have faith that right makes might, and in that faith let us to the end dare to do our duty as we understand it."

That night the great hall, and the next day the whole city, rang with delighted applause and congratulation, and he who had come as a stranger, departed with the laurels of a great triumph.

Alas! in five years from that exulting night we saw him again for the last time in this city, borne in his coffin through the draped streets. With tears and lamentations a heartbroken people accompanied him from Washington, the scene of his martyrdom, to his last resting place in the young city of the West, where he had worked his way to fame.

The great events and achievements of those five years, seen through the perspective of the forty that have since elapsed, have fixed his place in history forever. It is the supreme felicity of the American people, in the short period of their existence as a nation, to have furnished to the world the two greatest benefactors, not of their own time only, but of all modern history. Washington created the nation and is known the world over as the Father of his Country. Lincoln came to be its saviour and redeemer—to save it from self-destruction, and to redeem it from the cancer of slavery which has been gnawing upon its vitals from the beginning. If it had been put to the vote of the forty-four nations assembled at the Hague for the first time in the world's history, representing the whole of civilization, Christian and Pagan, to name the two men who in modern times had done the most to promote liberty, justice, civilization, and peace, I am sure that with one voice they would have acclaimed these two greatest of Americans. Let their names stand together for all time to come.

My Tribute to the Great Emancipator

REPUBLICAN CLUB OF THE CITY OF NEW YORK

WALDORF-ASTORIA HOTEL

FEBRUARY 12, 1909

For its part in the celebration of Lincoln's birthday, the Republican Club of the City of New York asked the prominent black leader, Booker T. Washington, president of Tuskegee Normal and Industrial Institute and one of the most popular American speakers of the period, to give its annual address on February 12, 1909. In an atmosphere in which racial prejudice was still in potent force, if only subtle, the invitation of this black leader represented a departure from the usual custom of calling upon a prominent white Republican to inspire the club and was the first instance of a black speaker.

Fully aware of his opportunity, Washington presented himself as the representative of ten million black Americans who owed their freedom to Lincoln.[1] Instead of reciting the events of Lincoln's life, Washington more appropriately chose to express "gratitude and appreciation" for Lincoln's contribution to a shackled race: the Emancipation Proclamation. Through this strategy, Washington was able to place Lincoln as the originator of black freedom and vocational and educational opportunities for blacks. Building around the scriptural text, "Though a man die, yet shall he live," Washington concluded that Lincoln "lives in the steady and unalterable determination of ten millions of black citizens to continue to climb year by year the ladder of the highest usefulness and to perfect themselves in strong, robust character."

By a topical organization Washington supported his main theme with two subthemes: Lincoln provided physical and moral freedom to blacks and "pushed back the boundaries of freedom everywhere, gave the spirit of liberty a wider influence throughout the world." The second theme was an adaptation of the Horatio Alger myth, often associated with Lincoln: that any poor man can be president. Washington saw in Lincoln a model: "In his rise from the most abject poverty and ignorance to a position of high usefulness and power, he taught . . . one of the greatest of all lessons. . . . Today, throughout the world, because Lincoln lived, struggled, and triumphed, every boy who is ignorant, is in poverty, is despised or discouraged, holds his head a little higher. . . . His ambition to do something and be something is a little stronger, because Lincoln blazed the way."

Washington, in a characteristic manner, inserted aphorisms into his speeches:

So often the keeper is on the inside of the prison bars and the prisoner on the outside.

Wherever in any country the whole people feel that the happiness of all is dependent upon the happiness of the weakest, there freedom exists.

One man cannot hold another man down in the ditch without remaining down in the ditch with him.

We should keep in mind that no one can degrade us except ourselves; that if we are worthy, no influence can defeat us.

It requires no courage for a strong man to kick a weak one down.

1. James S. Olson, "Booker T. Washington," in *American Orators before 1900,* ed. Bernard K. Duffy and Halford R. Ryan (Westport, Conn.: Greenwood, 1987), 399–405.

The speech is reprinted from Louis R. Harlan and Raymond W. Smock, eds., *The Booker T. Washington Papers,* 14 vols. (Urbana: University of Illinois Press, 1972-89), 10:33–39.

M*r. Chairman, Ladies and Gentlemen:* You ask that which he found a piece of property and turned into a free American citizen to speak to you tonight on Abraham Lincoln. I am not fitted by ancestry or training to be your teacher tonight for, as I have stated, I was born a slave.

My first knowledge of Abraham Lincoln came in this way: I was awakened early one morning before the dawn of day, as I lay wrapped in a bundle of rags on the dirt floor of our slave cabin, by the prayers of my mother, just before leaving for her day's work, as she was kneeling over my body earnestly praying that Abraham Lincoln might succeed, and that one day she and her boy might be free. You give me the opportunity here this evening to celebrate with you and the nation the answer to that prayer.

Says the Great Book somewhere, "Though a man die, yet shall he live" [John 11:25]. If this is true of the ordinary man, how much more true is it of the hero of the hour and the hero of the century—Abraham Lincoln! One hundred years of the life and influence of Lincoln is the story of the struggles, the trials, ambitions, and triumphs of the people of our complex American civilization. Interwoven into the warp and woof of this human complexity is the moving story of men and women of nearly every race and color in their progress from slavery to freedom, from poverty to wealth, from weakness to power, from ignorance to intelligence. Knit into the life of Abraham Lincoln is the story and success of the nation in the blending of all tongues, religions, colors, races into one composite nation, leaving each group and race free to live its own separate social life, and yet all a part of the great whole.

If a man die, shall he live? Answering this question as applied to our martyred President, perhaps you expect me to confine my words of appreciation to the great boon which, through him, was conferred upon my race. My undying gratitude and that of ten millions of my race for this and yet more! To have been the instrument used by Providence through which four millions of slaves, now grown into ten millions of free citizens, were made free would bring eternal fame within itself, but this is not the only claim that Lincoln has upon our sense of gratitude and appreciation.

By the side of [Samuel Chapman] Armstrong, and [William Lloyd] Garrison, Lincoln lives today. In the very highest sense he lives in the present more potently than fifty years ago; for that which is seen is temporal, that which is unseen is eternal. He lives in the 32,000 young men and women of the Negro race learning trades and useful occupations; in the 200,000 farms acquired by those he freed; in the more than 400,000 homes built; in the forty-six banks established and 10,000 stores owned; in the $550,000,000 worth of taxable property in hand; in the 28,000 public schools existing, with 30,000 teachers; in the 170 industrial schools and colleges; in the 23,000 ministers and 26,000 churches.

But, above all this, he lives in the steady and unalterable determination of ten millions of black citizens to continue to climb year by year the ladder of the highest usefulness and to perfect themselves in strong, robust character. For making all this possible, Lincoln lives.

But, again, for a higher reason he lives tonight in every corner of the republic. To set the physical man free is much. To set the spiritual man free is more. So often the keeper is on the inside of the prison bars and the prisoner on the outside.

As an individual, grateful as I am to Lincoln for freedom of body, my gratitude is still greater for freedom of soul—the liberty which permits one to live up in that atmosphere where he refuses to permit sectional or racial hatred to drag down, to warp and narrow his soul.

The signing of the Emancipation Proclamation was a great event, and yet it was but the symbol of another, still greater and more momentous. We who celebrate this anniversary should not forget that the same pen that gave freedom to four millions of African slaves at the same time struck the shackles from the souls of twenty-seven millions of Americans of another color.

In any country, regardless of what its laws say, wherever people act upon the idea that the disadvantage of one man is the good of another, there slavery exists. Wherever in any country the whole people feel that the happiness of all is dependent upon the happiness of the weakest, there freedom exists.

In abolishing slavery, Lincoln proclaimed the principle that, even in the case of the humblest and weakest of mankind, the welfare of each is still the good of all. In reestablishing in this country the principle that, at bottom, the interests of humanity and of the individual are one, he freed men's souls from spiritual bondage; he freed them to mutual helpfulness. Henceforth no man of any race, either in the North or in the South, need feel constrained to fear or hate his brother.

By the same token that Lincoln made America free, he pushed back the boundaries of freedom everywhere, gave the spirit of liberty a wider influence throughout the world, and reestablished the dignity of man as man.

By the same act that freed my race, he said to the civilized and uncivilized world that man everywhere must be free, and that man everywhere must be enlightened, and the Lincoln spirit of freedom and fair play will never cease to spread and grow in power till throughout the world all men shall know the truth, and the truth shall make them free.

Lincoln in his day was wise enough to recognize that which is true in the present and for all time: that in a state of slavery and ignorance man renders the lowest and most costly form of service to his fellows. In a state of freedom and enlightenment he renders the highest and most helpful form of service.

The world is fast learning that of all forms of slavery there is none that is so harmful and degrading as that form of slavery which tempts one human being to hate another by reason of his race or color. One man cannot hold another man down in the ditch without remaining down in the ditch with him. One who goes through life with his eyes closed against all that is good in another race is weakened and circumscribed, as one who fights in a battle with one hand tied behind him. Lincoln was in the truest sense great because he unfettered himself. He climbed up out of the valley, where his vision was narrowed and weakened by the fog and miasma, onto the mountain top, where in a pure and unclouded atmosphere he could see the truth which enabled him to rate all men at their true worth. Growing out of this anniversary season and atmosphere, may there crystallize a resolve throughout the nation that on such a mountain the American people will strive to live.

We owe, then, to Lincoln physical freedom, moral freedom, and yet this is not all. There is a debt of gratitude which we as individuals, no matter of what race or nation, must recognize as due Abraham

Lincoln—not for what he did as chief executive of the nation, but for what he did as a man. In his rise from the most abject poverty and ignorance to a position of high usefulness and power, he taught the world one of the greatest of all lessons. In fighting his own battle up from obscurity and squalor, he fought the battle of every other individual and race that is down, and so helped to pull up every other human who was down. People so often forget that by every inch that the lowest man crawls up he makes it easier for every other man to get up. Today, throughout the world, because Lincoln lived, struggled, and triumphed, every boy who is ignorant, is in poverty, is despised or discouraged, holds his head a little higher. His heart beats a little faster, his ambition to do something and be something is a little stronger, because Lincoln blazed the way.

To my race, the life of Abraham Lincoln has its special lesson at this point in our career. In so far as his life emphasizes patience, long suffering, sincerity, naturalness, dogged determination, and courage— courage to avoid the superficial, courage to persistently seek the substance instead of the shadow—it points the road for my people to travel.

As a race we are learning, I believe, in an increasing degree that the best way for us to honor the memory of our Emancipator is by seeking to imitate him. Like Lincoln, the Negro race should seek to be simple, without bigotry and without ostentation. There is great power in simplicity. We as a race should, like Lincoln, have moral courage to be what we are, and not pretend to be what we are not. We should keep in mind that no one can degrade us except ourselves; that if we are worthy, no influence can defeat us. Like other races, the Negro will often meet obstacles, often be sorely tried and tempted; but we must keep in mind that freedom, in the broadest and highest sense, has never been a bequest; it has been a conquest.

In the final test, the success of our race will be in proportion to the service that it renders to the world. In the long run, the badge of service is the badge of sovereignty.

With all his other elements of strength, Abraham Lincoln possessed in the highest degree patience and, as I have said, courage. The highest form of courage is not always that exhibited on the battlefield in the midst of the blare of trumpets and the waving of banners. The highest courage is of the Lincoln kind. It is the same kind of courage, made possible by the new life and the new possibilities furnished by Lincoln's Proclamation, displayed by thousands of men and women of my race every year who are going out from Tuskegee and other Negro institutions in the South to lift up their fellows. When they go, often into lonely and secluded districts, with little thought of salary, with little thought of personal welfare, no drums beat, no banners fly, no friends stand by to cheer them on; but these brave young souls who are erecting schoolhouses, creating school systems, prolonging school terms, teaching the people to buy homes, build houses, and live decent lives are fighting the battles of this country just as truly and bravely as any persons who go forth to fight battles against a foreign foe.

In paying my tribute of respect to the Great Emancipator of my race, I desire to say a word here and now in behalf of an element of brave and true white men of the South who, though they saw in Lincoln's policy the ruin of all they believed in and hoped for, have loyally accepted the results of the Civil War, and are today working with a courage few people in the North can understand to uplift the Negro in the South and complete the emancipation that Lincoln began. I am tempted to say that it certainly required as high a degree of courage for men of the type of Robert E. Lee and John B. Gordon to accept the results of the war in the manner and spirit in which they did, as that which [Ulysses S.] Grant and [William T.] Sherman displayed in fighting the physical battles that saved the Union.

Lincoln also was a Southern man by birth, but he was one of those white men, of whom there is a large and growing class, who resented the idea that in order to assert and maintain the superiority of the Anglo-Saxon race it was necessary that another group of humanity should be kept in ignorance.

Lincoln was not afraid or ashamed to come into contact with the lowly of all races. His reputation and social position were not of such a transitory and transparent kind that he was afraid that he would lose them by being just and kind, even to a man of dark skin. I always pity from the bottom of my heart any man who feels that somebody else must be kept down or in ignorance in order that he may appear great by comparison. It requires no courage for a strong man to kick a weak one down.

Lincoln lives today because he had the courage which made him refuse to hate the man at the South or the man at the North when they did not agree with him. He had the courage as well as the patience and foresight to suffer in silence, to be misunderstood, to be abused, to refuse to revile when reviled. For he knew that, if he was right, the ridicule of today would be the applause of tomorrow. He knew, too, that at some time in the distant future our nation would repent of the folly of cursing our public servants while they live and blessing them only when they die. In this connection I cannot refrain from suggesting the question to the millions of voices raised today in his praise: "Why did you not say it yesterday?" Yesterday, when one word of approval and gratitude would have meant so much to him in strengthening his hand and heart.

As we recall tonight his deeds and words, we can do so with grateful hearts and strong faith in the future for the spread of righteousness. The civilization of the world is going forward, not backward. Here and there for a little season the progress of mankind may seem to halt or tarry by the wayside, or even appear to slide backward, but the trend is ever onward and upward, and will be until someone can invent and enforce a law to stop the progress of civilization. In goodness and liberality the world moves forward. It goes forward beneficently, but it moves forward relentlessly. In the last analysis the forces of nature are behind the moral progress of the world, and these forces will crush into powder any group of humanity that resists this progress.

As we gather here, brothers all, in common joy and thanksgiving for the life of Lincoln, may I not ask that you, the worthy representatives of seventy millions of white Americans, join heart and hand with the ten millions of black Americans—these ten millions who speak your tongue, profess your religion—who have never lifted their voices or hands except in defense of their country's honor and their country's flag—and swear eternal fealty to the memory and the traditions of the sainted Lincoln? I repeat, may we not join with your race, and let all of us here highly resolve that justice, good will, and peace shall be the motto of our lives? If this be true, in the highest sense Lincoln shall not have lived and died in vain.

And, finally, gathering inspiration and encouragement from this hour and Lincoln's life, I pledge to you and to the nation that my race, in so far as I can speak for it, which in the past, whether in ignorance or intelligence, whether in slavery or in freedom, has always been true to the Stars and Stripes and to the highest and best interests of this country, will strive to so deport itself that it shall reflect nothing but the highest credit upon the whole people in the North and in the South.

PART FIVE

The Birthplace Celebration

The birthplace cabin of Abraham Lincoln, three miles south of Hodgenville, Kentucky, has become a much-visited spot on the Lincoln trail, which stretches from Kentucky to Indiana and into Illinois. Between 250,000 and 300,000 visitors from all over the world are attracted to the little cabin each year.[1] Five presidents, Theodore Roosevelt, William Howard Taft, Woodrow Wilson, Franklin D. Roosevelt, and Dwight D. Eisenhower, made pilgrimages there, and all, with the exception of FDR, came to make speeches about Lincoln.[2]

The alleged birthplace cabin was purchased in 1861 by Dr. George Rodman, who had it moved to his nearby farm to protect it. Alfred W. Dennett purchased it in 1894 and moved it back to Sinking Spring Farm, Thomas Lincoln's property. But in 1897 it was dismantled and carted around the country for display: first at the Tennessee Centennial Exposition, Nashville, 1897; Central Park, New York City, 1897; the Pan-American Exposition, Buffalo, New York, 1901; and the Louisville Homecoming, Kentucky, 1906. In 1907, Rodman transferred the title to the Lincoln Farm Association. The cabin was returned to Hodgenville, reconstructed, and placed under a Connecticut pink granite and Tennessee marble memorial building designed by John Russell Pope. The Lincoln Farm Association, under the leadership of Robert Collier and Richard Lloyd Jones and *Collier's Weekly,* persuaded 100,000 citizens to give $350,000 to pay for the construction.[3]

The memorial building stands on or near the original cabin site on a little knoll and is reached by fifty-six terraced steps, one for each year of Lincoln's life. Each of three sides of the memorial building is adorned by Doric columns. As visitors ascend the steps, they see the six front columns that make the portico that shields the stately double bronze doors. Inscribed on the facade are the words "With Malice Toward None With Charity For All," and engraved on bronze plaques on the interior and exterior walls are excerpts from Lincoln's speeches, including the Gettysburg Address. The memorial building is a most impressive cover for a crude little cabin and seems a little out of place in rural Kentucky.[4] As it now stands, the little cabin, thirteen by seventeen feet, is scrutinized by visitors who may walk around it. It must be admitted that what stands is probably not the actual Lincoln birthplace, but it makes no difference to the visitors who vicariously see in it a symbol of the developing West and the frontier and who associate this with Lincoln.

Two memorial events were held at what is now the Abraham Lincoln National Historical Park before the cabin and grounds were officially deeded to the United States by the Lincoln Farm Association. The first occurred February 12, 1909, at the laying of the cornerstone. The second took place November 9, 1911, when President William Howard Taft came for the formal dedication of the building. On Labor Day, September 4, 1916, President Woodrow Wilson delivered the acceptance speech when the Lincoln Farm Association formally presented the park to the United States.[5]

1. *Abraham Lincoln National Historical Park: Kentucky,* pamphlet (Washington D.C.: National Park Service, 1942), 3; letter to author from Patti Reynolds, park ranger, Jan. 20, 1988.

2. *Lincoln Lore* 1545 (Nov. 1966).

3. Richard Lloyd Jones, "The Lincoln Birthplace Farm," *Colliers* 42 (Feb. 10, 1906): 12–14; "A Park of Patriotism: The Lincoln Farm," *Review of Reviews* 33 (Mar. 1906): 293–95. The board of trustees included Joseph H. Choate, William Howard Taft, Horace Porter, Lyman J. Gage, Cardinal James Gibbons, Norman Hapgood, Henry Watterson, Augustus Saint-Gaudens, Jenkin Jerome, Richard Lloyd Jones, William Travers, Mark Twain, Albert Belmont, Edward M. Shepard, Ida M. Tarbell, Charles A. Towne, Thomas Hastings, Albert Shaw, Robert J. Collier, and Clarence H. Mackeyo; *Abraham Lincoln National Historical Park,* 13.

4. Mark E. Neely, Jr., *The Abraham Lincoln Encyclopedia* (New York: McGraw-Hill, 1982), 173–74; Roy Hays, "Is the Lincoln Birthplace Cabin Authentic?" *Abraham Lincoln Quarterly* 5 (Sept. 1948), 127–63; "His Old Kentucky Home," *Civil War Times* 22 (Feb. 1984), 36–37.

5. *Lincoln Lore* 826 (Feb. 1945); *Lincoln Lore* 1545 (Nov. 1966), 3–4.

The Supreme Vision of Lincoln

MEMORIAL BUILDING
HODGENVILLE, KENTUCKY
FEBRUARY 12, 1909

The one hundredth anniversary celebration of Lincoln's birth gave the state of Kentucky an opportunity to assert its place in the Lincoln aura. In a brief speech Governor Augustus E. Wilson declared, "Kentucky says, 'I am his own mother. I nursed him at my breast; my baby born of me. He is mine. Shall any claim come before the mothers.'" The governor had laid a primary claim to the Lincoln myth.[1]

What better place for a dramatic demonstration of this distinction than the laying of the cornerstone for the memorial building that would cover Lincoln's birthplace cabin at Hodgenville. A distinguished list of speakers assembled:

Invocation: E.L. Powell, Minister First Christian Church, Louisville, Kentucky.
Address on behalf of the United States of America: President Theodore Roosevelt.
Address on behalf of the State of Kentucky: Governor Augustus Wilson.
Address on behalf of Lincoln Farm Association: Governor Joseph Folk, President of Association.
Address on behalf of Federal Army: General James Grant Wilson.
Address on behalf of Confederate Army: General Luke F. Wright.[2]

Always a great admirer of Lincoln, President Theodore Roosevelt eagerly participated in this historic occasion.[3] In a letter to Rev. Duncan Milner dated November 30, 1908, Roosevelt had revealed, "Great Heart is my favorite character in allegory . . . and I think that Abraham Lincoln is the ideal Great Heart of public life."[4]

Roosevelt, who thought of himself as a "preacher militant," delivered a lay sermon, preaching what he called "realizable ideals." Obviously, he knew that in appearing at Hodgenville he had a bully pulpit and that what he said would be carried in full in newspapers throughout the country.[5] Departing from his usual extemporizing, Roosevelt read his address, which showed fine tuning of the rhetorical art, including apt comparisons and contrasts and an overall inspirational unity. In the scenario of the mythmaker, he portrayed Lincoln as "this homely backwoods idealist," an extension of the mythical western settler or idealized pioneer and rugged individualist. Roosevelt presented Lincoln as a model of the best American spirit and one to be imitated in 1904: "We can profit by the way in which Lincoln used both these traits ['indomitable resolution with cool-headed sanity'] as he strove for reform." Throughout his presentation Roosevelt mentioned the traits of the idealized hero:

> Saw into the future with prophetic imagination
>
> The practical man's hard common sense
>
> Never wavered in devotion to his principles
>
> Never went to extremes, he worked step by step
>
> The goal was never dim before his vision
>
> Could fight violently against what he deemed wrong
>
> Did not hate the man from whom he differed

At the climax of his eulogy Roosevelt turned the Lincoln image into an appeal for reconciliation. Aware that he was in Kentucky, where divisions still existed, Roosevelt suggested that Lincoln "saw clearly that the same high qualities, the same courage, and willingness for self-sacrifice, and devotion to the right . . . belonged both to the men of the North and to the men of the South."

The militant preacher brought his eulogy to a sweeping close, calling Lincoln "the mightiest of the mighty men who mastered the mighty days." These were exceedingly strong words, but Roosevelt's audience thought he was sincere. The editor of *Harper's Weekly* wrote: "So many speeches were made on the one hundredth anniversary of Lincoln's birthday that few found their way into print, but of those we have read that of President Roosevelt was incomparably the best . . . and will, in our judgment, stand out as the most satisfying effort Mr. Roosevelt has yet made."[6]

1. Nathan William MacChesney, *Abraham Lincoln: The Tribute of a Century, 1809–1909* (Chicago: McClung, 1910), 253.

2. *Lincoln Lore* 1545 (Nov. 1966), 4.

3. Theodore Roosevelt, *Review of Reviews* 39 (Feb. 1909), 1.

4. *Lincoln Lore* 1004 (July 5, 1948).

5. Owen Webster, *Roosevelt: The Story of a Friendship, 1880–1919* (New York: Macmillan, 1910), 232; *Works of Theodore Roosevelt,* 13: 615–28.

6. *Harper's Weekly* 53 (Feb. 27, 1909): 4.

The speech is reprinted from Herman Hagedorn, ed., *The Works of Theodore Roosevelt,* 20 vols. (New York: Scribner's, 1926), 11: 210–14. Reprinted with permission.

We have met here to celebrate the hundredth anniversary of the birth of one of the two greatest Americans; of one of the two or three greatest men of the nineteenth century; of one of the greatest men in the world's history. This rail-splitter, this boy who passed his ungainly youth in the dire poverty of the poorest of the frontier folk, whose rise was by weary and painful labor, lived to lead his people through the burning flames of a struggle from which the nation emerged, purified as by fire, born anew to a loftier life. After long years of iron effort, and of failure that came more often than victory, he at last rose to the leadership of the Republic, at the moment when that leadership had become the stupendous world-task of the time. He grew to know greatness, but never ease. Success came to him, but never happiness, save that which springs from doing well a painful and a vital task. Power was his, but not pleasure. The furrows deepened on his brow, but his eyes were undimmed by either hate or fear. His gaunt shoulders were bowed, but his steel thews never faltered as he bore for a burden the destinies of his people. His great and tender heart shrank from giving pain; and the task allotted him was to pour out like water the life-blood of the young men, and to feel in his every fibre the sorrow of the women. Disaster saddened but never dismayed him. As the red years of war went by they found him ever doing his duty in the present, ever facing the future with fearless front, high of heart, and dauntless of soul. Unbroken by hatred, unshaken by scorn, he worked and suffered for the people. Triumph was his at the last; and barely had he tasted it before murder found him, and the kindly, patient, fearless eyes were closed forever.

As a people we are indeed beyond measure fortunate in the characters of the two greatest of our public men, Washington and Lincoln. Widely though they differed in externals, the Virginia landed gentleman and the Kentucky backwoodsman, they were alike in essentials, they were alike in the great qualities which made each able to render service to his nation and to all mankind such as no other man of his generation could or did render. Each had lofty ideals, but each in striving to attain these lofty ideals was guided by the soundest common sense. Each possessed inflexible courage in adversity, and a soul

164

wholly unspoiled by prosperity. Each possessed all the gentler virtues commonly exhibited by good men who lack rugged strength of character. Each possessed also all the strong qualities commonly exhibited by those towering masters of mankind who have too often shown themselves devoid of so much as the understanding of the words by which we signify the qualities of duty, of mercy, of devotion to the right, of lofty disinterestedness in battling for the good of others. There have been other men as great and other men as good; but in all the history of mankind there are no other two great men as good as these, no other two good men as great. Widely though the problems of to-day differ from the problems set for solution to Washington when he founded this nation, to Lincoln when he saved it and freed the slaves, yet the qualities they showed in meeting these problems are exactly the same as those we should show in doing our work to-day.

Lincoln saw into the future with the prophetic imagination usually vouchsafed only to the poet and the seer. He had in him all the lift toward greatness of the visionary, without any of the visionary's fanaticism or egotism, without any of the visionary's narrow jealousy of the practical man and inability to strive in practical fashion for the realization of an ideal. He had the practical man's hard common sense and willingness to adapt means to ends; but there was in him none of that morbid growth of mind and soul which blinds so many practical men to the higher things of life. No more practical man ever lived than this homely backwoods idealist; but he had nothing in common with those practical men whose consciences are warped until they fail to distinguish between good and evil, fail to understand that strength, ability, shrewdness, whether in the world of business or of politics, only serve to make their possessor a more noxious, a more evil member of the community, if they are not guided and controlled by a fine and high moral sense.

We of this day must try to solve many social and industrial problems, requiring to an especial degree the combination of indomitable resolution with cool-headed sanity. We can profit by the way in which Lincoln used both these traits as he strove for reform. We can learn much of value from the very attacks which following that course brought upon his head, attacks alike by the extremists of revolution and by the extremists of reaction. He never wavered in devotion to his principles, in his love for the Union, and in his abhorrence of slavery. Timid and lukewarm people were always denouncing him because he was too extreme; but as a matter of fact he never went to extremes, he worked step by step; and because of this the extremists hated and denounced him with a fervor which now seems to us fantastic in its deification of the unreal and the impossible. At the very time when one side was holding him up as the apostle of social revolution because he was against slavery, the leading abolitionist denounced him as the "slave hound of Illinois." When he was the second time candidate for President, the majority of his opponents attacked him because of what they termed his extreme radicalism, while a minority threatened to bolt his nomination because he was not radical enough. He had continually to check those who wished to go forward too fast, at the very time that he overrode the opposition of those who wished not to go forward at all. The goal was never dim before his vision; but he picked his way cautiously, without either halt or hurry, as he strode toward it, through such a morass of difficulty that no man of less courage would have attempted it, while it would surely have overwhelmed any man of judgment less serene.

Yet perhaps the most wonderful thing of all, and, from the standpoint of the America of to-day and of the future, the most vitally important, was the extraordinary way in which Lincoln could fight valiantly against what he deemed wrong and yet preserve undiminished his love and respect for the brother from whom he differed. In the hour of a triumph that would have turned any weaker man's head, in the heat of a struggle which spurred many a good man to dreadful vindictiveness, he said truthfully that so long as he had been in his office he had never willingly planted a thorn in any man's bosom, and besought his supporters to study the incidents of the trial through which they were passing as philosophy from which to learn wisdom and not as wrongs to be avenged; ending with the solemn exhortation that, as the strife was over, all should reunite in a common effort to save their common country.

He lived in days that were great and terrible, when brother fought against brother for what each sincerely deemed to be the right. In a contest so grim the strong men who alone can carry it through are rarely able to do justice to the deep convictions of those with whom they grapple in moral strife. At such times men see through a glass darkly; to only the rarest and loftiest spirits is vouchsafed that clear vision which gradually comes to all, even to the lesser, as the struggle fades into distance, and wounds are forgotten, and peace creeps back to the hearts that were hurt. But to Lincoln was given this supreme vision. He did not hate the man from whom he differed. Weakness was as foreign as wickedness to his strong, gentle nature; but his courage was of a quality so high that it needed no bolstering of dark passion. He saw clearly that the same high qualities, the same courage, and willingness for self-sacrifice, and devotion to the right as it was given them to see the right, belonged both to the men of the North and to the men of the South. As the years roll by, and as all of us, wherever we dwell, grow to feel an equal pride in the valor and self-devotion, alike of the men who wore the blue and the men who wore the gray, so this whole nation will grow to feel a peculiar sense of pride in the man whose blood was shed for the union of his people and for the freedom of a race; the lover of his country and of all mankind; the mightiest of the mighty men who mastered the mighty days: Abraham Lincoln.

Lincoln the Orator

MEMORIAL BUILDING
HODGENVILLE, KENTUCKY
NOVEMBER 9, 1911

On November 9, 1911, the memorial building at the Abraham Lincoln National Historical Park was dedicated. President William Howard Taft was the featured speaker. Other speakers included ex-governor Joseph W. Folk of Missouri, who spoke for the Lincoln Farm Association, Governor Augustus E. Wilson, representing the state of Kentucky, John C. Black, a prominent attorney, Henry Watterson, editor of the Louisville *Courier-Journal,* and Senator William E. Borah of Idaho.[1] Borah, a rugged individualist, was invited because he was known as an eloquent ceremonial orator. An Illinoisan by birth, he had heard many Lincoln legends since boyhood in his home in rural Wayne County, where Lincoln was regarded as a saint.[2]

An articulate advocate for popular government, the Idahoan, like Bryan, centered his eulogy around Lincoln's speaking as the means for advancing the interests of the people, picturing Lincoln as one of the few "tribunes of the people," "its voice and conscience—a great apostolic figure" of democratic government. Of Lincoln's rhetorical art, Borah said: "I do not know of another figure in all the history of our free institutions so impressive as that of Lincoln as he stood before these vast throngs conducting his great propaganda of righteousness, and I do not know of one who ever spoke with greater power and effect."

It was evident that, like Bryan, Borah chose to concentrate upon *means* (not virtues) through which Lincoln achieved influence: "spoken thought," which Borah believed was "at times a most potent influence in the cause of liberty." For supporting material Borah drew upon primary Lincoln sources, including the lyceum lectures, the Lincoln-Douglas debates and the famous presidential utterances. In comparing

Edward Everett with Lincoln at Gettysburg, Borah aptly characterized Lincoln's rhetoric:

> The scholar with his wide range of words, his brilliant rhetoric, stood on the field of Gettysburg, beside the man whose school days could have been measured by the days of a single year. The one was the fruit of five generations of New England culture, the other took his diploma from the "university of nature." The one had mastered the logic of the books, the other understood perfectly the logic of the human heart. The one, slavish to his great art, clothed his theme in all the witchery of his inimitable style. The other, burdened with sorrow for those who had there given "the last full measure of their devotion," spoke with the abandon of a sorely chastened and over-wrought mind. The one had an oration, the other a message. The one was rhetoric, the other eloquence.

In Borah's view Lincoln had "crystallized the best there was in men, directed it through the channels of government, and at last embodied it into laws and constitutions." He made Lincoln the embodiment of the spirit of democratic government and the "inspiration of our free institutions."

1. *Lincoln Lore* 1545 (Nov. 1966), 4.
2. Claudius B. Johnson, *Borah of Idaho* (New York: Longmans Green, 1936), 5.

The speech is reprinted from William E. Borah, *American Problems: A Selection of Speeches and Prophecies,* ed. Horace Green (New York: Duffield, 1924), 31–42.

The life of no other public man is so well and so universally known as that of Abraham Lincoln. The hovel in which he was born, the loneliness of his childhood days, the poverty of his early manhood, the improvident and restless father, the sweet face which tradition gives his mother, the self-discipline, the hunger for knowledge, the rise from obscurity to power, the singular judgment and remarkable wisdom with which he exercised that power, his honesty, his great tenderness of heart, the marvel of his eloquence, the tragic close—these are the meager outlines of an epic from the simple homely life of American democracy, and the American people love and cherish it one and all, North and South. Fiction has no story so interesting as this. Poetry has not clothed its heroes with a mastery won over such obstacles and yet so complete as that which plain truth reveals in the sad and solitary career of this marvelous man.

Our government calls for a dual capacity in statesmanship—a combination of the apostle and the lawgiver. To frame and to successfully enact and execute our laws demands a high order of intellect; it involves a clear and comprehensive insight into the mechanism of our institutions. But there is another work which we can not neglect. So long as all sovereignty rests with the people, so long as the enactment of good laws and the enforcement of all law depend so largely upon the intelligence and conscience of the citizen, we cannot dispense with those who speak with wisdom and power to the multitude. Such are the men who keep alive that eternal vigilance which is the price of all we have. They are the tribunes of the people. Without them the public conscience would become sluggish and the wisest measures sometimes fail. They arouse public interest. They organize public thought. They call forth and direct the invincible moral forces of an entire nation. There is no higher duty than that of arousing to moderate and sustained action the minds of those with whom all power rests. There can be no graver responsibility than that of directing the people in the use of the instrumentalities of government.

Oratory has always been a factor in great movements. Spoken thought has been controlling in more than one crisis of human rights. There has seldom been a time when men were not to be moved to great deeds through the power of eloquence. It has been at times a most potent influence in the cause of liberty. If the time ever comes when it shall no longer have that influence, as many are fond to prophesy, it will be after selfishness and sensuality shall have imbruted or destroyed all the nobler faculties of the mind. The people have at different periods in their bewilderment and travail, when old beliefs were passing and old institutions crumbling, waited for some great leader, rich in human sympathy, to speak with that uncommon power with which it is given few men to speak. Lincoln was undoubtedly one of those few. He came from no school. He was the pride of no university. In spite of many obstacles he came to his own. Without the advantage of wealth, leisure or family prestige he outstripped all competitors. Accident or environment, necessity or chance may modify and color the fabric of life, yet purpose and will are masters also of these, and the strong and purposeful youth arose from his harsh and obscure surroundings to become the unchallenged voice of one of the most righteous of the world's great movements.

The first qualification of an orator is that he be master of his subject. The second, that his subject be master of him. This was singularly true with reference to Lincoln. His lyceum lectures and his speeches upon ordinary occasions do not rise above the commonplace. It was when the blight of slavery threatened the free soil of the North that his latent powers were given the energy and sweep of genius. This strange, untrained voice laden with sympathy but firm in tone rang through the land, tugging continuously at the consciences of men until the lethargy and selfishness of a century melted and fell away. He aroused public sentiment. He marshalled the righteousness of the nation. He crystallized the best there was in men, directed it through the channels of government, and at last embodied it into laws and constitutions. Through the power of speech he, more than anyone else, set in motion the moral forces which disenthralled a race. In the affairs of government and in the details of diplomacy he ranks among the great Presidents. But in this faith of ours which we call democracy he stands apart, its voice and conscience—a great apostolic figure. Who reads today his speech at Gettysburg, his second inaugural address or the letter to the brave mother who had lost five sons in battle, not to feel, to realize that here was a political gospel worthy of the faith which we profess, commensurate with the destiny for which as a

171

people we strive. In no other do we find such an unqualified acceptance of the basic truths of popular government.

The scholar with his wide range of words, his brilliant rhetoric, stood on the field of Gettysburg, beside the man whose school days could have been measured by the days of a single year. The one was the fruit of five generations of New England culture, the other took his diploma from the "university of nature." The one had mastered the logic of the books, the other understood perfectly the logic of the human heart. The one, slavish to his great art, clothed his theme in all the witchery of his inimitable style. The other, burdened with sorrow for those who had there given "the last full measure of their devotion," spoke with the abandon of a sorely chastened and overwrought mind. The one had an oration, the other a message. The one was rhetoric, the other eloquence. It is after all by reason of a profound conviction or the anguish of an all absorbing moral passion born amid the storms and tempests which sometimes sweep the soul that the heights of true oratory are obtained. Learning, culture, the training of the schools will aid, but these alone will not suffice. Paul before Agrippa, Phillips conquering the mob, O'Connell lifting a down-trodden people to the dignity of a nation, Burke aroused by the long line of indefensible crimes of Hastings, Webster pleading for the Union, Lincoln voicing the nation's compassion and the nation's courage at Gettysburg—these are the occasions and the themes which fuse and mould into one majestic and harmonious whole the varied powers of the gifted mind.

It is natural in speaking of Mr. Lincoln as an orator to recur to the occasions such as the second inaugural or the dedication of the field of Gettysburg, occasions upon which he spoke with such tenderness and pathos, such feeling, fitness and eloquence, such simple yet such searching power. But we cannot take his full measure as a public speaker without considering the great debate. This was the most crucial test of pure intellect to which he was ever subjected, for Stephen A. Douglas was "no mean" antagonist, no ordinary man. Endowed by nature with unusual mental power he had had the advantage of years of association with the strong minds of a most stirring period and a wide experience in the halls of legislation. Bold, resourceful, ambitious, he had no superior and few equals as a debater in the Senate of the United States, of which he was then the most interesting and striking figure. At the time of the debate he was at the very zenith of his popularity and in the full and imperious possession of all his great powers, both natural and acquired. He went into the contest with the spirit of victory strong upon him and inspired by the devotion of followers who thought it was not his to lose. The debate, as we know, took place in the open air in the presence of thousands of anxious followers. The theme, the surroundings, the momentous consequences which all dimly foresaw as soon to follow—for each spoke to and for a distinct civilization—make this debate unique, exceptional and profoundly interesting even now and must have made it vastly more interesting and absorbing to those who listened or who read of it as it progressed.

In the give and take of the close grip of the contest, in the finesse and brilliant fencing which sometimes seem essential in that kind of a deadly intellectual encounter, in the adroit and telling display of points for immediate effect before the great throng Douglas seems the superior. But in the calm and lucid statement of principles, in the remorseless arrangement of a great subject in order to hurl it with final effect upon the listener, in the use of that logic which is born of the wedlock of conscience and intellect, in the capacity to read out of the future the result of today's policies, in the prophetic sweep of a great mind, Lincoln was distinctly and unquestionably far the superior of his adversary. In fact, the great qualities which Lincoln possessed Douglas, with all his genius for debate, did not possess at all. There was no chance in such a duel of intellects for the false or specious arts of oratory. Each realized that "economy of expression" and integrity of thought must take the place of the diffuse and superficial entertainments with which men are prone to entertain popular assemblies. Never was more profound respect paid to the intelligence and patriotism of the people. I do not know of another figure in all the history of our free institutions so impressive as that of Lincoln as he stood before these vast throngs conducting his great propaganda of righteousness, and I do not know of one who ever spoke with greater power and effect.

The number of our public men who have sincerely accepted in full the principles of a democratic or republican form of government has not been so large as we sometimes suppose. Some of the ablest were never able to be free from an honest distrust in the self-governing capacity of those whom we so often style the common people. But

Lincoln's faith in our institutions and in the power of the people to rule was natural, simple and sincere. He had been and always continued to be one of them. Born in that lowly sphere where the anthem of human sympathy enriches the heart of childhood with compassion for all he learned to read the human heart, knew its emotions, its hopes and its longings far better than he knew books. But his speeches are wholly free from the protestations of loyalty to the people which so often characterize the addresses of public leaders. The insinuating and subtle self-laudation of an Alcibiades is in his speeches nowhere to be found. In all his public utterances there is no appeal to prejudice, no effort to mislead. Moderation is the constant surprise of every reader of his speeches—a rare quality indeed in political addresses. He never mistook anger for righteousness. In him there was nothing of the demagogue. He did not flatter, and in passion's hour he did not follow. He possessed in a remarkable way the capacity for intellectual solitude, even in the midst of the throng—yet he never lost faith in the throng. He paid the people the high compliment of speaking to them in the language of reason and true eloquence. He believed they would accept a great principle as a controlling basis for action, and time proved he was not mistaken. Some speakers seem to think it necessary to shriek, to exaggerate, to impugn, to resort to the cheap and common arts of public speaking when talking to the people at large. Lincoln never offered this challenge to their intelligence and manhood.

It is such qualities as these which make it difficult to speak of Lincoln as an orator or Lincoln as a lawyer or Lincoln as a political leader. There was in him a fulness, a completeness, a greatness, which seem to forbid an attempt to accentuate particular qualities. In the consideration of particular elements of strength we are soon lost in the contemplation of his massive figure as a whole. His life in all its wretchedness and glory, in all its penury and power intrudes itself upon us and seems as inexplicable and incomprehensible as the cunning of Angelo's chisel or the touch of Titian's brush. Sacred writers, had he lived in those days, would have placed him among their seers and prophets and invested him with the hidden powers of the mystic world. Antiquity would have clothed such a being with the attributes of deity. He was one of the moral and intellectual giants of the earth.

But we do not attempt to describe a painting of one of the old masters before which we stand in wonder and admiration. Millions

174

feel the inspiration of a great character, just as they feel the inspiration and thrill of a great poem, but in no wise seek or hope to tell the secret of the influence or power over them. We are dealing today as millions have dealt for fifty years with the life of one whose name and memory all revere. But even the most superlative masters of expression have not as yet portrayed in all its fulness the ever-growing greatness of his name. We see the awkward country boy in his cabin home in the midst of the trackless forest. We see him cover his mother's grave with winter's withered leaves and return to his cabin home to unconsciously enter the race for fame. We see him as he walks near the auction block in the slave market and hear his almost weird curse pronounced upon the institution of slavery. We see him in after years, when as the greatest ruler upon this earth, he walked with patience and compassion the paths of power—we hear men denounce him as a tyrant and a murderer while patiently he submits to it all. At last the storm begins to clear, the light breaks through the rifted clouds and we see him walking in the dawn of a new day and four million human beings are there unloosed of their fetters—and then the altar and the sacrifice. It seems like an exaggerated tale of oriental fancy, but it is not. The story is the product of our own soil. It is what happened here among a clean, liberty loving people, under the inspiration of our free institutions. It was and is in the fullest sense the guarantee which God and God alone gave, and, as we must believe every hour, gives, that no matter what the test, a government "conceived in liberty and dedicated to the proposition that all men are created equal shall not perish from the earth."

The Sacred Mystery of Democracy

MEMORIAL BUILDING
HODGENVILLE, KENTUCKY
SEPTEMBER 4, 1916

A third great ceremony at the Lincoln birthplace was held on Labor Day, September 4, 1916, when the Lincoln Farm Association presented the deed to the park to the government of the United States.[1] The program involved an impressive group of speakers, which included Joseph W. Folk, former governor of Missouri, who represented the Lincoln Farm Association; Mississippi Senator John Sharp Williams, who represented the South; Robert J. Collier of *Collier's Weekly*, who made the presentation; and Secretary of War Newton D. Baker, who accepted on behalf of the United States.[2] The featured speaker was President Woodrow Wilson.

The Democratic president was pleased to have another opportunity to speak about Lincoln. In 1909 and 1912 in Chicago he had delivered eulogies on the Illinoisan with whom, he said, he felt "the closest kinship in principle and in political lineament."[3] Richard N. Current has suggested that among the presidents, "Wilson had the truest empathy" with Lincoln and the "greatest insight" into his "qualities of leadership."[4] What Wilson pondered was how this spot could produce the immortal Lincoln. Speaking of "this little hut" as "a place . . . of mystery," "a shrine," "an altar upon which . . . [to] keep alive the vestal fire of democracy," the president saw in Lincoln the culmination of mysterious forces and insights, or what Wilson termed "the sacred mystery of democracy." "This strange child of the cabin kept company with invisible things," explained Wilson.

In his mythbuilding, Wilson, of course, re-echoed the Horatio Alger theme that every mother's son can become president: "No man can explain this [Lincoln's rise], but every man can see how it demonstrates the vigor of democracy, where every door is open . . . for the ruler to emerge when he will and claim his leadership in the free life."

Wilson goes beyond this to compare Lincoln with Christ, the cabin with the manger. Within the Wilson rhetoric about things that defy human understanding is a deification of Lincoln and the basis of a civil religion, perhaps the greatest praise a eulogist could bestow.

1. *Congressional Record,* 64th Cong., 1st sess., 1916. Vol. 53, pt. 6, 5974–85.

2. *Lincoln Lore* 1545 (Nov. 1966), 4.

3. Address before the Iroquois Club, Feb. 12, 1912; Arthur Link, ed., *The Papers of Woodrow Wilson,* 30 vols. (Princeton: Princeton University Press, 1977), 24: 151–62; "The Lincoln Centennial," *Collier's Weekly* 42 (Feb. 13, 1909): 12.

4. Richard N. Current, *Speaking of Abraham Lincoln* (Urbana: University of Illinois Press, 1983), 138.

The speech is reprinted from *Address of President Woodrow Wilson Accepting the Lincoln Homestead of Hodgenville, Kentucky,* Sept. 4, 1914, 64th Cong., 1st sess., S. Doc. 546. Reprinted with permission.

No more significant memorial could have been presented to the nation than this. It expresses so much of what is singular and noteworthy in the history of the country; it suggests so many of the things that we prize most highly in our life and in our system of government. How eloquent this little house within this shrine is of the vigor of democracy! There is nowhere in the land any home so remote, so humble, that it may not contain the power of mind and heart and conscience to which nations yield and history submits its processes. Nature pays no tribute to aristocracy, subscribes to no creed of caste, renders fealty to no monarch or master of any name or kind. Genius is no snob. It does not run after titles or seek by preference the high circles of society. It affects humble company as well as great. It pays no special tribute to universities or learned societies or conventional standards of greatness, but serenely chooses its own comrades, its own haunts, its own cradle even, and its own life of adventure and of training. Here is proof of it. This little hut was the cradle of one of the great sons of men, a man of singular, delightful, vital genius who presently emerged upon the great stage of the nation's history, gaunt, shy, ungainly, but dominant and majestic, a natural ruler of men, himself inevitably the central figure of the great plot. No man can explain this, but every man can see how it demonstrates the vigor of democracy, where every door is open, in every hamlet and countryside, in city and wilderness alike, for the ruler to emerge when he will and claim his leadership in the free life. Such are the authentic proofs of the validity and vitality of democracy.

Here, no less, hides the mystery of democracy. Who shall guess this secret of nature and providence and a free polity? Whatever the vigor and vitality of the stock from which he sprang, its mere vigor and soundness do not explain where this man got his great heart that seemed to comprehend all mankind in its catholic and benignant sympathy, the mind that sat enthroned behind those brooding, melancholy eyes, whose vision swept many an horizon which those about him dreamed not of,—that mind that comprehended what it had never seen, and understood the language of affairs with the ready ease of one to the manner born,—or that nature which seemed in its varied

178

richness to be the familiar of men of every way of life. This is the sacred mystery of democracy, that its richest fruits spring up out of soils which no man has prepared and in circumstances amidst which they are the least expected. This is a place alike of mystery and of reassurance.

It is likely that in a society ordered otherwise than our own Lincoln could not have found himself or the path of fame and power upon which he walked serenely to his death. In this place it is right that we should remind ourselves of the solid and striking facts upon which our faith in democracy is founded. Many another man besides Lincoln has served the nation in its highest places of counsel and of action whose origins were as humble as his. Though the greatest example of the universal energy, richness, stimulation, and force of democracy, he is only one example among many. The permeating and all-pervasive virtue of the freedom which challenges us in America to make the most of every gift and power we possess every page of our history serves to emphasize and illustrate. Standing here in this place, it seems almost the whole of the stirring story.

Here Lincoln had his beginnings. Here the end and consummation of that great life seem remote and a bit incredible. And yet there was no break anywhere between beginning and end, no lack of natural sequence anywhere. Nothing really incredible happened. Lincoln was unaffectedly as much at home in the White House as he was here. Do you share with me the feeling, I wonder, that he was permanently at home nowhere? It seems to me that in the case of a man,—I would rather say of a spirit,—like Lincoln the question *where* he was is of little significance, that it is always *what* he was that really arrests our thought and takes hold of our imagination. It is the spirit always that is sovereign. Lincoln, like the rest of us, was put through the discipline of the world,—a very rough and exacting discipline for him, an indispensable discipline for every man who would know what he is about in the midst of the world's affairs; but his spirit got only its schooling there. It did not derive its character or its vision from the experiences which brought it to its full revelation. The test of every American must always be, not where he is, but what he is. That, also, is of the essence of democracy, and is the moral of which this place is most gravely expressive.

We would like to think of men like Lincoln and Washington as typical Americans, but no man can be typical who is so unusual as these great men were. It was typical of American life that it should produce such men with supreme indifference as to the manner in which it produced them, and as readily here in this hut as amidst the little circle of cultivated gentlemen to whom Virginia owed so much in leadership and example. And Lincoln and Washington were typical Americans in the use they made of their genius. But there will be few such men at best, and we will not look into the mystery of how and why they come. We will only keep the door open for them always, and a hearty welcome,—after we have recognized them.

I have read many biographies of Lincoln; I have sought out with the greatest interest the many intimate stories that are told of him, the narratives of nearby friends, the sketches at close quarters, in which those who had the privilege of being associated with him have tried to depict for us the very man himself "in his habit as he lived"; but I have nowhere found a real intimate of Lincoln's. I nowhere get the impression in any narrative or reminiscence that the writer had in fact penetrated to the heart of his mystery, or that any man could penetrate to the heart of it. That brooding spirit had no real familiars. I get the impression that it never spoke out in complete self-revelation, and that it could not reveal itself completely to anyone. It was a very lonely spirit that looked out from underneath those shaggy brows and comprehended men without fully communing with them, as if, in spite of all its genial efforts at comradeship, it dwelt apart, saw its visions of duty where no man looked on. There is a very holy and very terrible isolation for the conscience of every man who seeks to read the destiny in affairs for others as well as for himself, for a nation as well as for individuals. That privacy no man can intrude upon. That lonely search of the spirit for the right perhaps no man can assist. This strange child of the cabin kept company with invisible things, was born into no intimacy but that of its own silently assembling and deploying thoughts.

I have come here today, not to utter a eulogy on Lincoln; he stands in need of none, but to endeavor to interpret the meaning of this gift to the nation of the place of his birth and origin. Is not this an altar upon which we may forever keep alive the vestal fire of democracy as upon a shrine at which some of the deepest and most sacred hopes of mankind may from age to age be rekindled? For these hopes must

180

con[s]tantly be rekindled, and only those who live can rekindle them. The only stuff that can retain the life-giving heat is the stuff of living hearts. And the hopes of mankind cannot be kept alive by words merely, by constitutions and doctrines of right and codes of liberty. The object of democracy is to transmute these into the life and action of society, the self-denial and self-sacrifice of heroic men and women willing to make their lives an embodiment of right and service and enlightened purpose. The commands of democracy are as imperative as its privileges and opportunities are wide and generous. Its compulsion is upon us. It will be great and lift a great light for the guidance of the nations only if we are great and carry that light high for the guidance of our own feet. We are not worthy to stand here unless we ourselves be in deed and in truth real democrats and servants of mankind, ready to give our very lives for the freedom and justice and spiritual exaltation of the great nation which shelters and nurtures us.

PART SIX

The Lincoln Memorial

The classical Lincoln Memorial, modeled on a Greek temple, stands at the west end of the Mall near the Washington Monument and two miles from the Capitol. Built of white Colorado Yule marble at a cost of $2,900,000 and positioned on a high terrace reached by wide steps, the magnificent structure is 204 feet long and 134 feet wide, enclosed by thirty-six Doric columns, 44 feet high, that represent the states in the Union in Lincoln's time. Within the front columns the central chamber is filled with the colossal marble figure of a seated Lincoln, the work of Daniel Chester French. The statue, nineteen feet high, rests upon a pedestal, eleven feet high. The massive chair in which Lincoln sits is nineteen feet across. Graven on the interior walls of the chamber are the Gettysburg Address and the Second Inaugural Address. The imposing figure of Lincoln towers thirty feet over the quiet stream of visitors who come, day after day. Each may think of a different Lincoln, the thoughtful president, Honest Abe, the Great Emancipator, Father Abraham, or the great martyr of freedom and liberty.[1]

The Lincoln Memorial, long in planning and execution, was considered as early as 1901 and debated in Congress. A bill sponsored by two of Lincoln's personal friends, Joseph C. Cannon and Shelby M. Cullom, led to the creation of a bipartisan Lincoln Memorial Commission, chaired by Chief Justice William Howard Taft. On May 30, 1922, at a public ceremony before three thousand invited guests and a vast gathering in the surrounding area, Taft presented the memorial to the government. In accepting it, President Warren G. Harding graciously responded, "This memorial edifice is a noble tribute, gratefully bestowed, and in its offering is the reverent heart of America; in its dedication is the consciousness of reverence and gratitude beautifully expressed."[2]

1. *Lincoln Memorial: A Guide to the Lincoln Memorial* (Washington, D.C.: 1986), 34–43; Maurine Whorton Redway and Dorothy Kendall Bracken, *Marks of Lincoln on Our Land* (New York: Hastings, 1957), 112–17.

2. *Congressional Record,* 67th Cong., 2d sess., 1922. Vol. 6, pt. 8, 8419–21; *New York Times,* May 31, 1923.

The People's National Tribute

LINCOLN MEMORIAL
WASHINGTON, D.C.
MAY 30, 1922

William Howard Taft, in a short but appropriate presentation speech, gave the salient facts about the significance of the Lincoln Memorial and made a tribute to Lincoln. The account of the construction, planning, and location magnified the mythic Lincoln, making the "aura about Lincoln's head at his death . . . into a halo of living light." Notable in the Taft presentation was religious symbolism. He spoke of Lincoln as "a Christlike character" and "the Nation's savior" and of the memorial as a place of worship and "a sacred religious refuge." He saw in the classical memorial the symbol to promote the unity of North and South "an altar upon which the sacrifice was made in the cause of liberty."

Taft simply followed the long tradition of glorifying Lincoln. From the time of the assassination, artists and orators were prone to hint at the near sainthood of Lincoln. A dramatic example appeared in 1865 in a lithograph by D. T. Wiest entitled *In Memory of Abraham Lincoln,* which was printed by William Smith in Philadelphia. Copying an earlier engraving by J. J. Barralet that depicted George Washington being lifted into heaven by angels, Smith simply inserted Lincoln in the place of Washington and changed some of the colors; hence, Lincoln's ascension was pictured.[1] Lincoln took his place alongside Washington, so that Washington, the father of his country, prepared the way for Lincoln, the savior of his country. Lincoln then became closely associated with Christ so that speakers suggested that Lincoln's birth in a rustic cabin was the same as Christ's birth in a manger, that the rail-splitter was almost the same as the carpenter, that the Lincoln opposition to slavery resembled Christ's ministry to the downtrodden, and that the assassination was a kind of crucifixion.

1. Harold Holzer, Gabor S. Boritt, and Mark E. Neely, Jr., *Changing the Lincoln Images* (Fort Wayne, Ind.: Louis A. Warren Lincoln Library and Museum, 1985), 72, plates 10 and 11.

The speech is reprinted from William Howard Taft, "The Lincoln Memorial," *National Geographic* 43 (June 1923): 597–602; also in *Modern Eloquence*, ed. Ashley Thorndike, 15 vols. (New York: Modern Eloquence Corp., 1923), 7:298–302. Reprinted with permission.

The American people have waited fifty-seven years for a national memorial to Abraham Lincoln. Those years have faded the figures of his contemporaries, and he stands grandly alone.

His life and character in the calmer and juster vista of half a century inspire a higher conception of what is suitable to commemorate him.

Justice, truth, patience, mercy, and love of his kind; simplicity, courage, sacrifice, and confidence in God, were his moral qualities. Clarity of thought and intellectual honesty, self-analysis and strong inexorable logic, supreme common sense, a sympathetic but unerring knowledge of human nature, imagination and limpid purity of style, with a poetic rhythm of the Psalms—these were his intellectual and cultural traits.

His soul and heart and brain and mind had all these elements, but their union in him had a setting that baffles description.

His humility; his self-abnegation and devotion; his patience under grievous disappointment; his agony of spirit in the burden he had to carry; his constant sadness, lightened at intervals with a rare humor all his own; the abuse and ridicule of which he was the subject; his endurance in a great cause of small obstructive minds; his domestic sorrows, and finally his tragic end, form the story of a passion and give him a personality that is as vivid in the hearts of the people as if it were but yesterday.

We feel a closer touch with him than with living men. The influence he still wields, one may say with all reverence, has a Christlike character. It has spread to the four quarters of the globe.

The oppressed and lowly of all peoples, as liberty and free government spread, pronounce his name with awe, and cherish his assured personal sympathy as a source of hope. Their leaders quote his glowing words of patient courage, of sympathy with the downtrodden, of dependence on God's wisdom and justice, and of his never-ceasing prayer for liberty through the rule of the people.

The harmony of his message with every popular aspiration for freedom proves his universality. It was this which Stanton was inspired to predict when, as Lincoln lay dead, he said, "He now belongs to the ages."

His own life without favoring chance in preparation for the task which Providence was to put on him, his early humble surroundings, his touch with the soil, his oneness with the plain people, and the wonder that out of these he could become what he was and is, give us a soul-stirring pride that the world has come to know him and to love him as we do.

We like to dwell on the fact that his associates did not see him as he was when on earth, and that it was for generations born after he was gone to feel his real greatness and to be moved by his real personality.

Not with the lowly only, but with all—rich or poor, ignorant or learned, weak or powerful, untutored or of literary genius—has this aura about Lincoln's head at his death grown into a halo of living light.

Therefore it is well that half a century should pass before his people's national tribute to him takes form in marble, that it should wait until a generation instinct with the growing and deepening perception of the real Lincoln has had time to develop an art adequate to the expression of his greatness.

The years immediately following the Civil War were not favorable to art, and the remains of that period in our Capital City and else-where show it.

But new impulses in the expansion of our country's energies were soon directed toward better things. Our expositions have marked the steps in that progress. They called together men who had been strug-gling singly to practice, preach, and bring home to us real conceptions of art and beauty in architecture and sculpture.

For fifteen years following the Centennial at Philadelphia, the nucleus there begun grew until at the Columbian Exposition at Chicago, in 1892 and 1893, there were gathered a group of artists who in the development of civic planning, landscape architecture, and monumental and sculptural beauty were the peers of any.

[Daniel W.] Burnham, [Charles F.] McKim, [Frederick Law] Olmsted the elder, [Augustus] Saint-Gaudens, [Charles B.] Atwood, and [Jesse] Millet were the leading figures. In 1894 they organized the American Academy in Rome for the graduate education of American students, where before entering upon their professional careers they should

188

study thoroughly that reservoir of Greek art, the greatest of antiquity, which is at Rome, where "the noble buildings are a forest, the animals of bronze, a herd; the statues, a population in marble."

In 1901, under the generous and farseeing favor of James McMillan, in charge in the Senate of the affairs of the District of Columbia, a commission was appointed to bridge over the period since Washington and L'Enfant's plan for the capital, and on the basis of that plan to enlarge and give greater scope to the beauty of this seat of government.

The four men who engaged in this work were, three of them, the creators of the "Court of Honor" and the "White City" at the Columbian Exposition, and the fourth, the younger [Frederick Law] Olmsted, was worthy of his sire. As a new feature in that plan, and referring to the place upon which we stand, they said in their report:

"Crowning the *rond-point,* as the Arc de Triomphe crowns the Place de l'Étoile at Paris, should stand a memorial erected to the memory of that one man in our history as a nation who is worthy to be named with George Washington—Abraham Lincoln.

"Whatever may be the exact form selected for the memorial to Lincoln, in type it should possess the quality of universality, and also it should have a character essentially different from that of any monument either now existing in the District or hereafter to be erected.

"The type which the Commission has in mind is a great portico of Doric columns rising from an unbroken stylobate. This portico, while affording a point of vantage from which one obtains a commanding outlook, both upon the river and eastward to the Capitol, has for its chief function to support a panel bearing an inscription taken either from the Gettysburg speech or from some one of the immortal messages of the savior of the Union."

Here, then, was the first conception of the Memorial we dedicate to-day. Not until 1911 was the idea carried forward. Then two sons of Illinois, Shelby M. Cullom and Joseph G. Cannon, fathered the bill for the creation of the present Commission, under whose official supervision this work has been done.

The Commission claims no credit for it except that it asked those who knew what to do, and did it. They consulted the Fine Arts Commission, made up of Burnham, Millet, Olmsted, [Daniel Chester] French, [Thomas] Hastings, [Cass] Gilbert, and [Charles H.] Moore, who urged the present site and recommended as the man to design and build it Henry Bacon, the student and disciple of McKim. McKim was the dean of the architects of this country, and did most among us to bring the art of Greece to appreciation and noble use. Bacon has been his worthy successor.

For ten years the structure has been rising. From the solid rock beneath the level of the Potomac, 50 feet below the original grade, it reaches a total of 122 feet above that grade.

The platform at its base is 204 feet long and 134 feet wide. The colonnade is 188 feet long and 118 feet wide, the columns 44 feet high and 7 feet 5 inches in diameter at their base. The memorial hall is 156 feet long and 84 feet wide.

The proportions of the memorial are so fine that its great mass and height and length and breadth are suppressed in its unity.

The outside columns are the simple Doric, the inside columns the simple Ionic. The marble of the structure is from the Colorado Yule mine, remarkable for its texture and the purity of its white, and for the size of the drums which make the columns noteworthy in the architecture of the world.

The colossal figure of the Beloved in Georgia marble, the work of another of the group of artists of whom I have spoken, Daniel Chester French, one of our greatest sculptors, fills the memorial hall with an overwhelming sense of Lincoln's presence, while the mural decorations of another great American artist, Jules Guérin, with their all-embracing allegory, crown the whole sacred place.

The site is at the end of the axis of the Mall, the commanding and noteworthy spine of the L'Enfant plan.

Burnham, McKim, and Saint-Gaudens, who followed this plan through to its triumph, took the Mall under their peculiar protection.

It was they who caused that wonderful group of the Silent Soldier and his battling armies to be put upon this axis at the foot of the Capitol which he did so much to defend.

It was they who struggled against encroachments upon this capital feature of our wonderful seat of government.

It was they who put this noble structure we celebrate to-day where it is.

They sought the judgment of John Hay, secretary and biographer of Lincoln, statesman and poet. He answered:

"The place of honor is on the main axis of the plan. Lincoln, of all Americans next to Washington, deserves this place of honor. He was of the immortals. You must not approach too close to the immortals. His monument should stand alone, remote from the common habitations of man, apart from the business and turmoil of the city—isolated, distinguished, and serene. Of all the sites, this one, near the Potomac, is most suited to the purpose."

And now, Mr. President, the ideal of these great American artists has found expression in the memorial as you see it. It is a magnificent gem set in a lovely valley between the hills, commanding them by its isolation and its entrancing beauty, an emblem of the purity of the best period of the Greek art in the simple Doric, the culmination of the highest art of which America is capable, and therefore fit to commemorate a people's love for the Nation's savior and its great leader.

Here, on the banks of the Potomac, the boundary between the two sections whose conflict made the burden, passion, and triumph of his life, it is peculiarly appropriate that it should stand.

Visible in its distant beauty from the Capitol, whose great dome typifies the Union which he saved; seen in all its grandeur from Arlington, where lie the Nation's honored dead who fell in the conflict, Union and Confederate alike, it marks the restoration of the brotherly love of the two sections in this memorial of one who is as dear to the hearts of the South as to those of the North.

The Southerner knows that the greatest misfortune in all the trials of that section was the death of Lincoln. Had he lived, the consequences of the war would not have been as hard for them to bear, the wounds would have been more easily healed, the trying days of reconstruction would have been softened.

Rancor and resentment were no part of his nature. In all the bitterness of that conflict, tried as he was, no word fell from his lips which told of hatred, malice, or unforgiving soul.

Here is a shrine at which all can worship. Here an altar upon which the sacrifice was made in the cause of Liberty. Here a sacred religious refuge in which those who love country and love God can find inspiration and repose.

Mr. President, in the name of the Commission, I have the honor to deliver this Lincoln Memorial into your keeping.

PART SEVEN

Lincoln as an
International Symbol

What David Lloyd George said in 1923 is still true today: "His fame is wider today than it was at the date of his tragic death, and it is widening every year" (204). This memorializing of Lincoln as a symbol of freedom and democracy commenced to spread abroad after the issuance of the Emancipation Proclamation and continues to this very day. In 1969 a traveling Lincoln exhibit attracted about half a million visitors in ten days in Tokyo, and one authority estimates that there are "more books on Lincoln in Japanese than any other language than English."[1]

Recently in November 1989, the Lincoln Society of Taiwan, Republic of China, held an international Lincoln conference. This group formed in 1984 attributes its inspiration to "Abraham Lincoln's 'with malice toward none, with charity for all.' " It states that it is "dedicated to his spirit of Honesty, Humility, Humanity and Holiness" and to seeking "to further the freedom, happiness and values of life of all the peoples of the world."[2]

Two speeches delivered in the early 1920s show the emergence of Lincoln as an international symbol: Elihu Root's speech of presentation of the Saint-Gaudens statue to the British people in 1920 and David Lloyd George's speech delivered in Springfield in 1923.

Augustus Saint-Gaudens unveiled his statue of Lincoln on October 27, 1887, on the shores of Lake Michigan in what is now Lincoln Park. The tall figure with its square shoulders, slightly drooped head, and its air of meditativeness and seriousness dominates its setting. The statue is mounted on an imposing pedestal placed in the middle of a high-backed, semicircular bench sixty feet across and thirty feet deep that rises six steps above the lawn. Replicas of it have been placed in Parliament Square in the shadow of Westminster in London, and in Lincoln Park in Palinco, a residential area of Mexico City.

1. *Lincoln Lore* 1672 (June 1977): 1–3.
2. Based upon published announcements, September 1987 and May 1988 from the Lincoln Society, Taipei, Taiwan, Republic of China.

Lincoln's Conceptions of Liberty and Justice

PARLIAMENT SQUARE
LONDON, ENGLAND
JULY 20, 1920

In London on July 20, 1920, Elihu Root formally presented the Augustus Saint-Gaudens statue to the British people as a symbol of unity, for the celebration of the centenary of the Treaty of Ghent, and the completion of one hundred years of peace between Great Britain and the United States. More than usual interest developed about the presentation of a Lincoln statue to the British people as a memorial of the amity of the two nations. After the committee had decided to send a replica of the Saint-Gaudens statue, Charles P. Taft offered to contribute a replica of George G. Barnard's statue of the frontier Lincoln that Taft had donated to Lytle Park in Cincinnati.[1] When the committee accepted the Taft offer, a public controversy developed because many considered the Barnard work ugly and gruesome. A referendum decided that the Saint-Gaudens statue would go to Parliament Square, and the Barnard statue was presented to Manchester for Platt Field.[2]

In the audience at the presentation were princes, government officials, prelates, soldiers, American boy scouts, artists, authors, and men and women of all ranks. To add dignity to the occasion, the guard of honor was fifteen veterans of the American Civil War. Root thought that his mission was to elucidate the significance of Lincoln appearing among the British officials "whose statues stand in Parliament Square."[3] The speaker found a common link between this simple man "full of sorrows" and those who fought for Anglo-Saxon freedom by suggesting that the American was "a representative of the deep and underlying qualities of his race—the qualities that great emergencies reveal, unchangingly the same in every continent; the qualities to which Britain owed her life in the terrible years of the last decade; the qualities that made both Britain and America great."

Of course Root knew that the British-American bond was strong after World War I. Root capitalized on this by firmly placing Lincoln in a British tradition linked by blood, speech, the Bible, Shakespeare, English prose masterpieces, and a common conception of justice and liberty. Touching deep sentiments, Root implied consubstantiality: "The souls of both Britain and America prove themselves of kin to the soul of Abraham Lincoln."

1. *Lincoln Lore* 414 (Mar. 15, 1937); Ibid., 1488 (Feb. 1962); Ibid., 1540 (June 1966); F. Lauriston Bullard, *Lincoln in Marble and Bronze* (New Brunswick, N.J.: Rutgers University Press, 1952), 28–89.

2. *Independent* 92 (Dec. 29, 1917): 599–601; Roy P. Basler, *The Lincoln Legend* (Boston: Houghton Mifflin, 1935), 292–93.

3. *New York Times,* June 29, 1920.

By authority of His Majesty's Government a statue of an American has been set up in the Canning Enclosure, where on one side Westminster Abbey and on another the Houses of Parliament look down upon it; where it is surrounded by memorials of British statesmen whose lives are inseparable parts of the history of the Kingdom and of the Empire; and where the living tides of London will ebb and flow about it. The statue is the work of Augustus St. Gaudens, son of a French father, native of Ireland, and greatest of American sculptors. The American commemorated is Abraham Lincoln, sixteenth President of the United States. In behalf of the American donors, I now formally present the statue to the British People.

Abraham Lincoln was born on the 12th of February, one hundred and eleven years ago, in a log cabin among the mountains of the State of Kentucky. He came into a frontier life of comparative poverty, labor, hardship, and rude adventure. He had little instruction and few books. He had no friends among the great and powerful of his time. An equal among equals in the crude simplicity of scattered communities on the borders of the wilderness, he rose above the common level by force of his own qualities. He was sent by his neighbors to the State Legislature, where he learned the rudiments of government. He was sent to the Congress at Washington, where he broadened his conceptions to national scope. He was admitted to the bar, and won high place as a successful and distinguished advocate.

He became convinced of the wickedness of African slavery, that baleful institution which the defective humanity of our fathers permitted to be established in the American Colonies. He declared his conviction that slavery was eternally wrong, with a power and insistence that compelled public attention. He gave voice to the awakened conscience of the North. He led in the struggle for freedom against slavery. Upon that issue he was elected President. In that cause, as President, he conducted a great war of four years' duration in which millions of armed men were engaged. When in his wise judgment the time was ripe for it, then upon his own responsibility, in the exercise of his authority as Commander-in-Chief, invoking the support of his country, the considerate judgment of mankind, and the blessing of

God upon his act, he set free the three million slaves by his official proclamation, and dedicated the soil of America forever as the home of a united liberty-loving commonwealth.

The act was accepted; it was effective; African slavery was ended; the war was won—for union and for freedom; and in the very hour of victory, the great emancipator fell at the hand of a crazed fanatic.

It was not chance or favorable circumstance that achieved Lincoln's success. The struggle was long and desperate, and often appeared hopeless. He won through the possession of the noblest qualities of manhood. He was simple, honest, sincere, and unselfish. He had high courage for action and fortitude in adversity. Never for an instant did the thought of personal advantage compete with the interests of the public cause. He never faltered in the positive and unequivocal declaration of the wrong of slavery, but his sympathy with all his fellowmen was so genuine, his knowledge of human nature was so just, that he was able to lead his countrymen without dogmatism or imputation of assumed superiority. He carried the Civil War to its successful conclusion with inflexible determination; but the many evidences of his kindness of heart toward the people of the South, and of his compassion for distress and suffering, were the despair of many of his subordinates; and the effect of his humanity and considerate spirit upon the conduct of the war became one of the chief reasons why, when the war was over, North and South were able during the same generation to join again in friendship as citizens of a restored Union.

It would be difficult to conceive of a sharper contrast in all the incidental and immaterial things of life than existed between Lincoln and the statesmen whose statues stand in Parliament Square. He never set foot on British soil. His life was lived and his work was wholly done in a far distant land. He differed in manners and in habits of thought and speech. He never seemed to touch the life of Britain.

Yet the contrast but emphasizes the significance of the statue standing where it does.

Put aside superficial differences, accidental and unimportant, and Abraham Lincoln appears in the simple greatness of his life, his character and his service to mankind, a representative of the deep and underlying qualities of his race—the qualities that great emergencies reveal, unchangingly the same in every continent; the qualities to which Britain owed her life in the terrible years of the last decade; the qualities that have made both Britain and America great.

He was of English blood; and he has brought enduring honor to the name. Every child of English sires should learn the story and think with pride, "Of such stuff as this are we English made."

He was of English speech. The English Bible and English Shakespeare, studied in the intervals of toil and by the flare of the log fire in the frontier cabin, were the basis of his education; and from them he gained, through greatness of heart and fine intelligence, the power of expression, to give his Gettysburg address and his second inaugural a place among the masterpieces of English prose.

He was imbued with the conceptions of justice and liberty that the people of Britain had been working out in struggle and sacrifice since before Magna Charta—the conceptions for which Chatham and Burke and Franklin and Washington stood together, a century and a half ago, when the battle for British liberty was fought and won for Britain, as well as for America on the other side of the Atlantic. These conceptions of justice and liberty have been the formative power that has brought all America, from the Atlantic to the Pacific, to order its life according to the course of the common law, to assert its popular sovereignty through representative government—Britain's great gift to the political science of the world—and to establish the relation of individual citizenship to the State, on the basis of inalienable rights which governments are established to secure.

It is the identity of these fundamental conceptions in both countries which makes it impossible that in any great world-emergency Britain and America can be on opposing sides. These conceptions of justice and liberty are the breath of life for both. While they prevail, both nations will endure; if they perish, both nations will die. These were Lincoln's inheritance; and when he declared that African slavery was eternally wrong and gave his life to end it, he was responding to impulses born in him from a long line of humble folk, as well in England as in America, who were themselves a product of the age-long struggles for the development of Anglo-Saxon freedom.

The true heart of Britain understood him while he lived. We remember the Lancashire workmen brought into poverty and suffering through lack of cotton. When the Emancipation Proclamation had dispelled all doubt as to the real nature of the struggle in America, six thousand of them met in a great hall in Manchester and sent to President Lincoln a message of sympathy and support. This was his answer:

> Under these circumstances, I cannot but regard your decisive utterances upon the question as an instance of sublime Christian heroism, which has not been surpassed in any age or in any country. It is indeed an energetic and reinspiring assurance of the inherent power of truth, and the ultimate and universal triumph of justice, humanity, and freedom. I do not doubt that the sentiments you have expressed will be sustained by your great nation, and on the other hand I have no hesitation in assuring you that they will excite admiration, esteem, and the most reciprocal feelings of friendship among the American people. I hail this interchange of sentiment, therefore, as an augury, that, whatever else may happen, whatever misfortune may befall your country or my own, the peace and friendship which now exist between the two nations will be, as it shall be my desire to make them, perpetual.[1]

We may disregard all the little prejudices and quarrels that result from casual friction and pinpricks and from outside misrepresentations and detraction, and rest upon Lincoln's unerring judgment of his countrymen and his race. We may be assured from him that whenever trials come, whenever there is need for assurance of the inherent power of truth and the triumph of justice, humanity and freedom, then peace and friendship between Britain and America will prove to be, as Lincoln desired to make them, perpetual.

This man, full of sorrows, spoke not merely for the occasions and incidents of his own day. He expressed the deepest and holiest feelings of his race for all time. Listen to the words of his Second Inaugural:

> Fondly do we hope, fervently do we pray, that this mighty scourge of war may soon pass away.
>
> Yet, if God wills that it continue until all the wealth piled by the bondman's two hundred and fifty years of unrequited toil shall be sunk, and until every drop of blood drawn by the lash shall be paid by another drawn with the sword, as was said three thousand years ago, so still it must be said, "The judgments of the Lord are true and righteous altogether."

---

1. To workers in Manchester, Jan. 19, 1863.

ELIHU ROOT

With malice toward none, with charity for all, with firmness in the right, as God gives us to see the right, let us strive on to finish the work we are in; to bind up the nation's wounds; to care for him who shall have borne the battle, and for his widow and for his orphan; to do all which may achieve and cherish a just and lasting peace among ourselves, and with all nations. [Mar. 4, 1865]

Consider this letter which he wrote to Mrs. [Lydia] Bixby of Boston:

I have been shown on the file of the War Department a statement of the adjutant general of Massachusetts, that you are the mother of five sons who have died gloriously on the field of battle. I feel how weak and fruitless must be any word of mine which should attempt to beguile you from the grief of a loss so overwhelming; but I cannot refrain from tendering to you the consolation that may be found in the thanks of the republic they died to save.

I pray that our Heavenly Father may assuage the anguish of your bereavement, and leave only the cherished memory of the loved and lost, and the solemn pride that must be yours to have laid so costly a sacrifice upon the altar of freedom [Nov. 21, 1864].

More than half a century has passed, but is this the voice of a stranger to the men and women of Britain in these later years?

Because under the direct tests of national character, in the stress of supreme effort and sacrifice, in the Valley of the Shadow of Death, the souls of both Britain and America prove themselves of kin to the soul of Abraham Lincoln, friendship between us is safe; and the statue of Lincoln, the American, stands as of right before the old Abbey where sleep the great of Britain's history.

Abraham Lincoln, the Inspirer
of Democracy

MIDDAY LUNCHEON CLUB
SPRINGFIELD, ILLINOIS
OCTOBER 18, 1923

The mecca of the Lincoln legend had long been Springfield, Illinois, where Lincoln lived from 1837 to 1861. Within a few blocks are the Lincoln home on the corner of Eighth and Jackson Streets, the reconstructed Old State House that contains the Illinois State Historical Society and Library, and the Lincoln-Herndon law office; not far away is the Lincoln tomb in Oak Ridge cemetery. About twenty miles northwest of Springfield, two miles from Petersburg, is the New Salem State Park, a reconstructed 1830s village of twelve log cabins, a tavern, ten shops, and a school. The little park represents what life was like when Lincoln lived there between 1831 and 1837.[1]

In 1923 the Right Honorable David Lloyd George, former prime minister of Great Britain, made a grand tour of Canada and the United States with at least fifteen stops along the way. He paused in the Illinois capital on October 19, 1923, to visit Lincoln's home, downtown Springfield, and Oak Ridge Cemetery.[2] Lloyd George had a vivid memory of personally accepting the Saint-Gaudens statue on behalf of Great Britain from Elihu Root three years before.[3] Lloyd George had his turn at eulogizing the American hero for the Midday Luncheon Club. He suggested that the Lincoln fame was "wider" that day "than it was at the time of his tragic death, and it is widening every year. His influence is deeper and is still deepening." His point of view was the same as that of British biographer Lord Charnwood who had suggested in 1917 that Lincoln belonged "not to one nation and one period, but to the world and to all time."[4]

It was quite evident that Lloyd George saw universality in the Lincoln legend, representing the Illinois lawyer as the inspirer of

202

Democracy who belonged "to mankind in every race, in every clime, and in every age." Much aware of how the two English-speaking nations had recently joined in World War I, Lloyd George suggested that the image linked "your great flag and our great flag" in the common cause of freedom. He predicted dangers that might happen in Russia, Italy, Spain, and Germany and suggested that the two nations might need to rally again in the cause of freedom.

1. Mark E. Neely, Jr., *The Abraham Lincoln Encyclopedia* (New York: McGraw-Hill, 1982), 221–22, 285–87.

2. London *Times,* Sept. 23, 1923, p. 14; A. J. Sylvester, *The Real Lloyd George* (London: Cassell, 1947), 130–31; Manchester *Guardian,* Oct. 20, 1923.

3. *New York Times,* July 29, 1920.

4. Roy P. Basler, *The Lincoln Legend* (Boston: Houghton Mifflin, 1935), 19; Lord Charnwood, *Abraham Lincoln,* 3d ed. (New York: Henry Holt, 1917), 455–56.

M r. *Chairman, Secretary of State, Your Honor the Governor, Your Worship the Mayor, Ladies and Gentlemen:* I have to thank the club for the honor they are conferring upon me and upon my wife and daughter and my comrades and colleagues who have accompanied us in entertaining us on our visit to Springfield. It is only part of the overwhelming kindness which we have received ever since we came to this great land, and it will be one of the most pleasing and memorable episodes in the whole course of our lives. But much as I wanted to see your great land, there was one spot above all others I was anxious to see, and that was the home of Abraham Lincoln, the inspirer of Democracy, not merely in your country, but in all lands.

I have come here today with one purpose and one purpose only. That is, to pay my humble and reverent tribute of respect to the memory of one of the great men of the world. It is difficult for me to express the feelings with which I visited the home and the last resting place of one of the noblest figures in the history of mankind; a man loved by the people in all lands, a man beloved by those who do love the people in all lands. There have been many great men whose names have been inscribed on the scroll of human history; there are only a few whose names have become a legend amongst men. Amongst those are conspicuously stamped the name of Abraham Lincoln. His fame is wider today than it was at the date of his tragic death, and it is widening every year. His influence is deeper and is still deepening. Even if this were the occasion, I do not feel competent to pronounce any judgment on the qualities that made him great and on the deeds and words that will make his name endure forevermore. Least of all would I presume to do so in the city where there are men still living who remember and knew him. All I know about him is that he was one of those rare men whom you do not associate with any particular creed, party, and, if you will forgive me for saying so, not even with any country, for he belongs to mankind in every race, in every clime, and in every age.

There are the great men of the party, and the great men of creeds. There are the great men of their time and there are the great men of all time of their own native land; but Lincoln was a great man of all time, for all parties, for all lands and for all races of men. He was the choice and champion of a party, but his lofty soul could see over and beyond party walls the unlimited terrain beyond. His motto was: "Stand with anybody who stands right. Stand with him while he is right and part with him when he goes wrong" [speech, Peoria, Ill. Oct. 16, 1854]. Those were his own words. No pure partisan would ever assent to so discriminating and disintegrating a proposition.

I have read many of his biographies. I read a very remarkable one which was published two years ago. Some one handed it to me at Niagara Falls, and I read it with deep and intense interest. His career was highly successful, judged by every standard of success—from the wretched log cabin at Kentucky, a picture of which I saw today, through that comfortable home I witnessed, and on to the official residence of the President of the greatest republic on earth. It seems a triumphal march enough for any ambition, and yet, his life is in many ways one of the saddest of human stories, and even the tragic end comes as a relief.

He once said, "I have not willingly planted a thorn in any man's bosom"—a great saying [response to serenade, Nov. 10, 1864]. And yet as soon as he reached the height of his ambition, this man who shunned hurt and scattered kindness on his path was doomed by a cruel destiny to send millions of his own fellow countrymen through the torturing experiences of a prolonged and fierce war against their own kith and kin. Thus, the tenderest soul who ever ruled over men was driven for five years by an inexorable fate to pierce the gentle hearts of mothers with anguish that death alone can assuage. And in this, the greatest and most poignant task of his life, he was worried, harrassed, encumbered, lassoed at every turn by the vanities, the jealousies, the factiousness and the wiles of swarms of little men. He was misrepresented, misunderstood, maligned, derided, thwarted in every good impulse, thought, or deed. No wonder his photographs—and I have studied most of them, became sadder and sadder and more and more tragic year by year up to the tragic end.

His example and his wise sayings are the inheritance of mankind, and will be quoted and used to save mankind from its follies to the end of the ages. The lessons of his statesmanship are as applicable today as they were sixty years ago. They will be as applicable a thousand years hence as they are today. Being dead, he still speaketh.

He has messages of moment for this present hour. I will give you two of them.

The messages of Abraham Lincoln to this day and this moment and this emergency in the life of man are: "Clemency in the hour of triumph." The doctrine of Abraham Lincoln was "Reconcile the vanquished."

It is a time for remembering that vengeance is the justice of the savage and that conciliation is the triumph of civilization over barbarism. Lincoln is the finest product in the realm of statesmanship of the Christian civilization, and the wise counsel he gave to his own people in the day of their triumph he gives today to the people of Europe in the hour of their victory over the forces that menace their liberties.

What is his next message? "Trust the common people." He believed in their sincerity, he believed in their common sense, he believed in their inherent justice, he believed in their ultimate unselfishness. The first impulse of the people may be selfish. Their final word is always unselfish. That was the doctrine that Abraham Lincoln thought and believed in, and today, when Democracy is in greater peril than it has probably been in your life time or mine, the message of Abraham Lincoln carries across the waves, and will, I hope, be heard in Europe and will impel the democracies of Europe to fight against the wave of autocracy that is sweeping over our continent. Russia, an autocracy; Italy for the moment a dictatorship; Spain, a dictatorship; Germany, slipping into dictatorship—most of Europe having abandoned confidence in the people. It is the hour of Abraham Lincoln's doctrine to be preached in the countries of Europe. His influence upon our democracy in England is deep, and I believe permanent, and if the peril reaches our shores, the words of Abraham Lincoln will be an inspiration and a strength for those who will be battling for the cause of the people.

A moment ago there were two flags here, your great flag and our great flag. They were intertwined. They have been ranged side by side in a great struggle in Europe for liberty, and they emerged triumphantly. I venture to say it is not the last time these two flags will be rallied to for the cause of freedom. A time will come, a time is coming, when the principles of Abraham Lincoln will have to be fought for again, and these two flags will be the rallying centers in that struggle; your great flag representing the stars that illumine the darkness that falls

206

upon the children of men, that is falling on them now in Europe, the bars that represent the shafts of sunlight that will dispel that darkness; our flag, with the cross that represents the hope of the earth in all its trials. These two flags standing together, rallying around them men taught in the principles of Abraham Lincoln, will yet save the world for liberty, for peace, for good will and honest men.

PART EIGHT

Reshaping the Lincoln Image

For about seventy-five years after Lincoln's death, those who memorialized the sixteenth president came from groups that had felt some direct personal involvement with their hero. Some had lived through the Civil War, perhaps had seen or heard Lincoln, or had read reminiscences by close observers. Offsprings of the war generation had also been touched by Lincoln's character, actions, mystique, or his example. Many homes displayed pictures, prints, or busts of the Illinois lawyer; repeating stories by or about him was a favorite conversation filler.

By the late 1940s original enthusiasms had found various outlets for expression. Over seventy-five bronze or marble statues graced city squares, museums, parks, schools, and public buildings in several states. Running through Kentucky, Indiana, and Illinois was the Lincoln Heritage Trail, which included the birthplace cabin at Hodgenville, Kentucky; the Indiana farm of Lincoln's father; the home and Old State Capitol in Springfield; and the reconstructed pioneer village of New Salem near Petersburg, Illinois. Lincoln Memorial University was established in 1897 and since February of 1938 has published the *Lincoln Herald* and has maintained the Historical Research Library and Museum since 1932. In Fort Wayne, Indiana, the Lincoln National Life Insurance Company maintained the Lincoln Library and Museum and published *Lincoln Lore,* a leaflet devoted to Lincoln.

Anyone who wished to had no difficulty locating a symbol or a shrine of the Illinois lawyer. But to large numbers these reminders of Lincoln had become commonplace, and in some instances even defaced or tarnished.[1] Many had become insensitive to what they viewed on weekends at the Lincoln sites. They participated in the Lincoln myth vicariously in that they drew their sentiments—if they had any—from what they had heard from teachers who had made them memorize the Gettysburg Address or from romantic plays or movies, television programs, or contemporary novels that often confused fiction with fact.

The speakers who now honor Lincoln have had a dual role of teacher and eulogist. Before they can praise, the speakers must overcome blind worship, ignorance, or distorted visions; they must find new ways to relate the historical Lincoln to the contemporary listener.

1. George Tice, *Lincoln* (New Brunswick, N.J.: Rutgers University Press, 1984), 7–9, 10, 25, 33, 56, 66.

Lincoln the Man

DEDICATION OF
ABRAHAM LINCOLN: THE HOOSIER YOUTH
FORT WAYNE, INDIANA
SEPTEMBER 16, 1932

One of the foremost Lincoln memorials is the Louis A. Warren Lincoln Library and Museum, endowed by the Lincoln National Life Insurance Company of Fort Wayne, Indiana. Established in 1928, this institution, located in spacious quarters in the home office building of its patron, has become one of the principal centers for Lincoln study. Its holdings include ten thousand books and pamphlets about Lincoln, six thousand photographs of contemporaries, and much manuscript material. It issues *Lincoln Lore,* the oldest continuously published periodical devoted to Lincoln. The directors, Louis A. Warren, R. Gerald McMurtry, and Mark E. Neely, Jr., have gained recognition among Lincoln scholars, and with their staffs they have encouraged and aided searchers in the Lincoln field.[1]

In 1928 Lincoln Life gave Paul Manship, a foremost American artist, a $75,000 commission to create a fitting statue to be placed in front of the home office.[2] The result was the bronze statue *Abraham Lincoln: The Hoosier Youth,* a figure twelve feet six inches in height, resting on a pedestal six feet seven inches high on a granite base. Departing from the traditional presidential figures, Manship chose to depict a youthful Lincoln at twenty-one. The figure, clean-shaven, is clad in a linsey-woolsey shirt, butternut trousers, and boots. Young Lincoln leans at ease against an oak stump, with an axe at his side, holding a book in his right hand and resting his left hand on a dog's head.[3]

Manship hoped to represent "a typical pioneer youth, not so much unlike the other boys who grew up at that time in . . . the West." The artist sought "not the descendant of 'poor white trash,' 'migratory squatters,' or 'drifting, roaming people struggling with poverty,' " but a "Hoosier youth . . . of respectable parents."[4] "Every part of the statue," says one critic, "is blended into a unified design . . . that leads upwards in an elongated pyramid to the noble head of the young Lincoln."[5]

The dedication, on September 16, 1932, was in the midst of a day-long impressive ceremony, which included the unveiling at 12:30 and a luncheon at 2 P.M. Among the eight luncheon speakers was Ida M. Tarbell, a well-known and popular author of several Lincoln biographies. Much in tune with the sculptor, she had emphasized in her writing the wholesome influence of the frontier, "raw and rude but . . . also buoyant and adventurous."[6] In her eloquent speech, she endorsed the artist's work. She gained rhetorical power through her command of simple language to personify the young frontier Lincoln. In her sensitivity she uttered what Manship hoped to portray: "This faith [freedom for all] illuminated his thoughts, shone through the words with which he clothed it, so that they live today—the most perfect expressions of democracy's dream the world knows. His words are simple, natural, like the man."

1. Mark E. Neely, Jr., *The Abraham Lincoln Encyclopedia* (New York: McGraw-Hill, 1982), 195–96.

2. *Addresses Delivered at the Dedication, of the Heroic Bronze Statue "Abraham Lincoln—the Hoosier Youth," September 16, 1932* (Fort Wayne: The Lincoln National Life Insurance Company, n.d.), 13.

3. F. Lauriston Bullard, *Lincoln in Marble and Bronze* (New Brunswick, N.J.: Rutgers University Press, 1952), 292–94.

4. *Lincoln Lore* 178 (Sept. 5, 1932).

5. Edwin Martha, *Paul Manship* (New York: Macmillan, 1957), 9.

6. Benjamin P. Thomas, *Portrait for Posterity: Lincoln and His Biographers* (New Brunswick, N.J.: Rutgers University Press, 1947), 185–87.

The speech is reprinted from *Addresses Delivered at the Dedication of the Heroic Bronze Statue "Abraham Lincoln—The Hoosier Youth," September 16, 1932* (Fort Wayne: The Lincoln National Life Insurance Company, n.d.), 10–11.

I count it a privilege and an honor to have the opportunity to congratulate Paul Manship and the Lincoln Foundation on the statue we are dedicating here today. It is the truest, as it is the most beautiful concept of Abraham Lincoln as a youth yet given this country.

Until now that youth has been the victim of over-much pitiless and unimaginative realism. Mr. Manship has stripped away the sordid and ugly details under which the real boy was all but buried, and by his simple, noble, truthful art has given us a Hoosier youth in whom we can see the man we know.

Here you have a son of the Republic, one who early dreamed its dream. Freedom for all men to be secured by the union of all men was the substance of Abraham Lincoln's faith. He put it into simple terms—the right of all men to eat the bread they earn. Coupled with that right was the responsibility to earn the bread they eat. As he saw the Republic there was no place in it either for slave or for parasite. This faith illuminated his thoughts, shone through the words with which he clothed it, so that they live today—the most perfect expressions of democracy's dream the world knows. His words are simple, natural, like the man.

And what a man he was. To begin with, a good worker; his hand always on his ax. "A good worker is so rare," Ralph Waldo Emerson commented, watching Lincoln with keen eye. Chiefly he labored to get at the core of his thoughts, and reaching it to preserve it in words, clear as light—no mistake in their meaning.

Labor, hardship, deprivation never clouded the kindliness of his nature. The man was friendly, easy to go to. The child, the youth, the man, sought him instinctively for help, counsel, companionship. Even in his lifetime this friendliness became a legend. Let a man be helped out of trouble, a child comforted, a youth set straight, and the doer unknown—it was Lincoln who did it.

His humor took on early this legendary quality—wise and witty comment—good stories—if the source was unknown, were his. Before his death, scores of which he probably never had heard were gathered into books; his name put to them. He was the universal friend—the universal humorist.

This friendliness, this humor, were so much a part of him that no burden, no sorrow, could check their natural flow. And he had no stronger allies in the dreadful days of the Civil War.

He knew his mind at the start of that tragedy. Had one purpose—to save the Union—since through union alone can man realize the oldest and noblest of his dreams—freedom to think and speak his own thoughts—find and follow the way of life for which he is suited. But this task must be done with men—all sorts of men. He saw early that he must not ask of them what was not in them to give. He must find what each could do; he must even, as he once said, use the meanness of men for the public good.

Men might fool him for a time, but never long. His insight into motives was uncanny. He sensed the contempt in which many a man held him on first sight—sensed jealousy—intrigue—treachery— and again and again outwitted them—established himself but kept his victory to himself. These men were necessary to the country. They were great men though they might not believe in his fitness, accept his judgments. With rare and unselfish humility and understanding he endured more than once the wrath of the country for losses, failures for which he was not responsible, rather than weaken popular faith in the man responsible.

Incredible his patience. It was the wisdom of the Hoosier youth who had learned and accepted the laws of nature, had learned that victory is a harvest which takes time; that haste and violence delay, and may destroy it.

So he could be patient, and as the years, with their torturing sorrows went by, he learned what was not easy for him—natural satirist and lampooner that he was—to speak no harsh or bitter word of any man, which meant he must think no harsh or bitter thought. Before the end he came to that supreme self-conquest.

"The things with which I deal are too great for malice," he told Horace Greeley.

There you have the best of him—the supreme thing he had learned in his long years of travail. When with victory in sight he asked the country to face it, "with malice towards none, with charity for all," he was but putting into words what he had come to believe to be the final, highest wisdom in man's relation with his fellows.

Lincoln's Faith in the People

RADIO ADDRESS
SPRINGFIELD, ILLINOIS
FEBRUARY 12, 1949

The Lincoln tomb makes Springfield, Illinois, a climactic place on the Lincoln trail. When he dedicated the memorial in 1874, Governor Richard J. Oglesby, a personal friend and political associate of Lincoln, delivered a noble epitaph: "And now under the gracious favor of Almighty God, I dedicate this monument to the memory of the obscure boy, the honest man, the illustrious statesman, the great Liberator, and the martyr President, Abraham Lincoln, and to the keeping of Time. Behold the image of the man."[1]

Annually after the dedication the American Legion sponsored Lincoln Day pilgrimages to the tomb to celebrate Lincoln's life and accomplishments. Governor of Illinois Adlai E. Stevenson spoke over the radio in 1949 from the Lincoln tomb as part of one of these pilgrimages. Stevenson paid tribute to Lincoln's "faith in the people."[2] Lincoln's faith sustained him and ultimately brought freedom to the United States.

1. Maurine Whorton Redway and Dorothy Kendell Bracken, *Marks of Lincoln on Our Land* (New York: Hastings, 1957), 107–11.
2. Chicago *Tribune*, Feb. 13, 1949.

The speech is reprinted from Walter Johnson, ed., *The Papers of Adlai E. Stevenson*, 8 vols. (Boston: Little Brown, 1972), 3:33. Reprinted with permission.

We come to the Tomb today to pay homage to the saviour of the Union, our fellow townsman of Springfield, Abraham Lincoln.

He was a good man and a brave man; he was gentle, friendly and loved the people. He took with him to the grave human slavery. He left behind him a nation indestructably united for the first time, and a world which had, because of him, a wider concept of freedom and of human rights.

Today everyone honors him, everyone everywhere. But it was not always so. In the Presidential election of 1860 he barely carried this his home town; all but three of the Springfield clergymen opposed him; he lost this county. In his time of severest trial during the Civil War, the leading Chicago editor wrote that complete success in the war "has become a moral impossibility" and that "Lincoln is only half awake and will never do much better than he has done." Bitterness, defeatism and the vengeful partisanship of little men were his lot. In 1864 he was defeated for reelection in this his home county by 400 votes.

No President, and probably few figures in history have been so mistrusted, reviled and hated.

But the abuse and ridicule is long since stilled. Today there is only applause. Today we stand by his side, our heads bowed in reverent homage to this man who loved the people—the fickle people, quick to condemn, who did not always make his path easier.

He never lost faith in the people and when the great decisions came he decided the great way, the hard way, because the disadvantages were patent and present, the advantages obscure and remote. It was his faith in us that sustained him—his faith that the people, once they understood him and his purposes, would support him, for his purposes were good, his purposes were their betterment and salvation, his purposes were to save the republic and expand human freedom, not only here but everywhere. In both he succeeded because he had faith in ultimate understanding and justice.

In death he has become an immortal leader of the people because in life he believed in the people. In the first inaugural address, while attempting to preserve the union by splicing the few common bonds

216

that remained between North and South, he turned to the people, asking, "Why should there not be a patient confidence in the ultimate justice of the people. Is there any better or equal hope in the world?" [First Inaugural Address, Mar. 4, 1861].

We legionnaires, we Americans, who have lived through two world wars against autocrats and dictators can well ask the same question when our hearts are faint—Is there any better hope in the world than the people? As long as our answer is Lincoln's answer we have nothing to fear—there will be no dictators in America.

ADLAI E. STEVENSON

The Struggle for Human Liberty

EIGHTY–EIGHTH ANNIVERSARY OF GETTYSBURG ADDRESS
GETTYSBURG, PENNSYLVANIA
NOVEMBER 19, 1951

Some grade school children who memorize the Gettysburg Address come to Gettysburg, Pennsylvania, in their yellow school buses to see the spot where Lincoln spoke. They are among a million and a half persons who view the historic sixteen-thousand-acre National Military Park with its two thousand monuments and markers, and particularly the Soldiers' National Monument where Lincoln spoke on November 19, 1863. Across the field at the west gate of the National Cemetery visitors may view the Lincoln Speech Memorial, reputed to be the only monument in the United States to an address. Erected in 1912, the granite monument with a bronze bust of Lincoln is flanked with two bronze plaques, one engraved with Lincoln's famous sentences. Aside from Gettysburg College, the town is mostly visited for its Civil War mementoes. The quiet southern Pennsylvania town with its statues, tours, wax museum, sideshows, the Cyclorama Center, and the National Visitor Center assumes symbolic importance in the myth of the man who spoke there for about two minutes.[1]

On the occasion of the eighty-eighth anniversary of the Gettysburg Address on November 19, 1951, Adlai E. Stevenson, governor of Illinois, came to Gettysburg to pay homage to "the tall gaunt man who . . . phrased in words clean of all ornament, the duty of the living to continue the struggle." During this period perhaps no American speaker was better qualified to interpret Abraham Lincoln than Stevenson, who was a member of a prominent Illinois family from Bloomington, a favorite town of Lincoln. The Illinois governor had grown up revering the Springfield lawyer and hearing speeches dedicated to him.[2]

What can the eulogist say about this most read and memorized speech? Stevenson recognized that what was demanded was to reassert

218

"the whole pith and substance of Lincoln's political philosophy"; he needed to reenergize the symbolic message for his listeners who perhaps had regarded Lincoln's address as empty ceremony.

The Illinois governor projected the Lincoln message into the future, saying "the struggle for human liberty goes on." In light of the recent battle with fascism in Europe, Stevenson aptly said: "The struggle must be re-fought by every generation and democracy is threatened not alone by hostile ideologies abroad, but by fear, greed, indifference, intolerance, demagoguery and dishonor here at home."

1. Maurine Wharton Redway and Dorothy Kendell Bracken, *Marks of Lincoln on Our Land* (New York: Hastings, 1957), 97–103; National Park Service, *Gettysburg National Military Park, Pennsylvania* (Washington D.C.: Government Printing Office, 1982).

2. Gettysburg *Times,* Nov. 19, 1951.

The speech is reprinted from Walter Johnson, ed., *The Papers of Adlai E. Stevenson,* 8 vols. (Boston: Little Brown, 1972), 3:468–71; also published in full in Gettysburg *Times,* Nov. 19, 1951. Reprinted with permission.

We are met here today on the field of a bloody, shattering battle. And we meet in reverence for the tall, gaunt man who, standing here 88 years ago, mindful of the dead and the cause for which they here died, phrased in words, clean of all ornament, the duty of the living to continue the struggle. The struggle did continue, the high fever that was Gettysburg passed, and the democratic experiment survived its mortal crisis.

More than the survival of the American Union was at issue here at Gettysburg. Upon the fate of the Union hung the fate of the new dream of democracy throughout the world. For in Lincoln's time the United States was the only major country of the world that enjoyed the democratic form of government, the only land where government was of, by, and for the people. America was democracy's proving ground. The masses of other lands looked to us with hope. If our experiment proved successful, they too might win self-government. But the cynics and the privileged, regarding our experiment with foreboding, identified it with mob rule and lawlessness, sneered and prophesied its doom. When civil war broke out they said: "We told you so."

But Lincoln saw the war in its global dimensions. He was a man of peace, yet even the horror of a brothers' war was not too great a price to save the Union and to demonstrate the viability and the superiority of government by the people.

As Lincoln saw it, the Confederate States had rejected two fundamental precepts of democracy. First, in refusing to accept him as their President and making his election their justification for withdrawing from the Union, they had violated the first rule of democratic government, the obligation of a minority to abide by the result of an election. Without such acquiescence democracy would not work. The Union must never be dissevered for any such reason as this.

Second, in making slavery the foundation stone of their new government, the Confederacy was renouncing the doctrine of the equal rights of man in favor of the creed of the master race, an idea that Lincoln abhorred. "The last, best hope of earth," in his view, was to be found in our Declaration of Independence which affirmed that all men are created equal, that they are endowed by their Creator with certain inalienable rights, among which are life, liberty, and the pursuit of happiness [annual message, Dec. 1, 1862].

Here, in fact, was the whole pith and substance of Lincoln's political philosophy. Here, in his deep reverence for the rights of man as proclaimed in our American charter of freedom, is to be found the explanation of most of his political actions. "I have never had a feeling politically," he said, "which did not spring from the sentiments embodied in the Declaration of Independence" [speech at Independence Hall, Feb. 22, 1861]. It was these principles, Lincoln believed, that would lift artificial weights from men's shoulders, clear the paths of laudable pursuit for all, and afford everyone an unfettered start and a fair chance in the race of life.

When we realize that Lincoln saw the dissolution of the Union as a threat to democratic aspirations throughout the world, his words at Gettysburg become more meaningful. Chancellorsville, Antietam, Chickamauga and Gettysburg were deciding more than the fate of these United States. Americans were dying for the new, revolutionary idea of the free man, even as they had died at Bunker Hill and Yorktown. They were dying to save the hope of all people everywhere.

So when Lincoln was asked to speak at the dedication of this cemetery, he welcomed the chance to tell the people what those three days of bloody battle meant and to explain what those men died for, as he saw it.

His thoughts went back four score and seven years to the revolutionary founding of this nation, conceived in liberty and dedicated to the proposition that all men are created equal. Then his mind came back to the war being fought to determine whether that nation, or any nation conceived in revolution and dedicated to such radical principles, could long endure—whether the people were capable of shaping their own destiny. He thought of the heroic dead, and of what the living owed them for their sacrifice. Mere words could not express it. The world, he thought, would little note nor long remember what was said that day. Then he looked ahead—not merely to the tomorrow, but into the far distant future, as he said: "It is for us, the living, rather to be here dedicated to the great task remaining before us . . . that these dead shall not have died in vain."

The war ended. The nation, reunited, once again offered hope for liberal yearnings everywhere. Inspired by the example of America, democracy made striking headway throughout the world, even among the so-called backward peoples of the earth. It seemed that the principles for which Lincoln fought and died would win world-wide acceptance. America took it for granted. To us it became merely a question of when and how. Busy building up a rich continent, America lost sight of its mission.

Then came the shock of World War I. But with victory, democracy took up its march again. Russia, most reactionary of all European countries, was in revolt against autocracy. Germany, Austria, Czechoslovakia, became republics. Woodrow Wilson, who, even as Lincoln, saw the fate of democracy as the prime issue of the war, went to Europe with a purpose to mark out new boundaries which would express, as nearly as possible, the people's will. Democracy was again in the ascendant. But America, mindless of her mission, following the soft voices of men of little vision, shrouded herself in isolation.

The rest is within the recollection of us all. Adolph Hitler resurrected the malevolent doctrine of the master race, and poised its ghastly death's head over Europe. And now comes imperial Communism, stalking freedom throughout the world.

The struggle for human liberty goes on. The great bearers of our tradition have believed in it not because they were born in it, but because they saw despotism as we have seen it and turned from it to rediscover the American faith in the free man.

The struggle must be re-fought by every generation and democracy is threatened not alone by hostile ideologies abroad, but by fear, greed, indifference, intolerance, demagoguery and dishonor here at home. Little men spread mistrust, confusion, fear. Careless inquisition and irresponsible accusation increase tensions, and tensions, repressions. The tyranny of organized opinion lifts its ugly head to mock the faith of the American Revolution.

No, Lincoln's fight is not finished. The far future into which he looked is here, and we are now the living. Eight and eighty years after he uttered here those immortal words, it is for us, the living, to be re-dedicated to our democratic faith; to be here dedicated to the great task, the same task, remaining before us. The fight goes on. Cemetery Ridge is shrouded in the mist of history. But American boys are dying today on Heartbreak Ridge far away for the last, best hope of collective security, of peace and of freedom for all to choose their way of life.

Proud of the past, [im]patient with what Washington called "the impostures of pretended patriotism," it is for us, the living, to rekindle the hot, indignant fires of faith in the free man, free in body, free in mind, free in spirit, free to hold any opinion, free to search and find the truth for himself; the old faith that is ever new—that burned so brightly here at Gettysburg long ago.

Unfinished Work of Emancipation

LINCOLN MEMORIAL
WASHINGTON, D.C.
SEPTEMBER 18, 1962

While he served as ambassador to the United Nations, Stevenson was invited to commemorate the Emancipation Proclamation about which so much of the Lincoln aura is associated and which has been called "the grand climax of his career."[1] The document has been the inspiration for poems, editorials, and orations. In fact, a popular 1865 collection from newspapers and periodicals contains sixty writings that traced their inspiration to the proclamation. Throughout the world Lincoln has become the symbol of freedom and has been remembered as the Great Emancipator. To add luster to the anniversary, the ceremony was scheduled at the Lincoln Memorial in Washington, a place that has become almost a sacred shrine to many American blacks.[2]

Following a strategy much like that at Gettysburg, the ambassador said, "The Proclamation of Emancipation meant *more* than it *said*" and "gave courage to the oppressed from the Thames to the Ganges; it inaugurated a *new* age of world-wide reforms." These remarks were most timely in light of the struggle for integration within the United States, but it also had a wider implication. He praised the proclamation as "a *beginning,* not an end . . . a call to a *new battle*—a battle which rages around us now in every part of the world in this *new* time of testing." Obviously Stevenson cast the Lincoln scenario upon a larger stage than the immediate occasion.

1. Richard N. Current, *The Lincoln Nobody Knows* (New York: Hill and Wang, 1958), 215.
2. Roy P. Basler, *The Lincoln Legend* (New York: Houghton Mifflin, 1935), 202–3.

224

The speech is reprinted from Walter Johnson, ed., *The Papers of Adlai E. Stevenson,* 8 vols. (Boston: Little Brown, 1972), 8: 292–94. Reprinted with permission.

This day just a hundred years ago, America reached a *turning* point.

It was five days after Antietam. In the South Mountain defiles and on the fields around Sharpsburg ghastly clumps of dead soldiers lay unburied. The foul weeds of *civil* war—*hatred, fury, cruelty*—grew ranker as the lists of slain and wounded filled the bulletin boards, and the hospital trains crept *North* and *South* between lines of harrowed watchers. In *Europe,* leaders pondered intervention; some ready to take harsh advantage of the New World's *agony;* some, like Gladstone, racked with anxiety to stop the slaughter.

And then came the *flash,* the lightning stroke that enables men to see the changes wrought by the storm. A haggard President told his cabinet and his *Maker* that if the foe was driven from Union soil, he would declare the slaves "forever free." Within *hours* headlines all over this land clamored with the word "Emancipation!" Within *days* every slave had heard the news. Within *weeks* people all over the world were hailing the redemption of young America's promise.

Like *all title deeds* of human progress, the Proclamation of Emancipation meant *more* than it *said.* Morally it meant that American civilization and human bondage were *irrevocably* incompatible. And a panoply of *larger* freedoms was bound up in that first small step. For the Proclamation touched not the fate of *Americans* alone; it gave courage to the oppressed from the Thames to the Ganges; it inaugurated a *new* age of world-wide reforms. It was an application of the basic tenets of the nation, tenets which gave promise, said Lincoln, that "in due time the weight[s] would be lifted from the shoulders of all men" [speech at Independence Hall, Feb. 22, 1861].

Since we admit so readily our *gratitude* and our *debt* to *other* nations for their enrichment of our national fabric, I hope it will not seem immodest to others that Americans take such pride in the momentous milestone we commemorate today, nor in the globe-circling spread of our spirit of *national* independence and *individual* freedom. During the past two centuries the two have walked *hand* in *hand.* Beside *national* independence in 1776 stood the goal of individual freedom; beside the preservation of the Union in 1862 stood the same great idea—planted there by the most *beloved* of American leaders.

And *today*—just a century later—freedom is *again* at stake. This time the whole world-wide society of men is perilously divided on the issue. *National* independence has swept the earth like wildfire, but *individual* freedom is *still* the great *unfinished* business of the world. Once more we doubt whether the human experiment can survive half *slave* and half *free*. Once more we *feel*, as men did in Lincoln's day, that the future of mankind itself depends upon the outcome of the struggle in which we are engaged.

In this *context*, with this *urgency*, with these *fears*, it would be easy enough to slip into the path of cloudy rhetoric. I could paint you a picture of this world struggle in which our *adversaries* would be *pitch black* and we—"the land of the free and the home of the brave"—would be *lily white*.

But since today we celebrate not only the *act* of Emancipation, but also the *Great Emancipator* (who sits brooding behind me,) it is well to point out that Lincoln, throughout all the *agonies* and *defeats*, and the breathtaking *triumphs* of the Civil War, *never* made such a speech. Never did he define his cause—this overwhelming cause of freedom—in terms of *white* and *black*, *good* and *bad*, *excellence* and *evil*. Abraham Lincoln of Ill. never stooped to cheap rhetoric. Instead, he continued, *obstinately* and *greatly*, to see human *affairs* and human *emotions* in all their *complexity* and *ambiguity*, and to *refuse* the snap judgments into which *self-righteousness* can so easily lead us all. If ever a leader *lived* by the Biblical injunction—"Judge not, lest ye be judged"—it was Lincoln. For him, *truth* was the groundwork of freedom, and you could no more build victory upon *delusion* than you could sustain society in *slavery*. And *this* is reason enough for his *saintly* rank among world statesmen.

So if today we wish to honor both the *act* of emancipation and the *man* who framed it, we have to follow in the *same* dedication to *truth*, and the *same* abhorrence for pretension and self-deceit. We *know* that we uphold the cause of *freedom*. Equally we *know* that we risk *betraying* it if we have any illusions about our *failures* and *insufficiencies*.

If the issue between North and South sometimes seemed ambiguous to Lincoln; if, as in the Second Inaugural, he recognized the equal complicity of *Northerners* organizing the slave trade and *Southerners* profiting by the results, so, too, today we must approach the theme of freedom in the *world* context with some of Lincoln's *modesty* and *accuracy.*

Are we the pure-souled defenders of freedom when Negro citizens are anywhere denied the right to *vote,* or to equal education, or to equal opportunity, to equal dignity? Can we be surprised if, abroad, *friends* with *sadness* and *enemies* with delight, observe the *inequalities* and *injustices* which still mar our American image?

In his day, Lincoln was bitterly attacked for this unwillingness to take the straight partisan line, to claim all *virtue* for the North, all *evil* for the South, to *praise himself* and his *cause,* to *damn* all his adversaries. His sense that issues might be relative and ambiguous roused men of rougher certitude to furies of denunciation, and Lincoln was accused of weakness, even of *treachery,* because he could not go along with the single-minded jingoism of much of the propaganda of his day.

So *Today,* there is a danger that those who do not see things in the *stark* contrasts of black and white will be denounced as *feeble* and even *treacherous.* It is therefore worthwhile recalling that Lincoln's sense of the complexity of all great historical issues did not hold him back for one hour from "doing the right" as God gave him to see the right, or deter him from emancipating the slaves and fighting a great war to its finish to ensure that the Union would be preserved and the Emancipation honored.

So today—that we make no claim to *final righteousness* will help us to keep open all the paths to *negotiation* and fruitful compromise. It does not—any more than it did for Lincoln—make us compromise with *violence, aggression* or *fraud.* We shall stand all the *firmer* for not standing in a *false* light. Our defense of freedom will be all the *stronger* for being based, not on *illusions* but upon the *truth* about *ourselves* and our *world.*

Freedom must be rooted in *reality* or it will *crumble* as *errors* are revealed and *faith* is shaken. Only the truth can make us free.

The *immortal* document that the Great Emancipator read to his advisers just one hundred years ago *closed* one era of American history and *opened* another. It freed the *Negro* from his age-old bondage; it freed the *white* people of the South from an outworn and crippling institution; it freed the *Republic* from the darkest stain upon its record. It gave freedom a *mighty* impulse throughout the globe. And it will surround the rugged features of President Lincoln with an *unfading* halo.

But it marked a *beginning,* not an end; it was a call to a *new battle*—a battle which rages around us now in every part of the world in this *new* time of testing.

Truth was never the enemy of liberty, and it is no coincidence that the greatest statesman of liberty, the greatest champion freedom has ever known, was also the man who claimed *least* infallibility for himself and for his cause. And *we* can be humble as he was humble, knowing that the *cause* of *freedom* is greater than its *defenders,* and can *triumph* in spite of all their shortcomings.

In this *spirit,* we dare declare that the *concern* and *dedication* of our Union is the freedom of *all* mankind. With this *candor,* we can claim to be Lincoln's heirs in the unfinished work of emancipation.

Abraham Lincoln and
Our Unfinished Business

ANNUAL DINNER, ABRAHAM LINCOLN ASSOCIATION
SPRINGFIELD, ILLINOIS
FEBRUARY 12, 1986

What Mario M. Cuomo said to the Lincoln Association is a most fitting closing selection for a book of Lincoln eulogies, for it offers the full-blown Lincoln myth in 1986 and demonstrates its continuing vigor and influence on American thinking.[1] Cuomo was quite correct in identifying Lincoln's personal mythology as "our national mythology."

Not departing from the traditional apocalyptic emphasis, the speaker suggested that Lincoln "consumed himself" in trying to give meaning to "the promise of equality and opportunity" and that "He could not escape the obligation of pursuing them [principles] despite the peril and pain that pursuit would inevitably bring."

Showing rhetorical finesse, Cuomo extended the Lincoln influence into the future, mentioning the continuing struggle to achieve Lincoln's ideals. In a deft touch, he warned of the loss of Lincoln influence by making him "a celebration, but not an *instruction;* a memory, but not a *model;* a legend, but not a *lesson*" [ital. added]. He argued that what Lincoln stood for should be applied to contemporary problems associated with discrimination involving class, race, sex, and ethnicity. "As individuals, as a people, we are still reaching up, for a better job, a better education, a better society, even for the stars, just as Lincoln did." Herein Cuomo incorporated the comparative degree ["better"] with the phrase "reaching up . . . for the stars," to achieve the sense of movement into the future. In this linguistic strategy he gave emphasis to the Lincoln idealism in such phrases as "lifting people up," "the leaving behind," "the reaching beyond," "extended the promise," "embrace grows wider," "to go forward," "enlarging the greatness of this nation." Such phrases achieved amplification, stirred in the listeners' minds hope and aspirations, and moved the thinking of the listeners toward the future.

The New York governor enhanced his persuasion considerably through a personal reference to his own background as "a first generation American" who knew the pain of being called a "wop." In what was a reflection of his political experience in New York politics he said, "We heard such voices again recently saying things like, Italians are not politically popular. Catholics will have a problem. He has an ethnic problem." Cuomo was able to overcome these prejudices and become successful. By invoking Lincoln's words Cuomo was able to prove to the American people that their country was not ruled by bigotry, that success was not contingent upon a person's country of origin, that Lincoln made it a country of freedom.

1. Owen Peterson, ed., *Representative American Speeches, 1985–1986* (New York: H. W. Wilson, 1986), 108–20.

The speech is reprinted with permission from Mario M. Cuomo.

Reverend Milkman, Justice Underwood, our distinguished awardee Justice Ward, Justice Miller, Distinguished Professor Robert Johannsen, General Herrero, Dr. Curtis.

Governor Thompson, I thank you for that generous introduction. It is a privilege for Matilda and me and Christopher to be in your great state and we appreciate your taking the time to be here to introduce me.

I would also like to thank Judge Harlington Wood for inviting me to be part of this celebration of one of the monumental figures of our history, whose words and life and legend have been for me, as they have for you I'm sure, an instruction and an inspiration for most of a lifetime.

I am also honored to be in the company of Representative Richard Durbin, who occupies the congressional seat Lincoln held, and Senator Paul Simon, himself an extraordinary success story, a man of intellect and integrity, whose distinguished works on the Lincoln theme have illuminated the man we honor tonight.

It is an intimidating thing to stand here tonight to talk about the greatest intellect, the greatest leader, perhaps the greatest soul America has ever produced. To follow such legendary orators as William Jennings Bryan and Adlai Stevenson. Only a struggling student myself, to face as imposing an audience as the Lincoln scholars—tough-minded, demanding, harsh critics, highly intelligent. And to face so many Republicans: tough-minded, demanding, harsh critics...

And I certainly wasn't encouraged after I learned that when another New York governor, Franklin D. Roosevelt, announced his intention to come here to speak on Lincoln, a local political stalwart threatened him with an injunction.

To be honest with you, I feel a little like the Illinois man from one Lincoln story. When he was confronted by a local citizens' committee with the prospect of being tarred and feathered and run out of town on a rail, he announced, "If it weren't for the honor of the thing, I'd just as soon it happened to someone else" [apocryphal].

I should tell you one more thing before I go on with my remarks. It would be foolish to deny that there has been some speculation surrounding this event about ambitions for the presidency. Let me be candid. I don't know anyone who wouldn't regard it as the highest possible political privilege to be President. And governors are, perhaps, better prepared than most to be President. Governors like Teddy Roosevelt and F.D.R. and even governors from places like Georgia and California, particularly governors of great industrial states with good records. That's because governors do more than make speeches. They have to make budgets and run things, and that's what Presidents do.

So, the truth is, despite what might be said about planning to run again for governor, the speculation about the Presidency is plausible. I wouldn't be a bit surprised—if the election goes well this year for him—if early next year you heard a declaration of interest from a reelected governor of a large state—Jim Thompson. Good luck, Jim!

But seriously, this is an event beyond the scope of partisan politics. When Lincoln gave his one and only speech in my capital, Albany, New York, he told the Democratic governor, "You have invited and received me without distinction of party" [N.Y. legislature, Feb. 1, 1861]. Let me second that sentiment, and thank you for inviting and receiving me in the same spirit.

To be here in Springfield, instead of at the memorial in Washington, to celebrate this "high holy day" of Lincoln remembrance, gives us a special advantage. In Washington, Lincoln towers far above us, presiding magisterially, in a marble temple. His stony composure, the hugeness of him there, gives him and his whole life a grandeur that places him so far above and beyond us that it's difficult to remember the reality of him. We have lifted Lincoln to the very pinnacle of our national memory, enlarged him to gargantuan proportions in white stone re-creations. We have chiseled his face on the side of a mountain, making him appear as a voice in the heavens.

There is a danger when we enshrine our heroes, when we lift them onto pedestals and lay wreaths at their feet. We can, by the very process of elevating them, strain the sense of connection between them and the palpable, fleshy, sometimes mean concerns of our own lives. It would be a terrible shame to lose Lincoln that way, to make of him a celebration but not an instruction; a memory, but not a model; a legend but not a lesson.

Here in Springfield there is less chance of that. Although he left

Springfield 125 years ago, here—where he practiced law, served as a legislator, and warned this nation of the dangers of a "house divided"—Lincoln, the man, still presides. Here we can remember that Lincoln—the miracle that we call Lincoln—worked within the hard, sometimes discouraging, sometimes terrifying, limits of time and place and chance. And by our so remembering, he can again begin to light our minds and move our hearts.

That is why I have come here, not just to light a candle to the apparition of him, but to remember his specific wisdom and goodness and to consider how it can continue to touch us, to teach us, to move us to the higher ground.

I have come to remember Lincoln as he was. The flesh and blood man, haunted by mortality in his waking and his dreaming life. The boy who had been uprooted from one frontier farm to another, across Kentucky and Indiana and Illinois, by a father restless with his own dreams.

To remember some of Lincoln's own words, which, taken altogether, are the best words America has ever produced. To remember the words that he spoke ten days after his lyrical, wrenching farewell to Springfield on his way to his inauguration as our sixteenth President. "Back in my childhood," he said then, "the earliest days of my being able to read, I got hold of a small book . . . Weems' *Life of Washington:*

> I remember all the accounts there given of the battlefields and struggles for the liberties of the country and the great hardships of that time fixed themselves on . . . my memory. I recollect thinking then, boy even though I was, that there must have been something more than common that those men struggled for. I am exceedingly anxious that the thing which they struggled for; that something even more than national independence; that something that held out a promise to all the people of the world for all time to come; . . . shall be perpetuated in accordance with the original idea for which the struggle was made. [N.J. senate, Feb. 21, 1861]

Here was Lincoln, just before his inauguration, reminding us of the source of his strength and eventual greatness, his compelling need to understand the meaning of things and to commit to a course that was directed by reason, supported by principle, designed to achieve the greatest good. He was a man of ideas, grand and soaring ones, and he

234

was cursed by the realization that they were achievable ideas as well, so that he could not escape the obligation of pursuing them, despite the peril and the pain that pursuit would inevitably bring.

Even as a boy he grasped the great idea that would sustain him—and provoke him—for the rest of his days, the idea that took hold of his heart and his mind, the idea that he tells us about again and again throughout his life. It became the thread of purpose that tied the boy to the man to the legend—the great idea—the dream, the achievable dream, of equality, of opportunity ... for all: "The original idea for which the struggle was made ... " The proposition that all men are created equal, that they are endowed by their creator with certain unalienable rights, that among these are life, liberty and the pursuit of happiness.

Even by Lincoln's time, for many, the words had been heard often enough so that they became commonplace, part of the intellectual and historical landscape, losing their dimension, their significance, their profoundness.

But not for Lincoln. He pondered them, troubled over their significance, wrestled with their possibilities. "We did not learn quickly or easily that all men are created equal," one Lincoln scholar has observed. No. We did not learn those words quickly or easily. We are still struggling with them in fact, as Lincoln did for a whole lifetime. From the time he read Weems' little book until the day he was martyred, he thought, and planned, and prayed to make the words of the declaration, a way of life. Equality and opportunity, for all. But truly, for *all*.

Lincoln came to believe that the great promise of the founding fathers was one that had only begun to be realized with the founding fathers themselves. He understood that from the beginning it was a promise that would have to be fulfilled in degrees. Its embrace would have to be widened over the years, step by step, sometimes painfully, until finally it included everyone.

That was his dream. That was his vision. That was his mission. With it, he defined for himself and for us the soul of our unique experiment in government: the belief that the promise of the Declaration of Independence—the promise of equality and opportunity—cannot be considered kept, until it includes everyone.

For him, that was the unifying principle of our democracy. Without it, we had no nation worth fighting for. With it, we had no limit to the good we might achieve. He spent the rest of his life trying to give the principle meaning. He consumed himself doing it. He reaffirmed Jefferson's preference for the human interest and the human right. "The principles of Jefferson," he said, "are the definitions and axioms of free society" [to Henry L. Pierce, Apr. 6, 1859].

But Lincoln extended those instincts to new expressions of equality. Always, he searched for ways to bring within the embrace of the new freedom, the new opportunity, all who had become Americans. Deeply—reverently—grateful for the opportunity afforded him, he was pained by the idea that it should be denied others, or limited.

He believed that the human right was more than the right to exist, to live free from oppression. He believed it included the right to achieve, to thrive, so he reached out for the "penniless beginner" [annual message, Dec. 2, 1861]. He thought it the American promise that every "poor man" should be given his chance. He saw what others would or could not see: the immensity of the fundamental ideas of freedom and self-determination that made his young nation such a radically new adventure in government.

But he was not intimidated by that immensity. He was willing to use the ideas as well as to admire them, to mold them so as to apply them to new circumstances, to wield them as instruments of justice and not just echoes of it.

Some said government should do no more than protect its people from insurrection and foreign invasion and spend the rest of its time dispassionately observing the way its people played out the cards that fate had dealt them. He scorned that view. He called it a "do nothing" abdication of responsibility [speech, June 20, 1848]. "The legitimate object of government," he said, "is to do for the people what needs to be done, but which they cannot, by individual effort, do at all, or do so well, for themselves. There are many such things...," he said [fragment, July 1, 1854?].

So he offered the "poor" more than freedom and the encouragement of his own good example: He offered them government, government that would work aggressively to help them find the chance they might not have found alone. He did it by fighting for bridges, railroad construction, and other such projects that others decried as excessive government. He gave help for education, help for agriculture, land for the rural family struggling for a start.

And always, at the heart of this struggle and his yearning was the passion to make room for the outsider, the insistence upon a commitment to respect the idea of equality by fighting for inclusion. Early in his career, he spoke out for women's suffrage. His contempt for the "Do-Nothings" was equalled by his disdain for the "Know-Nothings" [to editor, *Sangamo Journal,* June 13, 1836].

America beckoned foreigners, but many Americans—organized around the crude selfishness of the Nativist Movement—rejected them. The Nativists sought to create two classes of people, the old stock Americans and the intruders from other places, keeping the intruders forever strangers in a strange land.

Lincoln shamed them with his understanding and his strength. "I am not a Know-Nothing," he said. "How could I be? How can anyone who abhors the oppression of Negroes be in favor of degrading classes of white people? ... As a nation we began by declaring 'all men are created equal.'

"We now practically read it, 'All men are created equal except Negroes.' When the Know-Nothings get control, it will read 'All men are created equal except Negroes, and Catholics, and foreigners.'" Then he added: "When it comes to this I shall prefer emigrating to some country where they make no pretense of loving liberty— to Russia for instance, where despotism can be taken pure, and without the base alloy of hypocrisy" [to Joshua Speed, Aug. 24, 1855].

Had Lincoln not existed, or had he been less than he was and the battle to keep the nation together had been lost, it would have meant the end of the American experiment. Secession would have bred secession, reducing us into smaller and smaller fragments until finally we were just the broken pieces of the dream.

Lincoln saved us from that. But winning the great war for unity did not preserve us from the need to fight further battles in the struggle to balance our diversity with our harmony, to keep the pieces of the mosaic intact, even while making room for new pieces. That work is today, as it was in 1863, still an unfinished work ... still a cause that requires "a full measure of devotion."

For more than 100 years, the fight to include has continued:

—in the struggle to free working people from the oppression of a ruthless economic system that saw women and children worked to death and men born to poverty, live in poverty, and die in poverty—in spite of working all the time.

—in the continuing fight for civil rights, making Lincoln's promise real.

—in the effort to keep the farmer alive.

—in the ongoing resistance to preserve religious freedom from the arrogance of the Know-Nothing and the zealotry of those who would make their religion the state's religion.

—in the crusade to make women equal, legally and practically.

Many battles have been won. The embrace of our unity has been gradually but inexorably expanded. But Lincoln's work is not yet done.

A century after Lincoln preached his answer of equality and mutual respect, some discrimination—of class or race or sex or ethnicity—as a bar to full participation in America still remains. Unpleasant reminders of less enlightened times linger. Sometimes they are heard in whispers. At other times they are loud enough to capture the attention of the American people.

I have had my own encounter with this question and I have spoken of it. Like millions of others, I am privileged to be a first generation American. My mother and father came to this country more than sixty years ago with nothing but their hopes, without education, skills, or wealth. Through the opportunity given them here to lift themselves through hard work, they were able to raise a family. My mother has lived to see her youngest child become chief executive of one of the greatest states in the greatest nation in the only world we know.

Like millions of other children of immigrants, I know the strength that immigrants can bring. I know the richness of a society that allows us a whole new culture without requiring us to surrender the one our parents were born to. I know the miraculous power of this place that helps people rise up from poverty to security, and even affluence, in the course of a single lifetime. With generations of other children of the immigrants, I know about equality and opportunity and unity, in a special way.

And I know how, from time to time, all this beauty can be challenged by the misguided children of the Know-Nothings, by the short-sighted and the unkind, by contempt that masks itself as humor, by all the casual or conscious bigotry that must keep the American people vigilant.

We heard such voices again recently saying things like, Italians are not politically popular. Catholics will have a problem. He has an ethnic problem. An ethnic problem. We hear the word again, "Wop."

"We oftentimes refer to people of Italian descent as 'Wops'," said one public figure, unabashedly.

Now, given the unbroken string of opportunity and good fortune provided me by this great country, I might simply have ignored these references. I could easily have let the words pass as inconsequential, especially remembering Lincoln, himself the object of scorn and ridicule.

But the words, they took on significance because they were heard far beyond my home or my block or even my state, because they were heard by others who remembered times of their own when words stung and menaced them and their people. And because they raised a question about our system of fundamental American values that Lincoln helped construct and died for. Is it true? Are there really so many who have never heard Lincoln's voice, or the sweet sound of reason and fairness? So many who do not understand the beauty and power of this place, that they could make of the tint of your skin, or the sex you were born to, or the vowels of your name, an impediment to progress in this, the land of opportunity?

I believed the answer would be clear, so I asked for it by disputing the voices of division, by saying, "It is not so. It is the voice of ignorance and I challenge you to show me otherwise."

In no time at all the answer has come back from the American people, everyone saying the same things: "Of course it's wrong to judge a person by the place where his forebears came from, of course that would violate all that we stand for, fairness and common sense. It shouldn't even have been brought up. It shouldn't even have been a cause for discussion."

I agree. It should not have been. But it was. And the discussion is now concluded, with the answer I was sure of and the answer I am proud of as an American, the answer Lincoln would have given: "You will rise or fall on your merits as a person and the quality of your work. All else is distraction."

239

Lincoln believed, with every fibre of his being, that this place, America, could offer a dream to all mankind, different than any other in the annals of history: more generous, more compassionate, more inclusive.

No one knew better than Lincoln our sturdiness, the ability of most of us to make it on our own given the chance. But at the same time, no one knew better the idea of family, the idea that unless we helped one another, there were some who would never make it.

One person climbs the ladder of personal ambition, reaches his dream, and then turns and pulls the ladder up. Another reaches the place he has sought, turns, and reaches down for the person behind him. With Lincoln, it was that process of turning and reaching down, that commitment to keep lifting people up the ladder, which defined the American character, stamping us forever with a mission that reached even beyond our borders to embrace the world.

Lincoln's belief in America, in the American people, was broader, deeper, more daring than any other person's of his age—and, perhaps, ours, too. And this is the near-unbelievable greatness of the man, that with that belief, he not only led us, he created us.

His personal mythology became our national mythology. It is as if Homer not only chronicled the siege of Troy, but conducted the siege as well. As if Shakespeare set his playwrighting aside to lead the English against the Armada. Because Lincoln embodied his age in his actions and in his words:

—words, even and measured, hurrying across three decades, calling us to our destiny;

—words he prayed, and troubled over, more than a million words in his speeches and writings;

—words that chronicled the search for his own identity as he searched for a nation's identity;

—words that were, by turns, as chilling as the night sky and as assuring as home;

—words his reason sharpened into steel, and his heart softened into an embrace;

—words filled with all the longings of his soul and of his century;

—words wrung from his private struggle, spun to capture the struggle of a nation;

—words out of his own pain to heal that struggle;

—words of retribution, but never of revenge;

—words that judged, but never condemned;

—words that pleaded, cajoled for the one belief—that the promise must be kept—that the dream must endure and grow, until it embraces everyone;

—words ringing down into the present;

—all the hope and the pain of that epic caught, somehow, by his cadences: the tearing away, the binding together, the leaving behind, the reaching beyond.

As individuals, as a people, we are still reaching up, for a better job, a better education, a better society, even for the stars, just as Lincoln did. But because of Lincoln, we do it in a way that is unique to this world.

What other people on earth have ever claimed a quality of character that resided not in a way of speaking, dressing, dancing, praying, but in an idea? What other people on earth have ever refused to set the definitions of their identity by anything other than that idea?

No, we have not learned quickly or easily that the dream of America endures only so long as we keep faith with the struggle to include, but Lincoln—through his words and his works—has etched that message forever into our consciousness.

Lincoln showed us, for all time, what unites us. He taught us that we cannot rest until the promise of equality and opportunity embraces every region, every race, every religion, every nationality, and every class, until it includes, "the penniless beginner" and the "poor man seeking his chance" [speech, Chicago, Dec. 10, 1856].

In his time, Lincoln saw that as long as one in every seven Americans was enslaved, our identity as a people was hostage to that enslavement. He faced that injustice. He fought it. He gave his life to see it righted.

Time and again, since then, we have had to face challenges that threatened to divide us, and, time and again, we have conquered them. We reached out—hesitantly at times, sometimes only after great struggle, but always we reached out—to include impoverished immigrants, the farmer and the factory worker, women, the disabled.

To all those whose only assets were their great expectations, America found ways to meet those expectations and to create new ones. Generations of hard-working people moved into the middle class and beyond. We created a society as open and free as any on earth, and we did it Lincoln's way: by founding that society on a belief in the boundless enterprise of the American people.

Always, we have extended the promise, moving toward the light, toward our declared purpose as a people: "To form a more perfect union," to overcome all that divides us because we believe the ancient wisdom that Lincoln believed, "A house divided against itself cannot stand" [speech, Springfield, Ill., June 16, 1858].

Step by step, our embrace grows wider. The old bigotries seem to be dying. The old stereotypes and hatreds, that denied so many their full share of an America they helped build, have gradually given way to acceptance, fairness, and civility.

But still, great challenges remain. Suddenly, ominously, a new one has emerged.

In Lincoln's time, one of every seven Americans was a slave. Today, for all our affluence and might, despite what every day is described as our continuing economic recovery, nearly one in every seven Americans lives in poverty, not in chains—because Lincoln saved us from that—but trapped in a cycle of despair that is its own enslavement.

Today, while so many of us do so well, one of every two minority children is born poor, many of them to be oppressed for a lifetime by inadequate education and the suffocating influence of broken families and social disorientation. Our identity as a people is hostage to the grim facts of more than 33 million Americans for whom equality and opportunity is not yet an attainable reality, but only an illusion.

Some people look at these statistics and the suffering people behind them, and deny them, pretending instead we are all one great "shining city on a hill." Lincoln told us for a lifetime—and for all time to come—that there can be no shining city when one in seven of us is denied the promise of the declaration. He tells us today that we are justly proud of all that we have accomplished, but that for all our progress, for all our achievement, for all that so properly makes us proud, we have no right to rest, content; nor justification for turning from the effort, out of fear or lack of confidence.

We have met greater challenges with fewer resources. We have faced greater perils with fewer friends. It would be a desecration of our belief and an act of ingratitude for the good fortune we have had to end the struggle for inclusion because it is over for some of us.

So, this evening, we come to pay you our respects, Mr. Lincoln, not just by recalling your words and revering your memory, which we do humbly and with great pleasure.

This evening, we offer you more, Mr. President—we offer you what you have asked us for, a continuing commitment to live your truth, to go forward painful step by painful step, enlarging the greatness of this nation with patient confidence in the ultimate justice of the people.

Because, as you have told us, Mr. President, there is no better or equal hope in the world.

BANCROFT, GEORGE (1800–1891). Historian and diplomat. Born, Worcester, Massachusetts. He attended Phillips Exeter Academy; graduated from Harvard University in 1817; and pursued graduate study in Oriental languages, theology, and philology in Berlin and Göttingen, receiving a Ph.D. in 1820. In 1848 he was granted an honorary degree at Oxford University. He briefly taught at Harvard, and for eight years he was associated with Round Hill School in Northampton, Massachusetts. He held various government positions: collector of the port of Boston, 1837; U.S. secretary of navy under President Polk, 1845–46; U.S. minister to Great Britain, 1846–49; and to the German states, 1867–74. He is remembered for his ten-volume *History of the United States.*

BEECHER, HENRY WARD (1813–87). Clergyman. Born, Litchfield, Connecticut. He was the son of the well-known Presbyterian theologian Lyman Beecher and the brother of novelist Harriet Beecher Stowe, who wrote *Uncle Tom's Cabin.* Henry Ward graduated from Amherst College in 1834 and the Lane Theological Seminary, Cincinnati, in 1837. His first pastorate was at Lawrenceburg, Indiana, but after two years he moved to Indianapolis and finally to the Plymouth Congregational Church in Brooklyn, New York, where he served for forty years. He is reported to have drawn a weekly audience of 2,500, and his sermons were widely circulated in pamphlet form. He spoke on political and social issues as well as on religion. He also edited the *Independent* and the *Christian Union.* He was often considered the greatest pulpit orator of his time.

Beecher was an outspoken advocate of abolition, denounced slavery from his pulpit, and gave support to the antislavery forces in Kansas. He campaigned for John C. Fremont in 1856, and for Lincoln in 1860 and 1864.

BORAH, WILLIAM E. (1865–1940). U.S. Senator from Idaho. Born near Fairfield, Illinois. He was largely self-educated, but he attended the University of Kansas for parts of 1885 and 1886. He taught country schools in Kansas, was admitted to the Kansas bar in 1887, practiced law in Lyons, Kansas, from 1887 to 1890, and in Boise, Idaho, from 1890 to 1906.

In 1907 he entered the U.S. Senate and served there until his death in 1940. He is remembered as an isolationist and an independent Republican who opposed the participation of the United States in the League of

Nations and the World Court. From 1924 to 1933 he served as chairman of the Senate Committee on Foreign Relations. During his thirty-three years in the Senate, he was considered a great speaker. In Washington, on the campaign trail, and on radio he drew enthusiastic audiences.

BROOKS, PHILLIPS (1835–93). Episcopal clergyman. Born, Boston, Massachusetts. He graduated from Harvard University in 1855 and attended the Virginia Theological Seminary from 1856 to 1859. He was pastor at the Church of the Advent from 1859 to 1861 and at Holy Trinity Church in Philadelphia from 1861 to 1864. He moved to the Trinity Church, Boston, in 1869. In 1891 he was consecrated bishop of Massachusetts. He was recognized as the most famous Episcopal minister of his time, as well as the theologian who wrote the verses for "O Little Town of Bethlehem."

BRYAN, WILLIAM JENNINGS (1860–1925). Lawyer and political leader. Born, Salem, Illinois. He graduated from Illinois College in 1881. He moved to Lincoln, Nebraska, where he practiced law and edited the *Commoner,* a weekly paper. He was a member of the U.S. House of Representatives from 1891 to 1985; ran unsuccessfully as a Democrat for the presidency in 1896, 1900, and 1908; and served as the secretary of state from 1913 to 1915. He became a premier chautauqua lecturer and was considered a foremost orator. His most famous speech was the "Cross of Gold," delivered in Chicago in 1896.

CHOATE, JOSEPH H. (1832–1917). Lawyer and diplomat. Born, Salem, Massachusetts. He was a nephew of Rufus Choate, lawyer, orator, and U.S. representative. He graduated from Harvard University in 1852 and Harvard Law School in 1854, was admitted to the bar in 1855, and practiced in New York City for over fifty-five years, winning a reputation as an effective lawyer. He served as the U.S. ambassador to Great Britain from 1899 to 1905 and as head of the American delegation to the second Hague Conference in 1907. He was known for his charm as an after-dinner speaker, for his effectiveness as a jury lawyer, and for his eloquence at formal occasions.

CULLOM, SHELBY M. (1829–1914). Lawyer and politician. After his birth in Kentucky, his family moved to Illinois. He acquired an education at a subscription school and attended the Rock River Seminary at Mount Morris, Illinois. After two years of study in a law office in Springfield, he was admitted to the bar in 1855 and practiced law in Springfield for ten years. In 1858 he followed Lincoln, who was a friend of his father, into the Republican party, for which he worked faithfully for over fifty years. He served in the lower house of the Illinois legislature, in the U.S. House of Representatives, as Illinois governor, and in the U.S. Senate for thirty years. In the upper house he was a member of the Committee on Interstate Commerce and in 1901 moved to Committee of Foreign Relations. Because of his long tenure, he became an influential senator and party member. He was a life-long friend of John Hay, son of his one-time law partner and Lincoln's private secretary. Not a brilliant man, he was colorless, low-key, conservative, and conscientious.

CUOMO, MARIO M. (b.1932). Lawyer and politician. Born, Queens County, New York. He graduated from St. John's College in 1953 and St. John's Law School in 1956. He became the legal assistant to a judge of the New York State Court of Appeals from 1956 to 1958, later practiced law from 1958 to 1975, and taught at St. John's Law School. He was secretary of state of New York, lieutenant governor, and governor. He has written two books and contributed articles to legal publications.

DOLLIVER, JONATHAN P. (1858–1910). U.S. senator from Iowa. Born near Kingwood, West Virginia. After graduating from West Virginia University in 1875, he studied law in Morgantown and eventually moved to Fort Dodge, Iowa, where he practiced law and became involved in Republican politics. Almost immediately the Iowa Republican leadership recognized Dolliver for his oratorical ability and invited him in 1884 to deliver the keynote address at the state Republican convention in Des Moines and to campaign for the ticket. In 1888, under the tutelage of conservative William Boyd Allison, Dolliver served five terms in the U.S. House of Representatives.

In 1900 he was mentioned as a possible vice-presidential candidate. In 1901 he entered the U.S. Senate, joining the conservative Republicans who called upon him to be their speaker on numerous occasions. Soon he disagreed with the eastern party leadership, and by 1903 he had aligned himself with the insurgents: Robert M. LaFollette, Albert J. Beveridge, and Moses Clapp.

DOUGLASS, FREDERICK (1817?–95). Lecturer and journalist. Born, Tuckaloe, Maryland. He escaped from slavery in 1838 and served as a paid agent and lecturer for the Massachusetts Anti-Slavery Society. From money earned lecturing in England and Ireland he purchased his freedom and settled in Rochester, New York, where he edited the *North Star,* an antislave weekly, and other newspapers from 1847 to 1858. During the Civil War, he assisted in recruiting two black regiments and became an adviser to President Lincoln. Later he served as marshall and recorder of deeds of the District of Columbia from 1877 to 1881 and United States minister to Haiti from 1889 to 1891. His *Narrative of the Life of Frederick Douglass* has been called a classic autobiography.

EMERSON, RALPH WALDO (1803–82). American writer and philosopher. Born, Boston, Massachusetts, son of William Emerson, pastor of the First Unitarian Church of Boston. Ralph Waldo graduated from Harvard University in 1821, taught school briefly, attended the Harvard Divinity School from 1825 to 1829, and became the minister of the old South Church of Boston. After resigning from his pastorate in 1835, he settled in Concord and devoted the remainder of his career to public lecturing and writing. He is considered a premier figure in nineteenth-century American literature, particularly for his transcendental philosophical essays. He served as editor of the *Dial* from 1842 to 1844. His two most famous addresses are his Phi Beta Kappa oration "The American Scholar" and his Divinity School Address. Although he is remembered primarily as a philosopher and essayist, Emerson earned his living primarily on the lecture platform, traveling the circuit for almost forty years.

GARFIELD, JAMES A. (1831–81). Twentieth president of the United States. Born in Cuyahoga County, Ohio. He graduated from Williams College in 1856, taught at Hiram College from 1857 to 1861, and was admitted to the Ohio bar in 1860. In 1861 he organized an Ohio volunteer regiment, served in the field, fought in the battles of Shiloh and Corinth, and rose to the rank of major general. In 1863 he was elected to the U.S. House of Representatives, became a leader of the regular Republicans, and in 1880, as a compromise Republican candidate, was elected president over his Democratic opponent, W. S. Hancock. On July 2, 1881, he was shot by a disappointed officeseeker and died on September 19, 1881. He was considered an effective speaker and influential member of Congress, but his early death in office gave him little opportunity to demonstrate his leadership in the presidency.

LLOYD GEORGE, DAVID (1863–1945). First Earl of Dufor, British official. Born in Manchester, England, of Welsh parentage. He became a solicitor in 1884. He entered the House of Commons in 1890; served as president of the Board of Trade, chancellor of the exchequer, minister of munitions, and secretary for war. Replacing Herbert Henry Asquith, Lloyd George was appointed prime minister, becoming virtually a British dictator during the closing years of World War I and the settlement of peace in Europe. In 1919 he was honored with the Order of Merit. In the House of Commons he won recognition for his effective debating. He authored *War Memoirs* and *The Truth about the Peace Treaty.*

ROOSEVELT, THEODORE (1858–1919). Twenty-sixth president of the United States. Born, New York City. He graduated from Harvard University in 1880 and was elected to Phi Beta Kappa. He studied law, was a member of the New York legislature, the U.S. Civil Service Commission, president of the New York City Board of Police Commissioners, and U.S. assistant secretary of the navy. He served as a colonel of the Rough Riders in the Spanish-American War and governor of New York from 1898 to 1900. After being elected vice-president under William McKinley, Roosevelt became president on September 14, 1902, when McKinley was assassinated. In 1904 he won a second term, and in 1912 he ran unsuccessfully for the presidency on the Bull Moose ticket, receiving over four million votes. His publications include more than two thousand magazine articles and editorials, and his collected works encompass twenty volumes. He was constantly on the public platform as a campaigner, a lecturer, and an occasional speaker.

ROOT, ELIHU (1845–1937). Lawyer and diplomat. Born, Clinton, New York. Root graduated from Hamilton College in 1864, completed a law degree at New York University in 1867, and practiced law in New York City. He served as U.S. secretary of war from 1899 to 1904 and U.S. senator from New York from 1909 to 1915. He was president of the Carnegie Endowment for International Peace, a member of the Hague Tribunal, and was awarded the Nobel prize for peace in 1912. He authored several books on international relations.

SIMPSON, MATTHEW (1811–84). Methodist Bishop. Born, Cadiz, Ohio. He was largely self-educated, briefly attending an academy in Cadiz and Madison College in Unionville, Pennsylvania. He studied the printing business, law, and medicine in which after 1833 he was qualified as a practitioner. He turned to the Methodist ministry and was admitted to the Pittsburgh Conference in 1836. After preaching on a circuit at Cadiz, he gained an appointment in Pittsburgh. In 1837 he was appointed professor of natural science at Allegheny College; in 1839 he became president of Indiana Asbury University at Greencastle, Indiana, where he served until 1847. In 1852 he was elected Methodist bishop with his episcopal residences in Pittsburgh, Evanston, and, finally, Philadelphia, but his duties carried him all over the United States and to Mexico, Canada, and Europe. During the Civil War he spoke on behalf of the Union and had consulted with Edwin Stanton and Abraham Lincoln. He was not preeminent as a theologian or scholar, but he was an influential speaker and leader and revered among Methodists.

STEVENSON, ADLAI E. (1900–1965). Political leader. Born in Los Angeles, California. He was the grandson of Vice-President Adlai E. Stevenson, who served with Grover Cleveland. He graduated from Princeton University in 1922, studied law at Northwestern University in 1926, and practiced law in Chicago. He had a variety of appointments in the federal government, including special assistant to Secretary of the Navy Frank Knox and assistant to the secretary of state. He served as governor of Illinois from 1949 to 1953 and ran unsuccessfully for the presidency in 1952 and 1956. In 1961 President John F. Kennedy appointed him U.S. ambassador to the United Nations. In the twentieth century Stevenson won recognition as one of the most articulate and eloquent speakers for American liberalism. Among his best speeches are eulogies of Eleanor Roosevelt, John F. Kennedy, and Winston Churchill.

TAFT, WILLIAM HOWARD (1857–1930). Twenty-seventh president of the United States. Born, Cincinnati, Ohio. Taft graduated from Yale University in 1878, Cincinnati Law School in 1880, was admitted to the bar, and practiced law in Cincinnati. Benjamin Harrison appointed him U.S. solicitor general. He served as the first civil governor of the Philippines from 1901 to 1904. Under Theodore Roosevelt, he became secretary of war and defeated William Jennings Bryan for the presidency in 1908, but served only one term. After teaching law at Yale for eight years, he was appointed chief justice of the U.S. Supreme Court in 1921. After 1912, Taft lectured widely and became a favorite of the American people. His tenure as chief justice was more distinguished than that of his presidency.

TARBELL, IDA M. (1857–1944). Journalist and biographer. Born Hatch Hollow, Pennsylvania. She graduated from Allegheny College in 1880 and served on the editorial staffs of *The Chautauquan, McClure's,* and the *American Magazine.* She wrote many books, including a sensational exposé, *The History of the Standard Oil Company,* as well as *The Life of Abraham Lincoln* and *In the Footsteps of the Lincolns.* She also wrote biographies of Napoleon Bonaparte, Madame Roland, Judge Elbert H. Gary, and Owen D. Young. From 1920 through 1932, she annually toured the United States giving lectures.

WASHINGTON, BOOKER T. (1856–1915). Educational Leader. Born a slave in Franklin County, Virginia. After the Civil War the family moved to Malden, West Virginia. He gained his advanced education at Hampton Institute from 1872 to 1875. After graduating, he taught school for three years, attended Wayland Seminary, Washington, D.C., and then returned to Hampton for two years. In 1881 he founded Tuskegee Normal and Industrial Institute in Alabama to provide technical and practical education for blacks. During his tenure there he addressed many white audiences in the North to gain financial support. He became recognized as the foremost black leader. His most famous speech is the one he delivered before the Cotton States Exposition in Atlanta, Georgia, on September 18, 1895. His autobiography *Up from Slavery* became a best seller; later he wrote *The Story of the Negro.*

WILSON, WOODROW (1856–1924). Twenty-eighth president of the United States. Born at Staunton, Virginia. He was the son of a Presbyterian minister who preached in Georgia, South Carolina, and Virginia. He graduated from Princeton in 1879, studied law at the University of Virginia, and attempted to practice law in Atlanta, Georgia, in 1882. He completed a Ph.D. in government and history at Johns Hopkins University in 1886, taught at Bryn Mawr, Wesleyan University, and at Princeton. He became president of Princeton in 1902 and served in that position until 1910. He served as Democratic governor of New Jersey from 1911 to 1913 and as president from 1913 to 1921. He was a vigorous writer and speaker and is one of our best educated presidents. His fame rests on his leadership of the nation during World War I.

SELECTED BIBLIOGRAPHY

Addresses Delivered at the Lincoln Dinners of the Republican Club of the City of New York in Response to the Toast: Abraham Lincoln, 1887–1909. New York: Republican Club of the City of New York, 1909.

Addresses Delivered at the Lincoln Dinners of the National Republican Club in Response to the Toast: Abraham Lincoln, 1910–1927. New York: Republican Club of the City of New York, 1927.

The Assassination and History of the Conspiracy. With a foreword by Roy P. Basler. New York: Hobbs, Dorman, 1965.

Basler, Roy P. *The Lincoln Legend.* Boston: Houghton Mifflin, 1935.

Betts, William W., Jr., ed. *Lincoln and the Poets: An Anthology.* Pittsburgh: University of Pittsburgh Press, 1965.

Braden, Waldo W. *Abraham Lincoln: Public Speaker.* Baton Rouge: Louisiana State University Press, 1988.

Bullard, F. Lauriston. *Lincoln in Marble and Bronze.* New Brunswick, N.J.: Rutgers University Press, 1952.

Coggeshall, William T. *The Journey of Abraham Lincoln from Springfield, 1861 and from Washington to Springfield, 1865.* Columbus: Ohio State Journal, 1865.

Current, Richard N. *The Lincoln Nobody Knows.* New York: Hill and Wang, 1958.

Donald, David. *Lincoln Reconsidered.* 2d ed. New York: Knopf, 1959.

Holzer, Harold, Gabor S. Boritt, and Mark E. Neely, Jr., *Changing the Lincoln Image.* Fort Wayne: Louis A. Warren Lincoln Library, 1985.

——. *The Lincoln Image: Abraham Lincoln and the Popular Print.* New York: Scribners, 1984.

Lewis, Lloyd. *Myths after Lincoln.* New York: Harcourt, Brace, 1941.

MacChesney, Nathan William. *Abraham Lincoln: The Tribute of a Century, 1809–1909.* Chicago: McClung, 1910.

Monagham, Jay. "An Analysis of Lincoln's Funeral Sermons." *Indiana Magazine of History* 41 (March 1945): 31–44.

Morris, Benjamin F. *The Memorial Record of the National Tribute to Abraham Lincoln.* Washington: Morrison, 1865.

Neely, Mark E., Jr. *The Abraham Lincoln Encyclopedia.* New York: McGraw-Hill, 1982.

Redway, Maurine Whorton, and Dorothy Kendell Bracken. *Marks of Lincoln on Our Land.* New York: Hastings, 1957.

Searcher, Victor. *Farewell to Lincoln.* Nashville: Abingdon, 1965.

Shea, John Gilmary, ed. *The Lincoln Memorial: A Record of the Life,*

Assassination, and Obsequies of the Martyred President. New York: Bunce and Huntington, 1865.

Stewart, Charles J. "Lincoln's Assassination and the Protestant Clergy of the North." *Journal of the Illinois State Historical Society* 54 (Autumn 1961): 268–93.

——. "The Pulpit and the Assassination of Lincoln." *Quarterly Journal of Speech* 50 (Oct. 1964): 299–307.

——. "The Pulpit in Time of Crisis: 1865 and 1963." *Speech Monographs* 33 (Nov. 1965): 427–34.

Thomas, Benjamin. *Abraham Lincoln.* New York: Knopf, 1952.

Tice, George. *Lincoln.* New Brunswick, N.J.: Rutgers University Press, 1984.

Ward, Geoffrey C. *Lincoln and His Legend: The Lincoln Tomb.* Springfield: Sangamon State University, 1978.

Wilson, Rufus Rockwell. *Lincoln in Caricature.* New York: Horizon, 1953.

Index

255

Note on the Author

WALDO W. BRADEN is a Boyd Professor Emeritus of Speech, Louisiana State University. He has published over eighty articles in professional journals, several textbooks, and numerous books on American oratory, including *Abraham Lincoln: Public Speaker.*